CONSTITUTIONAL COURTS AS MEDIATORS

This book offers a new theoretical framework for understanding the mediator role played by constitutional courts in democratic conflict solving. The book proposes an informational theory of constitutional review in which constitutional courts obtain, process, and transmit information to parties in a way that reduces the uncertainty causing their conflict. The substantive focus of the book is the role of constitutional courts in democracies where the armed forces are fighting internal armed conflicts of different types: Colombia, Peru, and Mexico in Latin America and also Israel, Turkey, and Pakistan. Through detailed analyses of the political context, civil-military relations, and the constitutional jurisprudence on military autonomy and the regulation of the use of force the book shows that constitutional courts can be instrumental in striking a democratically accepted balance between the exercise of civilian authority and the legitimate needs of the military in its pursuit of order and national security.

JULIO RÍOS-FIGUEROA is Associate Professor of Political Science at Centro de Investigación y Docencia Económicas (CIDE), in Mexico City.

COMPARATIVE CONSTITUTIONAL LAW AND POLICY

Series Editors

Tom Ginsburg, *University of Chicago*
Zachary Elkins, *University of Texas at Austin*
Ran Hirschl, *University of Toronto*

Comparative constitutional law is an intellectually vibrant field that encompasses an increasingly broad array of approaches and methodologies. This series collects analytically innovative and empirically grounded work from scholars of comparative constitutionalism across academic disciplines. Books in the series include theoretically informed studies of single constitutional jurisdictions, comparative studies of constitutional law and institutions, and edited collections of original essays that respond to challenging theoretical and empirical questions in the field.

Books in the Series

Constitutional Courts as Mediators
Julio Ríos-Figueroa

Perils of Judicial Self-Government in Transitional Societies
David Kosař

Engaging with Social Rights
Brian Ray

Making We the People
Chaihark Hahm and Sung Ho Kim

Radical Deprivation on Trial
Cesar Rodríguez-Garavito and Diana Rodríguez-Franco

Unstable Constitutionalism
Edited by Mark Tushnet and Madhav Khosla

Magna Carta and its Modern Legacy
Edited by Robert Hazell and James Melton

International Courts and the Performance of International Agreements
Clifford Carrubba and Matthew Gabel

Reputation and Judicial Tactics
Shai Dothan

Constitutions and Religious Freedom
Frank Cross

Constitutionalism in Asia in the Early Twenty-First Century
Edited by Albert Chen

Social Difference and Constitutionalism in Pan-Asia
Edited by Susan H. Williams

Constitutions in Authoritarian Regimes
Edited by Tom Ginsburg and Alberto Simpser

Presidential Legislation in India
Shubhankar Dam

Social and Political Foundations of Constitutions
Edited by Denis J. Galligan and Mila Versteeg

Consequential Courts
Edited by Diana Kapiszewski, Gordon Silverstein and Robert A. Kagan

Comparative Constitutional Design
Edited by Tom Ginsburg

CONSTITUTIONAL COURTS AS MEDIATORS

Armed Conflict, Civil-Military Relations, and the Rule of Law in Latin America

JULIO RÍOS-FIGUEROA

Centro de Investigación y Docencia Económicas (CIDE), Mexico City

CAMBRIDGE
UNIVERSITY PRESS

CAMBRIDGE
UNIVERSITY PRESS

32 Avenue of the Americas, New York NY 10013

Cambridge University Press is part of the University of Cambridge.

It furthers the University's mission by disseminating knowledge in the pursuit of education, learning, and research at the highest international levels of excellence.

www.cambridge.org
Information on this title: www.cambridge.org/9781107079786

First published 2016

A catalogue record for this publication is available from the British Library.

Library of Congress Cataloguing in Publication Data
Names: Ríos-Figueroa, Julio, author.
Title: Constitutional Courts as Mediators. Armed Conflict, Civil-Military Relations, and the Rule of Law in Latin America / Julio Ríos-Figueroa.
Description: New York: Cambridge University Press, [2016] |
Includes bibliographical references.
Identifiers: LCCN 2015040746 | ISBN 9781107079786
Subjects: LCSH: Constitutional courts – Latin America. | Courts of last resort – Latin America. | Political questions and judicial power – Latin America. | Civil-military relations – Latin America. | Military law – Latin America.
Classification: LCC KG501.R56 2016 | DDC 347.8/035–dc23
LC record available at http://lccn.loc.gov/2015040746

ISBN 978-1-107-07978-6 Hardback

To Andrea, Inés, and Eva

CONTENTS

FIGURES

TABLES

ACKNOWLEDGMENTS

The difference between articles and books, someone said to me, is that when you write an article you know the starting and the end points. But when writing a book, research can take you in many different directions right after departing. I am not sure if the statement regarding articles is right, but in my case the comment about books could not be more accurate. Writing this book has been a long, hard, at many times uncertain, but always enriching journey in which I was privileged to have the support of many generous individuals and institutions in different capacities.

To keep the project moving at critical crossroads, dead-ends, and diversions Andrea Pozas-Loyo, Jeffrey K. Staton, and Rodrigo Uprimny were absolutely crucial. I simply would not have reached this final destination without your help. Thank you. Throughout the drive I was fortunate to get warning signs and alternative route suggestions from insightful friends and colleagues including Javier Angulo, Karina Ansolabehere, Luz Marina Arias, Allyson Benton, Carlos Bravo, Daniel Brinks, José Antonio Caballero, Tom Clark, Henar Criado, Luis de la Calle, Zachary Elkins, Tulia Falletti, Jennifer Gandhi, Tom Ginsburg, Juan González Bertomeu, Ezequiel González Ocantos, Hernán Gullco, Martha Liliana Gutiérrez, Gretchen Helmke, Francisco Herreros, Sandra Hincapié, Ran Hirschl, Christoph Hönnige, Gary Jacobsohn, Claudio López-Guerra, Noam Lupu, Ignacio Marván, Ximena Medellín, Pablo Mijangos, Gabriel Negretto, Roberto Niembro, Maria Popova, Xisca Pou, Sabrina Ragone, Javier Martín Reyes, Alejandra Ríos, María Paula Saffon, Ignacio Sánchez-Cuenca, Raúl Sánchez-Uribarri, Camilo Saavedra, Andreas Schedler, Gilles Serra, Hootan Shambayati, Udi Sommer, and Luis Daniel Vázquez. My heartfelt thanks to all of you.

In and on Colombia, Peru, and Mexico I benefited from the knowledgeable and generous advice of César Bazán Seminario, Yahayra Bernal, Camilo Castillo, José Ramón Cossío, Eduardo Dargent, Mauricio García Villegas, Pablo Kalmanotivz, Lilia Mónica López Benitez, David Lovatón Palacios, Gina Cabarcas Maciá, Manuel José Cepeda, Jaime Córdoba

Triviño, César Landa Arroyo, Alejandro Madrazo, Raúl Mejía, Aldo Ponce, César Rodríguez Garavito, Juan Carlos Rodríguez Raga, Edgar Saavedra Rojas, and the military and judicial officials who are mentioned in the respective chapters. A big thank you to several research assistants who participated at different stages of the project: Nancy Camacho Díaz, Camilo Castillo, Sicabí Cruz, Berta Díaz, María Fernanda Gómez Abán, Ana María Montoya, María Fernanda Nieto, Jimena Salazar, César Valderrama, and Javier Zúñiga Ramiro. Susan Thomae gracefully corrected the grammar and spelling of the manuscript.

I gratefully acknowledge the generous and continuous institutional support of my academic home, Centro de Investigación y Docencia Económicas (CIDE) and its División de Estudios Políticos, as well as to authorities who encouraged me and supported the project: Javier Aparicio, David Arellano, Enrique Cabrero, Guillermo Cejudo, Sergio López Ayllón, Andreas Schedler, and Ignacio Marván. I spent the academic year 2012–13 working on this project at the stimulating Instituto Juan March, now IC_3JM, partaking of the generosity of its director Ignacio Sánchez-Cuenca and its wonderful community. DeJusticia and the Universidad de los Andes in Colombia, and the Instituto de Defensa Legal/Justicia Viva and the Pontificia Universidad Católica in Peru, were hospitable and unsparing. I presented different versions and parts of the book at meetings, seminars, and conferences hosted by many institutions and organizations including the American Political Science Association, the Latin American Studies Association, the European Consortium for Political Research, the University of Chicago, the University of Houston, La Trobe University in Melbourne, the División de Estudios Políticos and the División de Estudios Jurídicos at CIDE, CIDE-Aguascalientes, the political science seminar at the Instituto Tecnológico Autónomo de México, the Universidad Diego Portales, the Fundação Getulio Vargas, GIGA-Hamburg, the Instituto de Investigaciones Jurídicas at the Universidad Nacional Autónoma de México, FLACSO-México, the Consejo Superior de Investigaciones Científicas and the Centro de Estudios Políticos y Constitucionales in Madrid, the Universidad de Salamanca, the Universidad de San Andrés in Buenos Aires, the Universidad de los Andes in Bogotá, the Pontificia Universidad Católica del Perú, the Center of Constitutional Studies at the Mexican Supreme Court, and the University of Oxford. A terrific book workshop organized by the series editors on Comparative Constitutional Law and Policy and hosted by the Department of Government at the University of Texas–Austin gave me the final push in the right direction to bring this book to what readers have in their hands. Thank you to the participants in these events.

Whatever this book is and is not has been influenced in direct and indirect ways by my professors at New York University: John Ferejohn, Barry Friedman, Stephen Holmes, Bernard Manin, Pasquale Pasquino, and Adam Przeworski. I have had the privilege to learn from them much more than what they formally teach in classes, seminars, talks, discussions, papers, and books, which already is an invaluable lot. Their intellectual curiosity, scholarly craftsmanship, and passionate commitment are examples that will be with me for the rest of my life.

In what has been a longer, at times harder and more uncertain, and yet more fulfilling journey my family and many dear friends with whom I have shared these years of life are the fuel that keeps the wheels moving. A special thank you to my parents, Amparo and Julio; and to my brother and his wife, Jorge and Mariví. Thank you also to my dear in-laws, Aurora, Ricardo, Julia, and Fernando. The book is dedicated to my life accomplice, Andrea, and our two new little passengers Inés and Eva in the hopes that our voyage is much longer and full of discoveries.

1

Constitutional Courts and the Armed Forces

Modern states need a corps of armed forces strong enough to provide security against external threats as well as to guarantee internal peace. But strong armies have also proven to be a threat to the regime and, specifically, to democratic stability, weakening the state and harming thousands of people. Powerful armies subordinated to democratic civilian governments are the puzzling exception where people with guns obey people without them (Przeworski 2011, 180). But how to create armed forces bounded by the democratic rule of law without jeopardizing its *sprit de corps* or its efficacy? In 1780 Thomas Jefferson said, "The freest governments in the world have their army under absolute government. Republican form and principles are not to be introduced into government of an army."[1] Absolutism is no longer an ideal model for organizing armed forces. True, they require strict discipline and a corporatist identity to work efficiently. But a history of military abuses, both within the armed forces as well as carried out by them, warns against prioritizing efficiency at the expense of accountability. Still the conundrum remains: How to obtain simultaneously the seemingly incompatible goals of having strong and efficacious militaries subjected to the rule of law?

Civilian governments and their armed forces clash over this quandary (cf. Barany 2012). When the dilemma is not dealt with successfully, an extreme outcome may be a coup d'état. Even if the generals seize power in the name of the rule of law "taking upon themselves the moral duty of deposing the illegitimate government," as the Chilean generals led by Augusto Pinochet declared in justifying the 1973 military takeover,[2] coups kill the democratic rule of law. The balance of authoritarian forces may produce something that resembles the engine force of constitutionalism (Barros 2002), or the courts may attempt to square the circle shedding some legality upon the usurpers (Mahmud 1994), but the democratic rule

[1] Thomas Jefferson, Notes Concerning the Right of Removal from Office, 1780. Papers 4: 282.

[2] Cited in Loveman and Davies (1997, 181).

of law simply does not mix well with military regimes. The recent examples of the brief democratic interlude in Egypt interrupted by a military coup in 2013, or the coup d'état in Thailand in 2014, confirm that democracy dies the day of the coup, despite the statements and press releases of the generals.[3]

Short of a coup, a fairly rare phenomenon these days, the dilemma posed by the need to have strong militaries bounded by law permeates civilian-military relations in every democracy. There is no easy and permanent solution; rather democracies deal with this dilemma in different ways depending on the context and specific circumstances. Sometimes the emphasis is put on the "strong armed forces" part of the dilemma, while other times the "bounded by law" part is stressed. Argentina, since its return to democracy, has moved toward the latter to the point of abolishing the military jurisdiction, making sure that the ordinary justice system processes all cases of all citizens including, of course, the members of the armed forces (see, e.g., Saín 2010). In contrast, after a Taliban terrorist attack in December 2014 the Pakistani democratically elected government empowered the military courts to try suspected Islamist militants, opening the way for a rapid but roughly hewed judicial process that could move defendants from arrest to execution in a matter of weeks (Walsh 2015). To strike a balance is a delicate act: too much transferring of power to the military and democracy may be hopelessly hurt; too much limiting of the military and democracy may be dangerously at risk. In short, finding a way to build limited but strong armed forces is difficult but key for democracies.

What can constitutional courts do about this? One view is that, essentially, courts cannot contribute anything useful in this domain because they are powerless or not well suited to intervene in these inherently political matters. According to Alexander Bickel, the rationale for the so-called political-question doctrine recommends judicial self-restraint and avoidance of issues when "the court's sense of lack of capacity is compounded by the strangeness of the issue and its intractability to principled resolution,

[3] In Thailand, three days after the coup, the National Council for Peace and Order junta issued order number 37, replacing civilian courts with military tribunals for trying some offenses. The order empowers the military court to prosecute all crimes in the Thai penal code, including *lèse majesté* crimes for insulting the monarchy and national security and sedition offenses. "The first person to be tried is former education minister Chaturon Chaisaeng. He has been denied bail and can be held for 12-day periods for a maximum of 84 days. There is a right to counsel but no right to appellate review" (note from the *Bangkok Post*, Friday, May 30, 2014, http://globalmjreform.blogspot.mx/; accessed October 16, 2015).

the sheer momentous of it, and the anxiety not so much that the judicial judgment will be ignored as that perhaps it should but will not be" (Bickel 1962, 184). More recently, Eric Posner and Adrian Vermeule argued that in times of security crisis "there is no reason to think that courts possessing limited information and limited expertise will choose better security policies than does the government" (Posner and Vermeule 2007, 12). The conclusion is clear: "In times of emergency, judges should get out of the government's way because government will choose good emergency policies and even when not, judicial intervention may only make things worse" (ibid.).

An alternative view suggests that constitutions and constitutional judges are devices to limit the arbitrary actions of governments (e.g., Sajó 1999; Stone Sweet 2012) and that, even in emergencies "governments should not be permitted to run wild, many extreme measures should remain off limits, because emergency measures have a habit of continuing well beyond their necessity" (Ackerman 2002, 16). When governments commit to not making arbitrary actions in exchange for taxes, investment, or support, giving autonomy to a court allowing it to punish deviances from previously made commitments is a device to make them credible (e.g., Ferejohn and Sager 2002; North and Weingast 1989). In this framework, courts' failure to impose limits on arbitrary actions undermines the credibility of the government, making judicial intervention a necessary condition.[4]

This book argues that the role of constitutional courts is neither to duck, leaving governments and militaries unconstrained, nor to strictly and systematically impose limits on them but rather that their role is to help these parties solve their own problems, in particular when they are informational. The book shows that under certain conditions constitutional courts' jurisprudence can provide information to civilian governments and their armed forces that reduces the uncertainty that surrounds their relations, helping them to cooperate and resolve their conflicts. Constitutional courts can be instrumental in striking a democratically accepted balance between the exercise of civilian authority and the legitimate needs of the military in its pursuit of order and national security, so that they can perform this function under conditions of security crises and emergencies. This role becomes even more relevant when the threats to the state come from within its borders.

[4] A similar debate can be found on whether and how courts should enforce socioeconomic rights (e.g., Dixon 2007; Motta Ferraz 2011; Rodríguez-Garavito 2011).

Informational Challenges in Civil-Military Relations

The constitutional dilemma of building efficacious armed forces bounded by law, and the consequent tension this generates between democratic civilian governments and their armed forces, is due in no small part to the ambiguous limits between the "military" and the "civilian" spheres. In this sense, Huntington argued, "the problem is not armed revolt but the relation of the expert to the politician" (Huntington 1957, 20). Should the military decide tactical or strategy questions only? What about tactical questions of special political importance such as nuclear tactics? What about tactics that involve the whole society, such as a mandatory draft? In countries that have never experienced a coup, notably the United States, the challenge of designing the proper division of labor between "military matters" and "civilian matters" has driven much of the civil-military conflict (Feaver 1999, 219).

The line becomes blurrier, and the stakes higher, in contemporary democracies with a history of military intervention in politics and where the armed forces' role is not confined to external defense but rather involves internal security. As Narcís Serra, former minister of defense in Spain from 1982 to 1991, one of the most contentious periods of the transition to democracy, puts it:

> One could study the adjustment of the armed forces to democracy in terms of the reduction of its reserve domains to areas of autonomy compatible with the democratic rule of law.... The demarcation of what are "military issues" or "civil issues" has generated a large number of conflicts between governments and the military. This is not surprising because it has direct implications for the scope for military autonomy and becomes embroiled in the debate about imprecise delineations of what is civil and what is military. (Serra 2010, 43, 202)

The fluid borders between the "civilian" and the "military" spheres create tension in their relation due to uncertainty. In particular, three types of uncertainties lie at the heart of the dilemma and are relevant to civilian-military relations: (1) uncertainty over the legal consequences of certain actions, (2) uncertainty over the bounds of the exceptions and emergencies permitted by the constitution, and (3) uncertainty about how to balance clashing constitutional principles or rules in particular cases. Consider the first type of uncertainty. In democratic countries where the armed forces are called on to face an internal security crisis, members of the military engage in combats and casualties take place. Are those casualties "homicides" that should be investigated and eventually punished, or simply "deaths in combat" that are acceptable in cases of armed conflict?

The answer depends on whether there is an officially declared internal armed conflict because that implies the use of the International Humanitarian Law (IHL) that recognizes "deaths in combat."[5] If an internal armed conflict is not officially declared, casualties are investigated and processed through the lenses of the national criminal law and thus we can have a "homicide." But whether there is an internal armed conflict, or who should declare one, is far from clear. Governments resist officially declaring an internal armed conflict because this implies greater international oversight and possibly also the recognition of the status of combatants to enemy armed groups. Members of the armed forces, in turn, urge the governments "not to tie their hands" with inadequate legal constraints. In contrast, what is crystal clear is that whether the facts are seen through the lenses of criminal law or the IHL is highly consequential. For one, serving soldiers may be charged with homicide in a civilian court and go to jail vis-á-vis facing no charge or a disciplinary sanction by a military court.

Consider now the uncertainty over the bounds of the exceptions allowed by the constitution. Many constitutions recognize the military jurisdiction as a separate body of law, prosecutors, and courts that are created to take into account the specifics of the armed forces' job in order to give stability to the institution and legal security to its members. But who can be investigated and tried in military courts, and under what circumstances? Military jurisdiction can be broader, including not only military officials but also civilians for diverse types of crimes, or narrower, including only military officials for strictly military crimes. At one extreme, one can find that broad military jurisdictions have often served as impunity mechanisms to cover crimes not related to the military service or the security of the country. At the other extreme, military justice can be abolished, creating a unitary justice system on the grounds that this exceptional body of laws and officers violates established rights and principles of constitutional due process.[6]

[5] To put it simply, the IHL is the law of war and it is applicable in situations of external or internal armed conflicts. The IHL, of course, sets limits as to what is permissible in armed conflicts based on principles that regulate the use of force such as proportionality, humanity, or necessity. Chapter 6 deals with IHL and the judicial regulation of the use of force in more detail.

[6] According to Serra, "the move to a unitary judiciary has an immediate consequence in the process of democratizing the armed forces: it gets rid of an autonomous power center that has been used to making its own rules and ordering itself, even ideologically, in opposition to the wishes of the duly constituted government" (Serra 2010, 244). Interestingly, this is a similar line of reasoning to that of the Argentine Supreme Court justices who argued

What is the right scope of the military jurisdiction is uncertain. Taking the jurisprudence on this issue of the Inter American Court of Human Rights (IACHR) as a standard, arguably a normative consensus around three points has been reached: civilians do not belong in military courts under any circumstance; only members of the armed forces for strictly military crimes committed under service can be investigated and tried in this special jurisdiction; and, when grave human rights violations are involved, even military officials should go to ordinary courts.[7] However, individual countries fall below/on/above the standard, and the timing, velocity, and historical patterns greatly differ among countries. In Brazil,

that the military justice system was unconstitutional in *Caso López* (Fallos 54:577; 310:1797, March 2007).

[7] The list of the IACHR's most notorious cases on the topic includes the following: (1) *Caso Loayza Tamayo v. Perú. Fondo.* Sentencia del 17 de septiembre de 1997, Serie C, núm. 33; (2) *Caso Loayza Tamayo v. Perú. Reparaciones y Costas.* Sentencia del 27 de noviembre de 1998, Serie C, núm. 42; (3) *Caso Castillo Petruzzi y otros v. Perú. Fondo, Reparaciones y Costas.* Sentencia del 30 de mayo de 1999, Serie C, núm. 52; (4) *Caso Cesti Hurtado v. Perú. Fondo.* Sentencia del 29 de septiembre de 1999, Serie C, núm. 56; (5) *Caso Durand y Ugarte v. Perú. Fondo.* Sentencia del 16 de agosto de 2000, Serie C, núm. 68; (6) *Caso Cantoral Benavides v. Perú. Fondo.* Sentencia de 18 de agosto de 2000, Serie C, núm. 69; (7) *Caso Bámaca Velásquez v. Guatemala. Fondo.* Sentencia del 25 de noviembre de 2000, Serie C, núm. 70; (8) *Caso Las Palmeras v. Colombia. Fondo.* Sentencia del 6 de diciembre de 2001, Serie C, núm. 90; (9) *Caso Myrna Mack Chang v. Guatemala. Fondo, Reparaciones y Costas.* Sentencia del 25 de noviembre de 2003, Serie C, núm. 101; (10) *Caso 19 Comerciantes v. Colombia. Fondo, Reparaciones y Costas.* Sentencia del 5 de julio de 2004, Serie C, núm. 109; (11) *Caso Lori Berenson Mejía v. Perú. Fondo, Reparaciones y Costas.* Sentencia del 25 de noviembre de 2004, Serie C, núm. 119; (12) *Caso de la Masacre de Mapiripán v. Colombia. Fondo, Reparaciones y Costas.* Sentencia del 15 de septiembre de 2005, Serie C, núm. 134; (13) *Caso Palamara Iribarne v. Chile. Fondo, Reparaciones y Costas.* Sentencia del 22 de noviembre de 2005, Serie C, núm. 135; (14) *Caso de la Masacre de Pueblo Bello v. Colombia. Fondo, Reparaciones y Costas.* Sentencia del 31 de enero de 2006, Serie C, núm. 140; (15) *Caso Almonacid Arellano y otros v. Chile. Excepciones Preliminares, Fondo, Reparaciones y Costas.* Sentencia del 26 de septiembre de 2006, Serie C, núm. 154; (16) *Caso La Cantuta v. Perú. Fondo, Reparaciones y Costas.* Sentencia del 29 de noviembre de 2006, Serie C, núm. 162; (17) *Caso de la Masacre de la Rochela v. Colombia. Fondo, Reparaciones y Costas.* Sentencia del 11 de mayo de 2007, Serie C, núm. 163; (18) *Caso Escué Zapata v. Colombia. Fondo, Reparaciones y Costas.* Sentencia del 4 de julio de 2007, Serie C, núm. 165; (19) *Caso Zambrano Vélez y otros v. Ecuador. Fondo, Reparaciones y Costas.* Sentencia del 4 de julio de 2007, Serie C, núm. 166; (20) *Caso Tiu Tojín v. Guatemala. Fondo, Reparaciones y Costas.* Sentencia del 26 de noviembre de 2008, Serie C, núm. 190; (21) *Caso Usón Ramírez v. Venezuela. Excepción Preliminar, Fondo, Reparaciones y Costas.* Sentencia del 20 de noviembre de 2009, Serie C, núm. 207; (22) *Caso Radilla Pacheco v. México. Excepciones Preliminares, Fondo, Reparaciones y Costas.* Sentencia del 23 de noviembre de 2009, Serie C, núm. 209; (23) *Caso Fernández Ortega y otros. v. México. Excepción Preliminar, Fondo, Reparaciones y Costas.* Sentencia del 30 de agosto de 2010, Serie C, núm. 215; (24) *Caso Rosendo Cantú y otra v. México. Excepción Preliminar, Fondo, Reparaciones y Costas.* Sentencia del 31 de agosto de 2010 Serie C, núm. 216.

for instance, civilians constituted 13.5 percent of defendants in military court cases in the period 2002–12 (some 2,555 cases).[8] In contrast, the Argentinean Congress in 2008 derogated the Code of Military Justice and the whole military jurisdiction, considering it unconstitutional.[9] In Pakistan, as mentioned, military jurisdiction has recently been substantially enlarged (see Chapter 7).

Consider, finally, the third type of uncertainty. How to balance clashing constitutional rights or principles in particular cases? For instance, discipline is often mentioned as a necessary condition for the effective operation of the armed forces. And discipline is based on obedience. But should soldiers obey whatever orders they are given? What if complying with an order implies violating human rights, like killing innocent civilians? What if complying with an order implies going against one's most deeply held beliefs? In these cases, the principle of discipline clashes with either the right to object based on conscience or with the duty of not violating human rights. Going back to military justice: accepting that military trials need to be expedient (especially in situations of combat), should basic due process rights such as the right to know the charges against you and the right to be tried before an independent judge be upheld nonetheless? Under what circumstances is expediency more important than the observance of these rights, or the other way around?

Constitutional Courts as Mediators

Constitutional courts help solve informational problems to the extent that their jurisprudence mirrors what mediators do in conflict resolution. The literature on conflict resolution offers two contrasting decision-making styles, that of the arbitrator and of the mediator. In essence, an *arbitrator* adjudicates responsibility based on the record and the disputing parties "are confined by traditional legal remedies that do not encompass creative, innovative, and forward-looking solutions to disputes" (Sgubini, Prieditis, and Marighetto 2013, 2). In contrast, mediators "facilitate dialogue in a

[8] "Julgamento Militar é posto em debate," *O Globo*, August 3, 2014.

[9] See *Caso López* (Fallos 54:577; 310:1797, March 2007), a case about the right of due process in criminal cases that took place in March 2007, where a dissenting opinion by judges Zaffaroni and Lorenzetti argued that the military jurisdiction was altogether unconstitutional because the principle of independence of its judges is not guaranteed – the president is commander in chief of the armed forces. Following the reasoning set forth in that dissenting opinion, Congress in 2008 derogated the code of military justice and the military jurisdiction.

structured multistage process assisting the parties in identifying and articulating their own interests, priorities, needs and wishes to each other," thus helping the parties reach a conclusive and mutually satisfactory agreement (ibid., 3).[10] Arbitration tends to be a better dispute-resolution mechanism when a conflict is an isolated instance, but when the parties' relation transcends the particular conflict mediation tends to be more effective. For instance, a dispute-settlement procedure that avoids clear winners and losers, and that considers relations between the actors in the future, would be better for a conflict of a divorcing couple with kids who will very likely continue seeing each other for the rest of their lives (Singer 1994, 55).

Constitutional courts often deal with conflicts that have more resemblance to a family dispute than to an isolated strife. The institutional parties before the court keep their relation after a specific conflict between the individual holders of a particular office has been solved. For instance, in *United States v. Nixon* the Supreme Court limited the powers of any U.S. president, not of Richard Nixon. In other words, in most cases the parties before constitutional courts will continue to have a relationship independent of the specific identity of the holder of the position at the time of the dispute. In these cases, the constitutional court's jurisprudence will be more effective at resolving conflicts to the extent that it aims at solutions that transcend the present conflict (i.e., the disposition of the case) and instead looks ahead to forging a creative solution (i.e., rule making) that integrates the views of the actual actors in the dispute with the more permanent roles of the institutions, groups, or principles that they represent (cf. Uprimny 2004, 73–5; see also Bush and Folger 2004).

Whether the jurisprudence comes nearer to the arbitrator or the mediator model is consequential for the parties whose conflict reaches the court. In Bolivia in 2003, after months of massive demonstrations, the government called the military to combat protesters. By the end of the year, after a series of confrontations, the death toll reached eighty people and the wounded were in the hundreds (Kyle and Reiter 2013, 389). Some military officials were accused of having used force disproportionately and of

[10] In the literature on conflict resolution, arbitrators can impose a solution to a conflict but mediators cannot. I argue that constitutional courts can be seen as a particular kind of mediator, a "mediator with power" (Uprimny 2004, 69), that share with regular mediators the goal of helping the parties in a conflict to reach an agreement, but at the same time share with regular courts and arbitrators the capacity to impose a legal solution to a conflict. In a nutshell, I argue that constitutional courts can be seen as *commanding mediators*, but I use the shorter phrase *mediators* for simplicity. More details on this aspect of the literature on conflict resolution can be found in Chapter 2.

having violated human rights. Should they be tried in military or civilian courts? For years, in Bolivia cases like these were sent to military courts.[11] But on May 6, 2004 the Bolivian Constitutional Tribunal ruled that military personnel allegedly responsible for human rights violations had to be tried in civilian courts (Sentencia Constitucional 0664/2004-R). In reaction to this ruling, the leaders of the military confined their troops to barracks and held an all-day meeting to decide on a response. In an open letter, the military threatened the court with "grave consequences," and in the ensuing political standoff, the Bolivian president and the high courts dropped their efforts to hold the military accountable (Pion-Berlin 2010, 537–9).

Interestingly, the Bolivian Constitutional Tribunal cited a decision by the Colombian Constitutional Court in support of its ruling, in which the latter argued that the link between a crime and military service, a requisite to be tried in military courts, is severed in cases of grave violations of human rights (C-358 1997 MP Eduardo Cifuentes Muñoz).[12] But in contrast to the Bolivian decision that came suddenly, without a warning, the Colombian one built on a jurisprudential trend of gradual but progressive limitation of the scope of military jurisdiction.[13] Again in contrast to what happened in Bolivia, the Colombian armed forces accepted a ruling that they knew was coming, and they have come to adopt the criteria that military courts should never investigate or try grave human rights violations. The bottom line is this: the question is not whether courts should intervene in these inherently political matters but rather how they should do it. The more they approach the mediator style, the more effective they will be in helping actors solving their own problems.

In this book I advance a *Theory of Constitutional Courts as Mediators* that specifies the conditions under which it is most likely to observe courts playing that role. Essentially, the theory posits that to the extent that constitutional courts are independent, accessible, and have ample powers of judicial review, they are more likely to obtain and credibly transmit relevant information to the actors in a conflict in a way that helps them address the underlying informational causes of their conflict. Constitutional

[11] "In Bolivia, since the transition to democracy in 1982, human rights cases involving members of the military were handled by military tribunals that protected its members and failed to advance cases.... Despite hundreds of deaths at the hands of security forces, there were no convictions from 1985 to 2003" (*Human Rights Watch World Report* 2013).

[12] MP stands for "Magistrado Ponente," the judge who writes the draft of a decision that is discussed by the court.

[13] Details on the jurisprudential line can be found in Chapter 3.

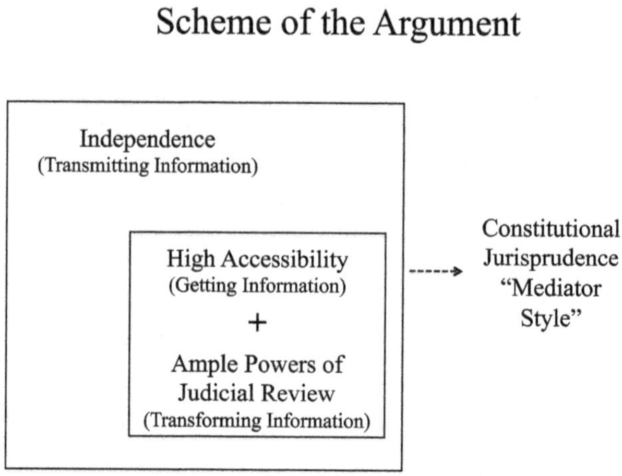

Figure 1.1. In the *Theory of Constitutional Courts as Mediators* judicial independence is a necessary condition. Given independence, more accessible courts with more powers of judicial review would be more likely to produce constitutional jurisprudence that mirrors what mediators do in conflict resolution.

courts that are more accessible gather more conflict-relevant information. Courts with higher judicial review powers – reviewing different types of cases, with higher levels of docket control and higher levels of discretion over how to decide cases – are more able to transform such information into creative and forward-looking jurisprudence. Courts that are more independent are more credible when transmitting such information. Independence is paramount because when judges lack independence they will tend to act as delegates of whoever controls them. Having independence, however, is not enough. Independent courts that are more accessible and that have more judicial review powers are more likely to produce mediator-like jurisprudence. In contrast, when courts do have independence, but they have meager judicial review powers and access to them is very limited, they would tend to behave more as arbitrators than as mediators. The general scheme of the argument is displayed in Figure 1.1.

The foundations of the *Theory of Constitutional Courts as Mediators* lie in the strategic account of judicial behavior. In this account, judges are strategic actors who realize that their ability to achieve their goals depends on the preferences of other actors, the choices they expect others to make, and the institutional context in which they act (Epstein and Knight 1998). The *Theory of Constitutional Courts as Mediators* accounts for the institutional conditions that make it more likely that judges produce jurisprudence of a certain type – what I call informative jurisprudence. Building on scholarship on conflict resolution, judicial politics, and constitutional law, Chapter 2 develops the theory, specifies the mechanisms through which the institutional variables affect judges' constitutional jurisprudence, and engages with concerns such as judges' motivations, alternative explanations of judicial behavior, endogeneity, reverse causality, and compliance with judicial decisions.

Empirical Strategy and Plan of the Book

To empirically evaluate the *Theory of Constitutional Courts as Mediators* I focus on constitutional courts' decisions that are related to military autonomy, the "military's decision making authority that ranges from military education to intelligence gathering to human rights" (Pion-Berlin 1992, 84). I look at cases that reach the constitutional court where some aspect of the military's decision-making authority is challenged. Sometimes these cases never reach the courts: in Chile, in many aspects the poster child for democracy in Latin America, despite the fact that several civilians are still tried in military courts and military autonomy is quite large, the constitutional tribunal has been largely absent from debates about military reform (Pereira and Zaverucha 2005). Other times, judges decide not to decide even in nonsensical ways: in 2009 the Mexican Supreme Court ruled that Ms. Reynalda Morales had no legal standing to petition that the case against the military officials who killed her husband be taken out of the military jurisdiction and transferred to a civilian court (AR 989/2009). The argument was that Ms. Morales lacked the "juridical interest" required to file an *amparo* suit because she was not directly affected by the agents of the state. Yes, the court essentially said that only Ms. Morales's dead husband could file the lawsuit. In short, based on the triad of conflict resolution, I look at cases in which a decision originally made within the armed forces is challenged by the civilian government, a group of legislators, a nongovernmental organization, a citizen, a member of the armed forces ... in general by anyone or any group with legal standing before the constitutional court (see Figure 1.2).[14]

[14] My sample consists of all the cases that reach the constitutional court in which the armed forces as an institution or a military officer are a part (either as plaintiff or defendant). I analyze quantitatively and qualitatively all these cases, and thus did not have to select a subsample of, for instance, "important" cases. However, I do not know the universe of judicial cases where the armed forces partake. In other words, while I analyze the universe

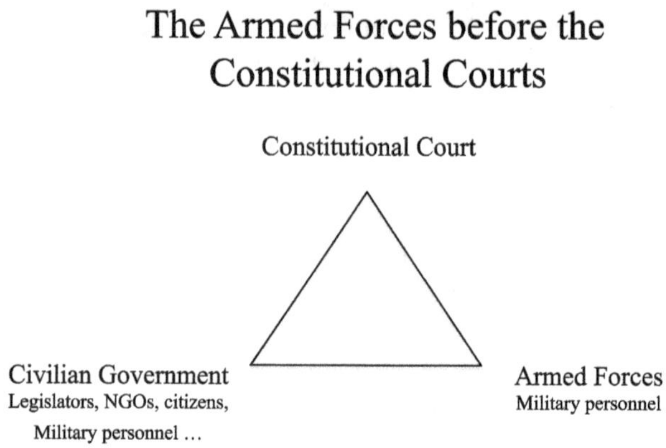

Figure 1.2. Based on the triad of conflict resolution, this book analyzes cases in which a decision originally made within the armed forces is challenged by anyone or any group with legal standing before the constitutional court.

The variable to be explained, therefore, is the constitutional jurisprudence on the armed forces, and more specifically, on military autonomy. In particular, I systematically analyze two types of decisions directly related to military autonomy: cases that reach the constitutional organ challenging a previous decision by a military authority (e.g., a military court, prosecutor, officer, or military administrative agency) and cases that reach the constitutional organ on the scope of the military jurisdiction: a separate body of law, prosecutors, and courts that are created to take into account the specifics of the armed forces' job in order to give stability to the institution and legal security to its members. In the first type of cases, the constitutional organ has to decide whether to uphold the previous decision by a military authority, thus respecting its autonomy, or rather to amend or repeal it, limiting such autonomy. In the second type of cases, the constitutional organ has to provide an answer to the question: Who can be investigated/judged in military courts, and under what circumstances?[15] As stated before, military jurisdiction can be broad, including not only military officials but also civilians, or narrow, including only military officials

of cases that reach the constitutional court, this is a sample of all the judicial cases where the armed forces are involved. I acknowledge this source of bias. When data are available, I offer proxies for the universe of cases. For example, in Mexico I contrast the number of complaints against the military filed before the National Commission of Human Rights with the number of cases that reach the Supreme Court.

15 These are not exclusive categories because sometimes a case on autonomy also touches on the issue of the scope of the military jurisdiction, and vice versa.

for strictly military crimes. In addition, I systematically analyze a subset of cases in which courts navigate the muddled waters of the regulation of the use of lethal force (this is the focus of Chapter 6).

Chapters 3, 4, and 5 systematically analyze the constitutional jurisprudence on military autonomy in Colombia (1958–2013), Peru (1979–2013), and Mexico (1917–2013), respectively.[16] These three countries were selected essentially for the variation they display in the independent variables (Seawright and Gerring 2008), not only within each country across time but also across countries. Specifically, in Colombia (1991), Peru (1993), and Mexico (1994) constitutional replacements or amendments significantly altered the institutional incentives on independence, access, and judicial review powers of the judges serving in the constitutional organ. This allows me to contrast the constitutional jurisprudence on military autonomy before and after such reforms, focusing on the mechanisms through which such institutional incentives produce (or not) mediator-like jurisprudence.[17] Whereas the theory developed in this book strictly applies to democracies, the quite long periods analyzed in the three cases include some nondemocratic periods, which are not excluded so that the narrative flows more naturally and also because they serve as a useful contrast to observe the jurisprudence produced when judicial independence is lacking.

Comparing two moments in time of a single unit implies being subject to the impact of variables that are not necessarily related to one's preferred cause. In general, three types of variables affect this comparison: processes external to the individuals but common to all of them (e.g., environmental factors); processes internal to the individuals such as maturity or learning; and a "bounce" effect produced by starting from a highly unfavorable situation (Glennerster and Takavarasha 2013). I acknowledge the presence and importance of regionwide environmental and learning factors,[18]

[16] The starting point in Colombia (1958) coincides with the end of the military rule, in Peru (1978) with the enactment of the constitution just before the end of a period of military rule, and in Mexico (1917) with the enactment of the constitution after the social revolution.

[17] In Ríos-Figueroa (2011) I present de jure indexes of judicial independence (0 to 6) and of judicial powers that include access (0 to 8). The values on independence before/after the judicial reforms are Colombia 4/4, Peru 4/1, and Mexico 5/5. The values on powers before/after the reform are Colombia: 4/5, Peru 2/3, and Mexico 2/3. There is thus variation across countries within time as well as variation across countries. As I explain in Chapter 2, I use these de jure indexes as a standard against which I compare the actual levels of independence as well as the jurisprudence on military autonomy produced by the constitutional courts. In the empirical chapters, I also take into account the political context that makes the institutional incentives included in these indexes more likely to be effective.

[18] Country-specific environmental factors are considered in the case-study chapters.

such as the tide toward *neoconstitutionalism* (Couso 2010) or the learning that takes place because courts are institutions that value consistency and coherence across time (actually, some historical patterns of interbranch relations have been unveiled, e.g., Kapiszewski 2012). However, the impact of environmental factors, learning, and sticky processes is highly differentiated across countries in Latin America because it is filtered by the political context and the institutional incentives that are the object of interest of this book. Thus, it is not rare to see jurisprudential U-turns (as in Peru) or critical junctures that break with historical patterns of interaction or jurisprudence (as in Colombia). This is not to deny the importance of transnational ideological currents, learned interactions, or principles and values relevant for the judges. The point is that, despite those factors, there is still considerable variation in judicial behavior across Latin American countries that needs to be explained.

In Chapter 7 I empirically evaluate the internal validity of the theory using a most-similar cases research design (Hirschl 2014; Przeworski and Teune 1970) on Colombia (since 1991), Peru (since 2002), and Mexico (since 2000) to investigate the constitutional courts' involvement in regulating the use of force under situations of internal security crisis. Taking advantage of a cross-country variation in the independent variables, I argue that while these countries are similar with regard to relevant variables that may lead to courts regulating the use of force, specifically an internal security crisis faced by the armed forces and competitive democratic elections, they differ in the variables that make it more likely that courts will act as mediators –most notably the level of accessibility to the constitutional court. This chapter is thus an exercise in comparative constitutional law and politics.

In this book, I thoroughly and systematically analyze constitutional jurisprudence in a single-issue area, military autonomy. As argued by Kapiszeweski (2012, 4), studying one policy realm is good as this removes "policy arena" as a potential cause of cross-case and cross-national variation (given that high courts are selectively assertive vis-á-vis national political authorities, and compliance also most likely varies across policy arenas). Of course, this policy realm is also politically relevant and thus a good test for courts. In fact, constitutional jurisprudence on military autonomy is a privileged window for analyzing the role of constitutional courts in a democracy. It is so not only because the dilemma about how to build efficacious armed forces bounded to the rule of law is inherent to democracy, but also because in this book I focus on a sample of cases in which the dilemma is present in its sharpest and most severe form: democracies where the armed forces are dealing with internal security crises. As former Israeli Supreme Court judge Aharon Barak puts it: "Matters of daily life constantly test judges' ability to protect democracy, but judges meet their supreme test in situations of war and terrorism" (Barak 2002, 106).

The three case-study chapters (3, 4, and 5) analyze constitutional courts' decisions on aspects of military autonomy in Latin American countries. This region was marked by military interventions and political instability in the period from the 1920s to the end of the 1970s, but in the last three decades has lived a period of democratic stability. Stability has permitted the region's democracies to exhibit interesting variation on several issues, including civilian-military relations and levels of military autonomy: specifically, the one related to the legacies of military interventions, highly autonomous armed forces, and broad military jurisdictions. Oftentimes, autonomy was exchanged for loyalty to governments, and thus it gave way to unaccountable militaries and impunity for members of the armed forces who committed crimes that had nothing to do with their specialized mission. But such high degrees of military autonomy and lack of accountability are not acceptable for the newly established democracies. Needless to say, some members of the armed forces were used to the previous situation and resist civilian attempts to limit their autonomy.

Constitutional courts, by and large institutional innovations of the last round of transitions to democracy in the Latin American region, enter the scene here: when specific cases on military autonomy reach the court, it is obliged to give reasons to uphold, expand, or limit military autonomy and the scope of this special jurisdiction. Through these decisions, constitutional courts may propose solutions within the democratic constitutional framework that are acceptable to civilian governments and to the armed forces. Moreover, they can also help overcome mutual misunderstandings about the specifics of each actor's preferences and requirements. Alternatively, of course, the constitutional court can evade the issue, simply adjudicate responsibility, and produce arbitration-like jurisprudence, or worse, deteriorate the relations between the civilian government and the armed forces. Latin America thus offers us great variation in the variables of interest, while allowing the researcher to control for general ideological changes, a civil law tradition, and a presidential system of government, all of which may be potential confounders in establishing the links between (1) levels of independence, access, and powers of judicial review and (2) the type of constitutional jurisprudence on the armed forces.

Nonetheless, to illustrate how the constitutional dilemma on the armed forces and the rule of law plays out outside Latin America, Chapter 7 suggests the transferability value of this book's theory (Slater and Ziblatt 2013) by analyzing general patterns of constitutional jurisprudence on the armed forces in cases outside this region that fall within the scope of the argument. Specifically, this chapter analyzes the cases of Israel, Turkey, and Pakistan. In these three countries, for different reasons and in different ways, the army has historically been an important actor in shaping democracy. Constitutional courts in these countries have intervened in military affairs and civilian-military relations, at times producing rich and intriguing jurisprudence. Interestingly, as Chapter 7 shows, variations in levels of independence, access, and powers of judicial review appear to be related to different styles of constitutional jurisprudence in these countries as well.

The last chapter of the book concludes with a discussion of the theoretical and normative implications of the analysis advanced in the book. The chapter argues and shows that the *Theory of Constitutional Courts as Mediators* can be used to analyze constitutional courts' intervention in other classes of conflicts that are also at least partly caused by the types of uncertainty discussed in the preceding text. Specifically, the chapter uses the theory to explain diverse jurisprudential lines in conflicts that involve the right to prior consultation, which essentially requires that indigenous and tribal peoples be consulted on issues that affect them and that trigger the same kind of uncertainties as internal armed conflicts. Finally, the chapter considers the implications of this research on normative debates about access to constitutional courts, judicial independence, and the role of courts in democratic conflict solving. This chapter highlights the role of accessibility to constitutional justice as the main element to trigger the production of mediator-like jurisprudence.

This book incorporates into a unified theoretical framework heretofore unconnected insights from the scholarship on conflict resolution, judicial politics, and constitutional law. By specifying how judicial independence, access to constitutional courts, and powers of judicial review combine to produce jurisprudence, this book builds on, and goes beyond, previous comparative efforts that link institutional incentives to judicial behavior (e.g., Hilbink 2007; Kapiszewski 2012). By specifying the conditions under which institutional incentives are most likely to be effective determinants of judges' behavior this book builds on works that point to the degree of political fragmentation and the public support for courts (e.g., Epstein, Knight, and Shvetsova 2001; Ginsburg 2003; Helmke 2005; Staton 2010;

Vanberg 2005). Finally, by taking jurisprudence seriously this book builds on the suggestions of constitutional law scholars to evaluate the role of a court, taking into account the trajectory of jurisprudence over longer periods of time, as well as the quality and style of this jurisprudence: not whether or not judges should intervene, but rather how they should do so (Hirschl 2014; López Medina 2009; Whittington 2001).

2

A Theory of Constitutional Courts as Mediators

What Do Constitutional Courts Do?

The basic social logic of courts and judges is rooted in the triad for conflict resolution: whenever two actors come into a conflict that they cannot solve themselves, they call upon a third for assistance (Shapiro 1981, 1). According to this simple but universal view of courts, the effectiveness and efficiency of the third party are related to the extent that she is impartial to the issue in dispute and neutral regarding the parties in conflict, as well as to the extent to which she applies preexisting legal norms after adversary proceedings (Shapiro 1981). The immediate role of courts would then be to arbitrate specific disputes of various sorts within a political community.

But courts are also means for achieving other, more general or proximate, normatively appealing goals through the resolution of those specific disputes. For instance, according to modern political thinkers, along with the other branches of government, courts partake in creating a moderate or balanced system of rule. This is what Montesquieu famously called "the liberty of the constitution" in *The Spirit of the Laws*. Montesquieu argued that judges should be either the "mouthpiece of the law … mere passive beings incapable of moderating either its force or rigor" (VI 6), or political actors that "deliberate, communicate their thoughts, argue [… and …] change their minds" (VI 4).[1] There is no contradiction: for Montesquieu the role of judges and of the judicial organ depends on how close a given regime is to the desired moderate government. In republics, where nonarbitrary government is already established by the separation of executive and legislative powers, judges should play a minimum role and the judiciary should be so weak as to become a "null power." But in monarchies, where the executive and legislative powers are concentrated in the king, a

[1] Quotations refer to the book and chapter (e.g., XI, 6) of the English edition of *The Spirit of the Laws* cited in the reference section (Montesquieu 1977).

permanent judicial organ and deliberative judges are necessary for checking power and preserving the balance of government.[2]

Moreover, recent political science scholarship on courts and judges has gone one step further: courts not only check the government, disabling arbitrary actions, but they can also enable the government to reach other goals. Specifically, recent scholarship theorizes on the role that courts play in bringing about normatively appealing outcomes such as regime stability, human rights protection, or investment and economic growth by helping solve commitment, coordination, or cooperation problems. Courts, one argument goes, are devices to make previously made commitments credible, such as constitutional promises to protect property rights, because they can punish deviances from the original commitment (e.g., Ferejohn and Sager 2002; North and Weingast 1989). Courts signaling government misconduct in a highly public fashion, another argument states, enable the people to coordinate their responses in an informed manner in order to control their government (e.g., Law 2009, 730; see also Sutter 1997; Weingast 1997). Courts, finally, can help in solving cooperation dilemmas by receiving and transmitting information in order to reinforce the reputation system, reduce transaction costs, and promote honest exchanges among actors (e.g., Blomquist and Ostrom 2008; Carrubba 2009; Milgrom, North, and Weingast 1990).

Constitutional scholars, by contrast, emphasize that constitutional courts are deliberative institutions that occupy a privileged position in the political system. Judges in constitutional courts weigh reasons for and against an action, they deliberate both internally – among themselves in order to agree on their decisions, and externally – offering reasons for their decisions to the public (Ferejohn and Pasquino 2003, 2010). Judges deliberate and interpret the constitution from a vantage point: at the intersection between a horizontal dimension linking them to the other branches of government and a vertical dimension linking them to citizens. On the horizontal dimension, constitutional judges are in charge of overseeing the functioning of the institutional checks and balances that are the hallmark of the moderate exercise of political power. On the vertical dimension, constitutional judges are responsible for protecting the rights of citizens. In this perspective, constitutional review serves as a catalyst

[2] The great innovation of Hamilton in Federalist 78 is to argue for independent and powerful judicial institutions *in a republic*: "In a monarchy it [the judiciary] is an excellent barrier to the despotism of the prince; in a republic it is a no less excellent barrier to the encroachments and oppressions of the representative body."

to debate as a polity some of the most difficult and fundamental issues that confront them. It forces a people, and its government, to work to reach answers to these questions in order to find solutions and compromises that obtain broad and lasting support (Friedman 2009, 16; see also Rodríguez-Garavito 2011).

The deliberative or dialogical view of constitutional courts emphasizes the fact that constitutional judges are able to weigh in and mix different points of view, asking for opinions and discussion about the possibilities of constitutional interpretation in order to integrate popular, governmental, and other actors' views into constitutional interpretation (cf. Friedman 1993). Recognizing different points of view on the same issue, in turn, makes congressmen, the executive, and other governmental or nongovernmental actors better justify and potentially review their policy decisions. This smoothens the relation between branches of government and other political actors because the court does not just have a resolution about a case but also promotes the analysis and the reconsideration of other political actors' points of view (cf. Gargarella 2008). The dialogue between the court, the public, and the political actors runs both ways, because the court sometimes sets the public debate going, but other times it starts from what the majority, a minority, or a specific political actor raises as a critical issue. In this perspective, in sum, "constitutional judges deliberate through concrete cases that come before them, inviting the political actors and also the public at large to deliberate and reflect on similar issues" (Ferejohn and Pasquino 2010, 358).

But how exactly, and under what conditions, do constitutional courts promote public deliberation and other normatively appealing outcomes? To be clear, constitutional courts can help obtain those goals but they do so through the solution of specific disputes. What makes the difference between courts simply solving specific disputes and courts that in addition contribute to obtaining larger goals is *how* the court goes about solving them. The literature of third-party intervention in conflict resolution describes a very interesting figure, the mediator, who is helpful in answering these questions. In the most general formulation, there is a conflict between two (or more) actors when their manifest pretensions to a certain object or issue are mutually incompatible; thus from the point of view of each one of them the position of the other is an obstacle to making his wish happen (Uprimny 2004, 23). Conflict settlement processes are varied and depend, for instance, on how consensual or adjudicative the process is, how formal or informal, how confidential or public, depending as well as on whether a third party participates in solving a dispute and how much

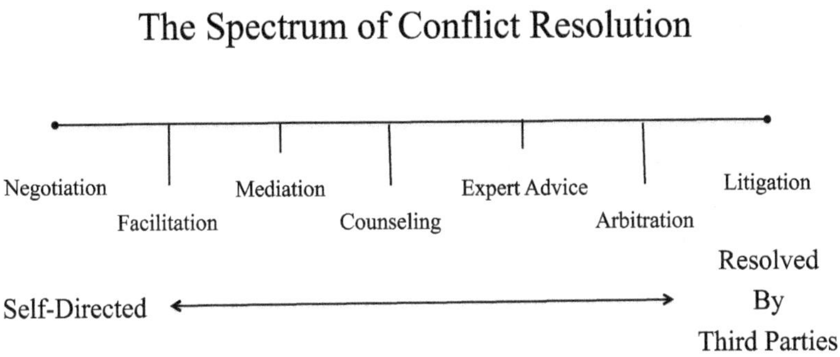

Figure 2.1. Conflict-resolution mechanisms placed along a single dimension that captures the degree of control over the process retained by the parties.

control over the outcome this third party has (cf. Uprimny 2004, 67–9. See also Singer 1994).

When actors have total control over the solution of their conflict the process approaches the ideal of a direct negotiation between the actors. When a third party helps the actors in a conflict to reach a solution but the actors retain much of the control over the process, we find mechanisms such as facilitation, mediation, counseling, or expert advice (see Figure 2.1). As control over the process and the outcome switches from the conflicting parties to the third party, we find mechanisms such as arbitration and ordinary litigation where the third actor listens to presentations made by both sides, examines written materials and other evidence relating to a case, and then makes a determination of who is right and who is wrong, or how a conflict should be settled (see Goldberg et al. 2012; Singer 1994).

Consider the difference between arbitrators and mediators. In contrast to arbitrators that impose a solution based on their assessment of the record, mediators suggest a structure and a process on the discussions that is designed to move the parties toward mutual understanding and win-win agreements. Far from imposing a solution, mediators facilitate agreements by helping each party to understand the other party's views about the nature of the problem and how they think it might best be solved. By clarifying the divergent views and reasons for those views, mediators can get the parties to develop a common understanding of the situation. To do so, mediators often try to get the disputants to focus on underlying interests (the things they really need or want) more than their initial opening positions (what they initially say they need or want) (see Bush and Folger 2004).

As the literature on third-party mediation in international conflicts clearly puts it, the mediator faces two key challenges: "First, there is the problem of the mediator's acquisition of conflict-relevant information. Second, there is the problem of credibly communicating this relevant information to the parties to the conflict" (Fey and Ramsay 2010, 530; Kydd 2003, 600). By and large, the literature of international relations has focused on the issue of credibility and left behind the question of how the mediator obtains relevant information (Fey and Ramsay 2010, 530). What makes a mediator credible in transmitting information has in fact generated interesting debates. Some authors argue that the mediator needs to be impartial in the sense of not sharing completely the preferences of any of the actors in the dispute (Kydd 2006; Smith and Stam 2004).[3] Other authors add that whereas mediators may share the preferences of one of the parties, it is critical that they are neutral to the issue in dispute, that is, that they do not strongly prefer a particular solution to the conflict (Rauchhaus 2006). In contrast, how the mediator acquires conflict-relevant information has been largely resolved by assuming that she somehow gets it, an assumption that "may be acceptable if the mediator has independent sources of information, but many mediators have no obvious source of reliable information external to the negotiations themselves" (Kydd 2010, 117).

I build on the argument that successful third-party mediators should be impartial to the parties in dispute, in the sense of not sharing the preferences of one of the parties in the conflict (Uprimny 2004, 73–5; see also Bush and Folger 2004; Fisher, Ury, and Bruce 2011), because this addresses the two key challenges that mediators face. First, this impartiality is critical to a mediator's capacity to obtain relevant information from the parties, who would not trust a biased mediator with conflict-relevant or private information. Second, impartiality is also a source of credibility for the mediator at the moment of transmitting information. In sum, impartiality is essential for successful mediation because it addresses how the mediator gets conflict-relevant information and how the mediator effectively and credibly transmits such information.

Because the mediator's role essentially consists of receiving, processing, and transmitting information, he or she is most successful when the cause of conflict between two actors is uncertainty, simply because in those cases a third-party mediator can facilitate cooperation by providing relevant information that reduces such uncertainty (cf. Gilligan and Johns

[3] However, Kydd had argued that in a bargaining context a mediator biased toward a party can be credible (Kydd 2003; see also Favretto 2009). For example, in the conflict between Egypt and Israel over the Sinai Peninsula in 1978, Egypt accepted the United States as a mediator "because being an ally of its adversary made it credible that it could make Israel negotiate and settle an agreement" (Uprimny 2004, 87).

2012; Kydd 2006). Of course, there can be uncertainty over different things. For instance, actors can be uncertain about whether the other side prefers to reciprocate cooperation or to exploit it (Kydd 2006, 454). Asymmetric information can also be a cause of conflict: actors can have private information about their own resolve, relative power, or costs for conflict. For instance, if one or both sides overestimate their own chance of winning or their opponent's costs of conflict, they may stick to positions that are irreconcilable.[4] Finally, there can be uncertainty over the appropriate solution to their conflict, assuming there is one. For instance, actors may not know or understand well all the alternatives to the conflict because of their unilateral view of the problem and a misperception of the other actor's interests or point of view (cf. Kydd 2006, 2010). In sum, it is critical to identify the specific type of uncertainty so that the mediator can effectively reduce it.

Constitutional Courts as Mediators

The dialogical or deliberative literature on constitutional courts illuminates the role of constitutional courts in a democracy, but it falls short when we want to identify the conditions under which we can find such a rich exercise of constitutional review. The literature of political science on the role of courts in producing appealing outcomes, such as regime stability or economic growth, illuminates the theoretical function that courts play in producing those proximate outcomes, but forgets about the actual immediate role of courts resolving specific disputes. The literature on third-party involvement in conflict resolution describes a specific figure, the mediator, whose function is strikingly similar to that of a deliberative court, and specifies the conditions under which third-party mediation is more likely to be effective. However, unlike mediators, judges do have the capacity to impose decisions on the conflicting parties based on their reading of the law. Whereas each body of literature fails to provide by itself a full account of the role of constitutional courts, each one provides valuable insights that I combine into a *Theory of Constitutional Courts as Mediators*.

Specifically, I argue that constitutional courts can be seen as a particular kind of mediator, a "mediator with power" (Uprimny 2004, 69), that shares with regular mediators the goal of helping the parties in a conflict to reach an agreement, but at the same time share with regular courts and

[4] Asymmetric information also creates incentives to bluff, to claim to be strong and unmoved by the costs of war in order to persuade the other side to make further concessions (Kydd 2010, 106).

arbitrators the capacity to impose a legal solution to a conflict. This *commanding mediator* uses resources at his or her disposal (such as argumentation, incentives, and sanctions) to actively influence the actors to reach an agreement. Constitutional courts as mediators reduce a specific type of uncertainty that is related to constitutional disputes between actors that involve interpreting the principles, values, and "rules of the game" that undergird a particular democratic regime.[5] In particular, constitutional courts can contribute to reducing (1) the uncertainty on the legal consequences of certain actions, (2) the uncertainty on the bounds of the exceptions and the weight of extraordinary circumstances, and (3) the uncertainty about how to balance clashing constitutional principles or rules in particular cases.

In a nutshell, the *Theory of Constitutional Courts as Mediators* posits that constitutional courts that are independent, are accessible, and have ample powers of judicial review can obtain, process, and credibly transmit relevant information to reduce the uncertainty that is causing a conflict between two or more actors.[6] Specifically, independence is linked to the court's credibility. Access is related to the court's capacity to get information. And powers of judicial review are related to the court's capacity to transmit such information in an effective manner. In this theory, independent, accessible, and powerful constitutional courts transmit information through their jurisprudence, which has to have certain characteristics for reducing uncertainty and enhancing cooperation. Let us look closer, define with precision, and operationalize the concepts of judicial independence, judicial access, and powers of judicial review and explain how they combine to produce informative, mediator-like jurisprudence.

Judicial Independence: Credibility in Obtaining and Transmitting Information

In the most basic scheme of courts as third-party dispute settlers (Shapiro 1981) "independence" is the bedrock for judges' legitimacy before the

[5] As Oliver Wendell Holmes put it, "Behind the logical form of judicial decisions lies a judgment as to the relative worth and importance of competing legislative grounds, often an inarticulate and unconscious judgment, it is true, and yet the very root and nerve of the whole proceeding" (Holmes 1992, 167).

[6] Not all conflicts are caused by one of the types of uncertainty described. Some conflicts are more distributional in nature. Others are more related to identity concerns where some kind of recognition is sought after. Moreover, some conflicts have informational, distributional, and identity-related causes. The *Theory of Constitutional Courts as Mediators* directly applies to conflicts caused primarily by uncertainty.

parties in the dispute, the political actors, and the public at large (see, e.g., Bybee 2010). Without independence judges are delegates of those who control them, undermining the credibility of the information they could transmit because it will tend to be biased toward the views of the controllers. At the broadest level, "independence" of judicial institutions and actors "expresses the aspiration that judicial decisions should not be influenced in an inappropriate manner by considerations judged to be normatively irrelevant" (Vanberg 2009).[7] A familiar distinction in the literature involves the difference between de facto and de jure concepts. The latter deals with formal rules designed to insulate judges from undue pressure, either from outside the judiciary or from within. The concept of de facto judicial independence is behavioral and involves both the idea that judges are the "authors of their own opinions" (Kornhauser 2002, 42–55), that his or her decisions reflect his or her preferences, and also that judges' decisions are enforced in practice (Cameron 2002).

In order to gauge independence I look at de jure incentives that allegedly motivate judges to decide based on his or her preferences. These incentives are of two types. The first impact on whether the preferences of a judge diverge from those of the parties in the case and are contained in appointment mechanisms. The second set of incentives, contained in tenure and removal mechanisms, impact on the extent to which judges can evaluate the cases before them free from undue pressures. Consider the first type: constitutional judges decide over a wide diversity of issues with a similarly wide diversity of parties, but one of the main parties before them is the government. The government, that is, the executive branch, many times is a defendant or a plaintiff in cases before the constitutional court; but many other times when it does not directly appear before the court, it is an indirect party (together with the legislative branch) because the result of the decision involves them (e.g., if they have to pass legislation, appropriate funds, or exercise the authority of the state in some other form). Thus, I focus on incentives that promote divergence of preferences between the judges and the government.[8]

The appointment mechanism works in various ways. For instance, it affects the chances that judges with preferences distinct from those of the executive and the legislative arrive at the court. Consider the distinction

[7] Of course, political authorities always apply some pressure when they are parties to a case or when they file briefs as interested parties (e.g., *amicus curiae* briefs and other similar institutions). The key here is that this pressure is acceptable within the rules of the legal system.

[8] This would capture the impartiality required for successful mediation as described in the conflict-resolution literature.

between "veto players" and "quota" appointment mechanisms. Veto-player judicial appointments require the consent of at least two actors (e.g., the president and the majority of the senate), and they tend to produce more "centrist" judges if the preferences of those actors differ. However, quota appointments give a certain number of the seats in the court to different organs that fill them unilaterally (e.g., the president and the senate each appoint three judges). Notice that while "quota" mechanisms would tend to produce more "extreme" judges, judges who share the preferences of their appointers, the court overall could be "moderate" or "balanced" to the extent that the preferences of the appointing actors diverge.

The institutional and partisan identity of the appointer also matters. When the executive is the appointer, she would tend to appoint persons identified with, or closer to, the executive's agenda that is influenced both by the executive's personal characteristics and also by those of the party to which she belongs. In contrast, legislative-appointed judges are selected through a bargaining process among parties with representation in congress and thus would more closely reflect the interests, ideology, and bargaining power of the parties. Finally, when a court or a judicial organ is the appointer, it would tend to propose candidates identified with the interests of the judicial branch, interests that are related to the legitimacy of the organ, the protection of its institutional interests, and the development of jurisprudence. Of course, in veto-player appointment systems the preferences of the appointers are subject to the restriction of what the organ that ratifies is willing to accept. The effects of the appointment method on the type of judges may be reinforced if the constitutional organ is located outside the judiciary. Notice also that the so-called co-optation method, that is, when courts appoint judges unilaterally, may promote divergence of interests between the judicial and the elected branches; but this depends on how the first set of judges is selected (their preference will tend to persist).[9]

Appointment mechanisms vary considerably (Malleson and Russell 2003). In a general way, for judges' preferences to diverge from the executive's preferences the appointment procedure should meet the following condition:

(i) At least two different organs of government with different interests (e.g., president and congress from different parties; the supreme court

[9] This method may also pose obstacles to the injection of new ideas and creative jurisprudential approaches from outside of the judiciary, producing a sort of crystallization of the jurisprudence. Whether co-optation systems promote divergence of preferences, thus, should be analyzed in each particular case.

and the president; a judicial council and congress, etc. . . .) appoint constitutional judges, or in quota systems a single organ does not appoint a majority of judges.

Consider now the second type of incentives, those contained in tenure and removal mechanisms and that foster judges' being the "authors of their own opinions" (Kornhauser 2002, 42–5). If tenure is too short, constitutional judges face incentives to curry favor with both the current and the incoming government with an eye on their next employment. Their views on issues, therefore, will likely be unduly influenced by what these parties prefer. Tenure need not be for life, but it should give judges a sufficiently long time horizon so that autonomous behavior is incentivized. A long tenure also allows judges to have broader horizons, which is key to their not only thinking about the specific interaction between the actors in the case before them, but also about the future relation between them. If judges' tenure is short they are incentivized to proceed with urgency, whereas a longer tenure and greater access allows them to proceed gradually, knowing that they will probably have more opportunities in the future to decide on a certain issue. Similarly, if removal procedures are too easy judges face a credible threat of removal if they vote their mind, given that their preferences diverge from those of the executive and the legislative.[10] A credible threat of removal, in other words, also encourages judges' views on the cases that they decide to be unduly influenced by the interests of those who can remove them.

In general, tenure and removal mechanisms should meet the following conditions in order for judges to have incentives to sincerely and autonomously evaluate cases:

(ii) The length of tenure of judges is at least longer than the appointer's tenure; and
(iii) The process to remove judges is initiated by at least two-thirds of the legislature where a single party does not control such supermajority, and never by the executive.

In sum, theoretically, independence is a necessary condition for judges to be credible third-party mediators. They need this to be true so that

[10] See Helmke and Staton (2011, 332–24). Notice that the length of tenure and the removal mechanism could also indirectly affect the type of judges that arrive at the court (e.g., judges' preferences) through a self-selection mechanism. For example, some judges who value things other than simply being a member of the constitutional court (e.g., their reputation as a neutral and balanced judge) would not even want to be considered for this position as tenure is too short or removal procedures too easy.

parties bring cases to them; otherwise the solution to the dispute would be a foregone conclusion. And judges also need this independence so that parties accept the court's decision without suspicion of systematic bias or undue influence. Without independence, judges would act as delegates of those who appoint or can remove them, making any information that the judges may transmit noncredible.

Access to Constitutional Courts: Acquisition of Conflict-Relevant Information

Access to constitutional courts is directly related to how courts get information, how much and how good information, and also to how often they can decide on the same issue. This is a critical element of the *Theory of Constitutional Courts as Mediators*. Constitutional courts are in a privileged position to learn how existing rules work in application through reviewing how they work in individual controversies (e.g., Clark and Staton 2013; Rogers 2001; Whittington 2003). For example, when the court gets cases challenging a particular actor's respect for fundamental human rights, the court gets important information about the general degree of discretion such actor should be granted. More access also implies that more actors can more easily sound the "fire alarm" (McCubbins and Schwartz 1984) so that the court learns where things are departing from the proper constitutional bounds.

In a nutshell, access is crucial because the more cases reach the court, the more the court learns about the conflict and the performance of the actors, and the more information it can transmit. Notice that the constitutional court receives information not only about how the law is being applied, but also on the conflict that is driving the parties to the court. Moreover, this conflict-relevant information comes from both parties in the case, plaintiff and defendant, which allows the court to learn both sides of the same issue.[11] In addition, the constitutional court also directly gets information on a particular topic or actor from amicus briefs, other government actors (e.g., the solicitor general or the *procurador*), international court rulings, or experts who can be summoned

[11] Note that this is not necessarily private information of the parties, but rather each party's argumentation, views, and assessment of the issue in dispute. Moreover, courts receive amicus briefs, experts' assessments, and so on. In this sense, courts have sources of information that are independent of the parties' own private information and thus could solve the acquisition and transmission of information problems simultaneously (see Fey and Ramsay 2010).

by the court.[12] Notice that I include the jurisprudence by international courts, such as the Inter American Court of Human Rights (IACHR), as additional information that the national courts can use (or not). The reason is that national courts and litigants will tend to use international court rulings that behoove them, and try to ignore, delay, or minimize those that do not (cf. Hunneus 2012).

Constitutional judges with a continuous flow of cases will not only get more and more varied information, but will also be more able to express their jurisprudential preferences under more favorable circumstances (cf. Epstein, Knight, and Shvetsova 2001; Graber 1998; Scheppele 2003). If judges receive only a few scattered cases, the lack of information is compounded by the fact that the chances that these cases arrive under nonfavorable political circumstances are relatively higher. Moreover, wide and easy access to instruments of constitutional review implies that more and more diverse cases on the same issue reach the judges, allowing them to make subtler distinctions. On the contrary, when legal standing is restricted to state actors, not only the court gets fewer cases but this also implies fewer external sources of information. Notice that while some institutional elements other than standing requirements augment the flow of cases, such as the automatic constitutional review of certain governmental decisions, still others reduce it, such as time restrictions for challenging laws or certain government actions.

To assess the degree of access to constitutional courts I focus on the scope of legal standing before the courts as is established in the constitutional text. In other words, I look at how many instruments of constitutional review there are in a country and who are the actors that can use them. For instance, in some countries such as Mexico only political authorities can file constitutional challenges against laws in the abstract, but in other countries such as Colombia any citizen can file this type of suit. The logic of the indicator is simply that the more instruments for constitutional review with broader legal standing, the more accessible the court is.

[12] In *Ex parte Peterson*, 253 U.S. 300 (1920), the U.S. Supreme Court stated: "Courts have, in the absence of prohibition, inherent power to provide themselves with the instruments required for the performance of their duties, which include the authority to appoint fact-finding referees, to issue injunctions to the parties in a case, and require discovery of information and documents, etc." (cited in Blomquist and Ostrom 2008, 186). Blomquist and Ostrom argue that "courts' use of these powers in water resource disputes, for instance, has enabled water users and other interested parties to develop information about resource conditions and to negotiate rules allocating resource use" (186).

Powers of Constitutional Review: Processing and Transforming Information

The powers of constitutional review of a court are directly related to how the court processes and transmits the information that it gets. In other words, they are directly related to whether the court can produce informative and creative, that is, mediator-like, jurisprudence. Powers of constitutional review are related to how many different types of cases the court gets (e.g., abstract or concrete, a priori and a posteriori), to how much control over its docket a court has,[13] and to how much discretion a court has over the particular way in which a decision is processed and framed. A court that has discretion over its docket and sentencing guidelines can avoid cornering one actor, asking her or him to comply with a resolution that is highly unlikely to be complied with, strategically managing conflict between the actors, and avoiding setbacks for its own decisions. Discretion in picking cases also matters for efficiency, especially when the flow of cases to the court is very high (Clark and Strauss 2010).

Docket control and discretion on how to decide cases allow judges to better transmit information to the actors involved in a dispute and to better manage confrontation levels with and among them. Constitutional judges who can pick their legal battles can reduce the costs associated with their decisions. Flexibility on how to decide cases is greater when, for instance, there are no limits on time to disposition of cases, no limits on the topics that can be challenged with a given instrument, or no instrument-dependent effects of judicial decisions.[14] This last type of flexibility also helps judges to tailor their sentencing guidelines in order to reduce the likelihood of noncompliance, promote deliberation and cooperation, and minimize the chances of setbacks for their decisions. Supermajority or unanimity requirements for reaching a decision of unconstitutionality impose constraints on how courts decide cases, especially in internal deliberation.

[13] The writ of certiorari in the case of the United States is the obvious and most famous example. Most countries do not give to constitutional judges something like the certiorari power but some recognize the possibility of choosing which cases to hear from one type of instrument but not others (e.g., the *tutela* in Colombia). Other countries give judges the possibility to take on some cases that are heard in lower courts when they consider them important enough (e.g., Mexico and Argentina).

[14] For example, instruments of concrete review usually produce *inter partes* effects while instruments of abstract review generate *erga omnes* effects. Notice also that constitutional judges who enjoy more flexibility on how to decide on cases are also regularly freer to use international court rulings to reduce the levels of confrontation.

To assess powers of review of constitutional courts I look at the incentives set in formal mechanisms of judicial review. These incentives impact the flexibility judges have in picking and choosing which cases to hear, as well as how they go about debating and deciding them. These incentives are contained in the characteristics of the instruments for judicial review available in a country (e.g., the *amparo* suit, the action of constitutionality, or constitutional controversy), including how hard it is to file these instruments, whether the court is legally obliged to decide on the case once it has been filed, who is affected by decisions on them, whether there are any supermajority requirements implied in making decisions, or whether they are part of the original jurisdiction of the constitutional court or reach the court through an appeals process.

Caveats with Using De Jure Indicators

I assess levels of independence, access, and powers of judicial review by looking at formal rules established in constitutions. I am not interested in the formal rules per se but rather, as explained before, in the incentives they are likely to place on judges. De jure measures are good because they are comparable across countries, comparable across time within the same country, and reproducible by any person who looks at the legal texts and follows the coding rules. They also allow getting proxy measures of specific concepts of interest distinguishing, for instance, access from independence and powers. However, de jure measures also present important challenges (see, e.g., Ginsburg and Melton 2013; Ríos-Figueroa and Staton 2012). At least two are critical and should be addressed. First, the incentives that formal rules allegedly establish are not directly observable and thus depend upon a theoretical framework that makes them plausible. I have tried to specify theoretically why and how certain incentives on independence, access, and powers are likely to induce judicial behavior that is more sincere, forward looking, and cautious.

Second, the actual operation of the formal rules may diverge from what they are intended to produce. In this regard, it is important to note that I use the de jure incentives as a standard about what is expected regarding judicial decisions and then I contrast against this standard a pattern of actual decisions in the countries under study (see Pozas-Loyo and Ríos-Figueroa 2007). In addition, I take into consideration the political context under which the institutional incentives are likely to be more effective (e.g., Epstein, Knight, and Shvetsova 2001; Scheppele 2003). Specifically, because institutions do not work in a vacuum (the social, political, and economic contexts in which they operate condition their effectiveness), it has been argued that the extent to which the executive and legislative branches can coordinate against a judicial decision that affects them, and the public support for the court, increases de facto judicial independence. Larger government's share of legislative seats, to the point that the government enjoys a majority in congress, means that governments could more easily react against an unwelcome judicial decision, thus making judges behave strategically, falsifying their preferences (when they diverge from the executive's) to prevent a backlash.[15] In addition, public support can back the court even in the contexts of unified government, lowering the costs for the court of making decisions against the executive and legislative, and serving as a kind of backing force in case of retaliation by a threat to punish politicians in the next election (e.g., Gibson, Caldeira, and Baird 1998; Staton 2010; Vanberg 2005). (Because public opinion also affects compliance with judicial decisions, I discuss it in more detail in the following text.)

In the particular case of access, we also know that it is only partially determined by the requirements on legal standing before the court because it is also influenced by the capacities of actors to actually bring cases to the constitutional court. Specifically, the literature on judicialization argues that for cases to reach the court the following are necessary: a structure of legal opportunity, a structure of support for legal mobilization, and also an institutional framework that facilitates litigation (e.g., Epp 1998; Smulovitz 2010; Wilson 2006). Moreover, actual judicial decisions can encourage or disincentive potential litigants with similar cases (Gauri and Brinks 2008; Helmke and Staton 2011). In the chapters on case studies, I trace these aspects of access to justice and judicialization more closely.

What Does "Informative Jurisprudence" Look Like?

Regular mediators provide information using their communication skills, in formal and in informal meetings with one or both of the actors in a dispute. Constitutional judges do not do this: they produce written decisions, taking into account the facts of the case, previous decisions on similar cases, the constitution, the arguments of the parties, and other relevant

[15] For a discussion on the effect of fragmentation on judicial behavior see (Aydın 2013; Hilbink 2012; Leiras et al. 2015; Popova 2012; Ríos-Figueroa 2007). The expectation of alternation in office in a sufficiently competitive political environment also incentivizes the political actors to maintain judicial review (Stephenson 2003).

sources of information. In a word, constitutional judges produce jurisprudence. Still, I argue that courts can act as *commanding mediators*. It is thus important to specify some of the characteristics that should be present in jurisprudence so that it approaches the informational role played by regular mediators. The literature on conflict resolution, coupled with the deliberative literature on constitutional courts, is a useful guide in this endeavor.

Mediator-like constitutional jurisprudence should reflect the fact that the actors that are parties in a given case are likely to maintain a relationship afterward. As discussed in Chapter 1, this jurisprudence should aim at solutions that transcend the present conflict and look forward to forging a creative solution that integrates the views of the actual actors in the dispute with the more permanent roles of the institutions, groups, or principles that they represent. Moreover, mediator-like jurisprudence should be aimed at transforming not only the actors' behavior but also their attitudes and preferences because these are more stable and last longer.

Successful mediators distinguish between the particular issue that created the conflict, its underlying causes, and the specific actors that are involved in it (Fisher, Ury, and Bruce 2011). Constitutional courts' jurisprudence should mirror what successful mediators do. Specifically, mediator-like jurisprudence should be clearly argued and based on the constitutional principle, right, or norm that is behind the issue in dispute. Mediator-like jurisprudence should use the most objective criteria available to search for mutually acceptable solutions, or at least to discuss the terms of the potential agreement. For constitutional courts, this means providing a robust interpretation of constitutional principles and rules as the standard that drives the suggested solutions.

Mediator-like jurisprudence should avoid producing clear winners and losers and shaming actors. One way to do this is for a court to present its reasoning on a certain issue in advance of deciding against the party whose behavior is not compatible with that reasoning. Announcing in advance the view of the court on a certain issue, when the court knows that the issue will come before it again in the future, is one way to help prepare the actors for a decision that will force them to modify their behavior. This is not unfamiliar to courts and can be traced back to the famous *Marbury v. Madison* decision in which Justice Marshall conceded the outcome of the case to the defendant but the ruling to the plaintiff. A related way to avoid shaming actors is for courts not to ask for strict compliance in cases in which this will be difficult to get, but instead to provide a road map for the actors involved in a conflict so that they can adapt their behavior and eventually fully comply with the courts' decision (see Dixon 2007; Gargarella 2008; Rodríguez-Garavito 2011).

Finally, another way to avoid producing winners and losers is for the court to "give and take." In other words, to study in detail and comprehend the positions of the actors in order to suggest that actors interchange concessions of diverse priority in such a way that both actors obtain satisfaction on points that they consider most important (cf. Fisher, Ury, and Bruce 2011). For instance, in the conflict between Egypt and Israel, much used in the literature on international relations, Egypt wanted to recover sovereignty over the Sinai Peninsula as a matter of national dignity, whereas Israel wanted to partially control the peninsula as a matter of national security. The solution was to cede complete sovereignty to Egypt but creating a demilitarized zone under international supervision (Uprimny 2004). Constitutional courts can also "give some" to an actor in a conflict while "taking some" from him or her. This is more easily done when actors are recurrent parties before the court, which is often the case once the court is able to distinguish between the specific identity of the actor and the institution, group, or principle that she or he represents.

In a nutshell, mediator-like jurisprudence is not case circumscribed; it is creative, forward looking, nonshaming, and transparent in its argumentation that should be robustly grounded on constitutional principles and norms. The argument of this book is that this kind of jurisprudence is more likely to be produced by courts that are more independent, broadly accessible, and have ampler powers of constitutional review. In contrast, when courts do have independence but they have meager powers of judicial review and access to them is very limited, they would tend to act as "arbitrators," not as mediators. A court behaving as an arbitrator simply determines the outcome of a case based on the record adjudicating responsibility between disputing parties. In other words, arbitrator-like jurisprudence lacks the characteristics of mediator-like jurisprudence. Finally, when courts are not independent they tend to reflect the viewpoint of the actor to whom they are subordinated, and they would act as mere delegates. Table 2.1 summarizes the propositions of the *Theory of Constitutional Courts as Mediators* when the variables take extreme values.

Judges' Motivations and Alternative Explanations for Judicial Behavior

The foundations of the *Theory of Constitutional Courts as Mediators* lie in the strategic account of judicial behavior. On this account, judges are strategic actors who realize that their ability to achieve their goals depends on

Table 2.1. *Conditions of different roles for constitutional courts*

Courts as ...	High level of independence	Wide access	Ample powers of judicial review
Delegates	NO		
Arbitrators	YES	NO	NO
Mediators	YES	YES	YES

the preferences of other actors, the choices they expect others to make, and the institutional context in which they act (Epstein and Knight 1998). The *Theory of Constitutional Courts as Mediators* accounts for the institutional conditions that make it more likely that judges will produce jurisprudence of a certain type, what I have called *informative jurisprudence*. The theory's emphasis on institutions that constrain and enable judges to interpret the constitution assumes that judges' preferences or motivations are a complex mix of policy influence, satisfaction of both personal and professional goals, and institutional building (see Epstein and Knight 2013). The levels of independence, access, and powers of judicial review thus allow or hinder judges in carrying out their motivations. The idea is that, given independence, the higher the level of access and powers of judicial review enjoyed by judges, the better able they would be to completely carry out the fullest potential of a judge's job, which is to solve conflicts and provide some greater public goods through conflict resolution.[16]

James Gibson's dictum still serves as a basic guide for determinants of judges' decisions, which are "a function of what they prefer to do, tempered by what they think they ought to do, but constrained by what they perceived is feasible to do" (Gibson 2008, 516). In other words, to explain judicial decisions one needs to look at the constraints and capabilities expressed in the institutional and political context ("what judges perceive is feasible to do," the focus of this book), at judges' ideological

[16] To be clear, I am not arguing that institutional incentives automatically produce a certain type of jurisprudence. Rather, the institutional environment in which judges work make it more likely that they will produce a certain type of jurisprudence. If we could have the exact same judge (having a specific ideology, concerns for the judicial branch, preferences over leisure and work, etc.) working in two different institutional environments, we could see differences in his or her jurisprudence developed over time that could be in principle attributed to the institutional incentives. An analogy would be a professor moving from one academic department where a certain kind of research is incentivized to another where the incentives point toward different research topics, methodologies, or outlets.

predispositions (i.e., "what they prefer to do," which is the focus of the attitudinal model [Segal and Spaeth 2002]), and at judges' perception of the law and their ideas about how a judge should do his work (i.e., "what they think they ought to do," which is the focus of the legal model).

The attitudinal model argues that policy preferences summarized in the liberal-conservative continuum largely determine judges' decisions. So, even if the appointment, tenure, and removal mechanisms meet the requirements mentioned in the preceding text, the ideological composition of the court may be such that judges' personal views are strong and consistent enough to determine most decisions (and, of course, they may be very close to those of, say, the executive). This is a stronger explanation to the extent that a single ideological dimension underlies the political space, making ideology a good predictor of behavior across many different issues and branches of government. In the countries analyzed in depth in this book a single ideological space underlying politics is the exception rather than the rule.[17] Moreover, the attitudinal model depends on institutional and historical characteristics of the U.S. Supreme Court that are difficult to find elsewhere, such as appointments for life, close to zero probability of removal, and absence of a higher or more prestigious court or position. In Latin America, in contrast, we find shorter tenures, frequent constitutional changes that imply reshuffling in courts, a history of arbitrary removals, and the existence of higher or more prestigious positions either in politics or in places such as the IACHR (e.g., Castagnola and Pérez-Liñán 2009). Even in the United States, studies show that ideological attitudes alone do not completely explain patterns of judicial decisions (see Epstein and Knight 2013). Nonetheless, in the chapters on Colombia, Peru, and Mexico I look specifically at whether the ideological composition of the constitutional courts is a variable that systematically explains judges' behavior.

The impact of ideas about how judges should do their work or what they actually do is another factor that explains constitutional jurisprudence.[18] I acknowledge the presence and importance of these ideas but I think they do not determine my outcome of interest, that is, the constitutional jurisprudence on military autonomy. Specifically, an ideological factor that

[17] For example, the ideological position on economic matters in many cases tends to diverge from the ideological position on moral issues. The federal/national versus state/local cleavage oftentimes also appears as a relevant dimension that influences judicial behavior.

[18] In Mexico, e.g., what can be called the "self-conception of the role of judge" is an ideological dimension that has been shown to be relevant for Supreme Court Judges (Magaloni, Sánchez, and Magar 2011).

affects all individuals in the countries included in my study is the move toward what has been called *neoconstitutionalism* (Couso 2010). In contrast to the positivist/formalistic position that for decades was dominant in Latin American judiciaries, in the last three decades a new approach that acknowledges the open nature of legal texts and rules has gained acceptance, making courts loosen their formalist straitjackets. However, the impact of *neoconstitutionalism* on jurisprudence is highly differentiated across countries in Latin America because it is filtered through the political context and the institutional incentives that are the object of interest of this book (cf. Hilbink 2007). A case in point is Venezuela, once a leading country in ideological matters of the justice system and nowadays a country where nonindependent judges act as delegates of the government (Pérez-Perdomo 2010).

Finally, the legal model provides another explanation for constitutional jurisprudence that is, not surprisingly, the constitution: if the interpretation of the constitution changes the primary cause should be that the constitution changes. Interestingly, in the cases under study, the articles of the constitution that specify military autonomy and the scope of military jurisdiction (the two topics analyzed in detail in this book) are remarkably constant even among different constitutions within the same country. Nonetheless, as I will show, jurisprudential patterns do vary, suggesting that something other than "the (constitutional) law" is driving these changes. Of course, when other articles of a new constitution change, this may affect how judges interpret a specific article that remains the same. But to engage in such "systemic interpretation" of the constitution, or something along these lines, actually implies that judges enjoy not only independence but also broad powers of judicial review and probably broad access, too, which is the point of this book.

Endogeneity, Reverse Causality, and Compliance

It is worthwhile to address these concerns theoretically, even if they are addressed again in the following empirical chapters. As explained in Chapter 1, to evaluate empirically the *Theory of Constitutional Courts as Mediators* I take advantage of cross-country and within-country variations in the institutional conditions that make the production of mediator-like constitutional jurisprudence more likely. In other words, I see if a change from less to more independence, access, and powers of judicial review is accompanied by a change in judicial behavior that approaches the analogy of the mediator. I use key judicial reforms to identify the before and after periods, because in these reforms it is possible to look at the constitutional changes on the incentives analyzed in this book. The assumption here is that institutional changes are related to the behavioral changes observable in judges' decisions. This raises an endogeneity concern that can be stated as follows: Is it possible that a third variable Z is causing both X (institutional reforms on the judiciary) and Y (judge's constitutional interpretation)?

What variable Z can cause both X (institutional design of constitutional justice) and Y (constitutional jurisprudence)? A clear candidate for Z in this book is democratization, which we know drives the enacting of new constitutions or amendments to existing ones, oftentimes including judicial reforms, and also impacts the working of the new institutions in a politically competitive context. However, notice first that not all democratic transitions are accompanied by new constitutions. Actually, the replacement and amendment of constitutions is itself determined by a complex set of factors (Negretto 2013). Moreover, whereas democratization may promote the empowerment of judges at the constituent moment, we do observe diversity in institutional design and in jurisprudence. In other words, while democratization may be related to judicial reform and to judges' behavior the influence is not unidirectional and determinant.[19]

In particular cases, there may be other variables related to both the institutional reform of constitutional justice and the judges' interpretation of the constitution. For instance, in Colombia one such variable is the violence that during the 1980s was so critical that it was partly addressed with the creation of the Constitution of 1991. This constitution, which created an independent, accessible, and powerful constitutional court, started to be enforced in the 1990s in a context in which violence was still at critical levels, arguably influencing how judges interpreted the constitution. I address case-specific underlying variables in the chapters on case studies. Suffice

[19] Political competition is a more concrete version of the "democratization" variable. The argument would be that, once the factors that trigger constitutional replacement and amendment are in place, higher levels of political competition would lead to a "multilateral constitution-making process," which in turn is correlated with more independent, powerful, accessible courts (Pozas-Loyo and Ríos-Figueroa 2010). Interestingly, once a court with those characteristics is created, political competition (aka fragmentation) produces coordination costs for the executive and the legislative to react to a court decision they dislike, thus opening a space for judges to decide what they think best – it implies neutrality. Political competition also would allow demands by the public to say limit the military, but also demands by public to expand and protect the military may be raised and implemented. Therefore, the effects of political competition, a variable that actually influences the X and the Y of this study, cannot reasonably be expected to push in a single identifiable direction.

it to say for now, regarding the Colombian case, that the Constitutional Court's jurisprudence varies from issue to issue and that I find no identifiable pattern that can be reliably related to the context of violence.

Another endogeneity concern, reverse causality, can be stated as follows: because politicians are constrained by institutions but at the same time design these institutions themselves, wouldn't we expect the institutional design to serve their interests? This takes us to the constitution-making process that can be controlled by either a single political actor that unilaterally replaces or reforms the constitution or at least two actors who do so in a multilateral bargain. Specifically, "multilateral" constitution-making processes tend to produce reforms that diffuse power across the different political groups, lowering the stakes of winning/losing future elections, such as those that meet the conditions for independence and review powers for judges (Pozas-Loyo and Ríos-Figueroa 2010). Thus, the very nature of these multilateral processes make it harder for constitution makers to predict who will be sitting in the constitutional court and whom will the judges' future decisions favor, assuming that the fragmentation of the constituent assembly continues in the first elected legislature.[20] On the contrary, in "unilateral" constitution-making processes the appointment, tenure, and removal mechanisms of judges will more likely be designed in such a way that there is more proximity of preferences between the political group in control of constitution making and the future judges. But, of course, this assumes that the "unilateral" character of the constituent moment persists in the first elected legislature.[21] Moreover, when looking at the specific topic of this book, reverse causality seems rather unlikely: it is hard to imagine politicians creating a court in order to obtain a very specific policy regarding military autonomy, simply because they can just go right ahead and do that.[22]

[20] For example, the appointment procedures of judges designed under "multilateral" or fragmented constitution making bodies usually give at least two actors (e.g., the president and the Senate) the possibility to veto nominations of judges. The result is the appointment of judges who are acceptable to all the actors with a capacity to veto, and thus judges who will not directly represent the interests of one of such actors in court.

[21] To be sure, even in multilateral constitution-making processes there are a variety of appointment and removal mechanisms that in combination with the composition of the legislature may produce more/less proximity of preferences and may be more/less effective.

[22] Now, it can be argued that if there is a correlation between *how* the court decides cases regarding the military and *how* it decides other issues, then the politicians may have created the court to get exactly that type of judicial decision making. But, again, courts decide differently across different areas of issue. Moreover, if there is a correlation, that type of decision making may also sometimes hurt politicians.

Finally, judges are strategic actors who want their decisions to be implemented, but having neither purse nor sword they depend on other actors' compliance for that. How are courts' decisions affected by uncertainty about compliance? First, in the framework of the *Theory of Constitutional Courts as Mediators* the conditions under which we know compliance is more likely to take place also apply. Specifically, public support for the court, and public opinion in particular cases, are key to compliance with judicial decisions. To be clear, public support is understood here as "diffuse" support, which consists of a "reservoir of favorable attitudes of goodwill that helps members to accept or tolerate outputs to which they are opposed or the effects of which they see as damaging to their wants" (Easton 1975, 144). As Gibson and Caldeira argue, "diffuse" public support is a necessary condition for the effective judicial control of a state's constitution (Gibson and Caldeira 1995), and it (plus other conditions such as transparency) is key to compliance with judicial decisions especially when they go against the preferences of the executive or the legislative. In other words, it is less costly for politicians not to comply if the public does not oppose these actions (Helmke and Staton 2011; Staton 2010; Vanberg 2005).

But notice also that in the framework of the *Theory of Constitutional Courts as Mediators* the problem of compliance takes on a somewhat different form. Specifically, informative jurisprudence implies that courts tailor decisions that do not shame, do not create sharp winners and losers, and that underscore the iterated relation between the parties. Therefore the likelihood of all the parties' compliance increases vis-à-vis the decisions made by courts-as-arbitrators. Moreover, in this framework compliance goes hand in hand with the transmission of information. For instance, courts-as-mediators can make use of forums where the parties in the conflict develop responses to the problems. These forums provide information to the parties about their preferences and viewpoints on the conflict, but they also increase public awareness and increment the costs for the parties for not complying (Botero 2014, 30). Transmitting information effectively does not assume compliance, but arguably simply issuing creative and forward-looking jurisprudence would incentivize the actors in the conflict to apply the solution suggested by the mediator.[23]

[23] In contrast to arguments of credible commitment, arguments of coordination do not assume that government actors comply with judicial decisions. The reason is, in part, that these arguments posit that citizens can make use of judicial signals to help coordinate their responses to a government that has exceeded its constitutional limits. In other words, these arguments deal precisely with the issue of government compliance with constitutional boundaries (Ríos-Figueroa 2015, 200; Ríos-Figueroa and Staton 2012).

Nonetheless, in addition to these theoretical considerations, because compliance is such a complex and crucial issue in the scholarship of judicial politics, it is empirically assessed in the case studies.

Constitutional Courts as Mediators in Cases Dealing with the Armed Forces

The construction of a "democratic army," an army that unconditionally supports democratic governance, involves striking a delicate balance between ensuring the loyalty of the military to the popularly elected politicians while granting the military sufficient autonomy and strength to successfully discharge its functions and execute its missions (cf. e.g., Agüero 1995; Barany 2012; Serra 2010).[24] This dilemma is inherent to democracy, and sometimes the views and pretensions of the members of the armed forces and those of politicians are incompatible (Huntington 1957, 20). The stakes are higher, and the tensions more acute, in democracies where the armed forces are called upon to perform activities related to internal security, such as fighting terrorism, drug trafficking, organized crime, and sometimes even regular street crime. Tense civilian-military relations do not necessarily produce a coup or an intervention, but they certainly can hollow out democracies.[25]

The constitutional dilemma of the armed forces under democracy involves three relevant actors: the civilian government, the armed forces, and the citizens or general public. As Roberth Dahl eloquently puts it: "In order for a state to be governed democratically, evidently two conditions are required: 1) If military and police organizations exist, as they surely will, then they must be subject to civilian control.

[24] Experts on civilian-military relations often express the same idea in somewhat different ways. For example, Feaver (1999, 215) argues that "the civil-military *problematique* is a simple paradox: The very institution created to protect the polity is given sufficient power to become a threat to the polity.... On the one hand, the military must be strong enough to prevail in war.... On the other hand, just as the military must protect the polity from enemies, so must it conduct its own affairs so as not to destroy or prey on the society it is intended to protect." Brunneau, in an article on civilian-military relations in Latin America, states that "civil-military relations should be conceptualized not only in terms of democratic civilian control but also for effectiveness in implementing a spectrum of roles and missions" (Brunneau 2013, 143).

[25] As a former Spanish defense minister puts it, "striking a balance between controlling the military and maintaining discipline on the one hand, and inspiring motivation and necessary collaboration in order to construct and apply a new framework of relationships on the other, is one of the most difficult challenges in a period of consolidation of democracy" (Serra 2010, 153).

But civilian control, while necessary, is not sufficient, for many non-democratic regimes also maintain civilian control. Therefore, 2) the civilians who control the military and police must themselves be subject to the democratic process" (Dahl 1985, 245). In transitional contexts in which military subordination to civilian government is in construction, Dahl's normative point turns into a strategic calculation for civil politicians who, on the one hand, need to survive in office by winning votes and, on the other, need to subordinate the military and provide for defense. As David Pion-Berlin argues, "depending on context, these may or may not be compatible goals. The military, on the other hand, is concerned first and foremost with its institutional well-being, including material interests, career aspirations, and organizational cohesion" (Pion-Berlin 2012, 77).

It can be argued that the constitutional dilemma disappears in contexts where the civilian government's and the military's goals are compatible. For example, there would not be incompatible pretensions in those places where civilian governments and the armed forces agree, for instance, that military autonomy in most or all of its dimensions should be extensive. This can happen in a country suffering from guerrilla movements or organized crime where the civilian government calls upon the armed forces to fight them. In exchange for its participation in such unconventional tasks, the military demands broad autonomy. And the civilian government grants it. Such an agreement, the argument goes, would dissolve the constitutional dilemma.

However, such a scenario is unlikely to last for long under democracy: the agreement is between a particular government and the armed forces but these two actors do their job under a legal and political framework that conditions their actions, that is, a constitution, a series of international treaties and commitments, promises, and public statements. In a democracy, these frameworks produce expectations in the public that can demand coherence and exert pressure on the government to limit the military. Thus, even if the specific persons holding the executive office wanted to grant them more autonomy, such autonomy can come only at a large political price. In other words, restating Dahl, civilian-military relations in a democracy involve not two but three actors and the public's legitimate expectations trigger the constitutional dilemma even if there is agreement between the armed forces and the civilian government.

As advanced in Chapter 1, relations between civilian governments and the armed forces are plagued with lack of clarity on what belongs to the "civilian" or to the "military" spheres, which creates different types of uncertainty.[26] First, as Pion-Berlin has argued, "there exists a perceptual gap between the military and government: the two sides have different angles of vision, which has sometimes obscured the boundaries between their respective spheres of influence" (Pion-Berlin 1992, 99).[27] Second, military autonomy is complex and multidimensional[28] and thus not easily reduced to a simple bargaining problem where the armed forces always prefer more, and the civilian government less.[29] For instance, at its recent 100th anniversary, the Mexican military publicly asked for new legislation that clearly delimits its faculties vis-à-vis the war on drugs: they no longer want the ambiguous bounds and blank checks that have rendered members of the armed forces vulnerable to arbitrary interpretations of their duties and rights, as well as vulnerable to diffuse blames that affect the perceived legitimacy of their acts.

26 Some scholars of civilian-military relations have actually argued that this lack of clarity should be the bedrock upon which to build a democratic theory of civilian-military relations. For example, Rebecca Schiff's *Theory of Concordance* (1995) argues that it should not be assumed that separate civilian and military spheres are required in order to prevent domestic military intervention, but rather that cooperation and involvement among the military, the political institutions, and the society at large should be encouraged (Schiff 1995, 15). Also Bland's *Theory of Shared Responsibility* (1999) argues that, "civil control of the military is managed and maintained through the sharing of responsibility for control between civilian leaders and military officers … [which assumes that] the sole legitimate source for the directions and actions of the military is derived from civilians outside the military/defense establishment, and that civilian control is a dynamic process susceptible to changing ideas, values, circumstances, issues, and personalities, and to the stresses of crisis and war" (Bland 1999, 10).

27 "Because they perceive their professional reputations to be at stake, the armed forces have obstructed judicial proceedings even though civilians contend these lie squarely within the political realm. Similarly, the armed forces (and the army in particular) have not entirely abandoned the view that internal security lies within their purview, while the democratic leaders believe such operations fall under the auspices of the police and internal security forces" (Pion-Berlin 1992, 99).

28 For example, the military can enjoy more or less autonomy regarding the internal control of the profession (recruitment, promotions, etc.), the preparation and administration of its budget, the planning of its missions and strategies, or the scope and extent of the military jurisdiction.

29 There are few attempts to measure military autonomy. In a 1992 article, Pion-Berlin assessed autonomy across eleven areas (personnel decisions, force levels, military education, doctrine, reform, budgets, arms production and procurement, defense organization, intelligence gathering, internal security, and human rights), and found that "overall the armed forces are weaker in Argentina, Uruguay, and Peru than in Brazil and Chile. Once disaggregated by function it is also clear that autonomy is greater in certain areas and less so in others. On the one hand, the armed forces exhibit firm control over education, doctrines, and reform. On the other hand, they have much less control over budgets, force levels, and defense organization" (Pion-Berlin 1992, 87).

Moreover, civil-military relations vary across democratic regimes and across time within the same democratic regime. Particular situations (e.g., internal unrest produced by guerrillas, terrorist groups, or organized crime) may be better suited for higher levels of autonomy in some areas and lower levels in others, and this combination may change with the circumstances. In a nutshell, the lack of *prima facie* clarity about the "civilian" and "military" spheres generates (sometimes severe) conditions of uncertainty of different types. The former minister of defense in Spain puts it this way, "The aim cannot be to reach a state in which problems in civilian-military relations do not exist, but to achieve a situation in which civil supremacy is not questioned and problems are located within the parameters established in already established democracies" (Serra 2010, 157).

The main message of this book is that constitutional courts' jurisprudence can serve as a road map guiding the behavior of relevant actors under conditions of uncertainty by stipulating causal patterns or by providing compelling ethical or moral motivations for action (cf. Goldstein and Keohane 1993, 16). Specifically, constitutional courts can reduce three types of uncertainties that lie at the heart of the constitutional dilemma of the armed forces: (1) uncertainty over the legal consequences of certain actions, (2) uncertainty over the bounds of the exceptions and emergencies allowed by the constitution, and (3) uncertainty about how to balance clashing constitutional principles or rules in particular cases. By providing such a constitutional road map for driving through uncharted territory, courts help political actors determine their own goals and alternative political strategies by which they may reach these goals within the bounds of the constitution and the laws.

Informative jurisprudence by constitutional courts can ease relations between the armed forces and the military. This jurisprudence can serve as a searchlight that guides these two actors, and the public, toward the normalization of relations. On the one hand, the military develops attitudes of loyalty to the democratic system when they can see that there is a light at the end of the tunnel of loss of privileges and changes in their professional profile: new missions carried out within the democratic framework and a professional profile that guarantees their corporate future and efficacy. On the other, informative jurisprudence serves the civilian government in developing competency on military affairs and rules of engagement and in assessing priorities to the demands of the armed forces. Moreover, easily accessible courts serve as a monitoring mechanism by bringing the government's and the military's conduct to the attention of organized civilian society and citizens in general. Constitutional courts essentially participate in the enforcement of the constitutional/legal provisions under which both the civil government and the armed forces perform their job (cf. Feaver 1999, 230).

In democracies, and even more so in processes of transition to and consolidation of democracy, the military and the government have to learn to understand each other. It is not merely a question of controlling the military or reducing their previous prerogatives. As Serra argues, "one must define its tasks in the new democratic context and its role in the new state administration" (Serra 2010, 52). Both actors are crucial to this redefinition of roles. The military cannot perform its duty, nor can civilians exercise their authority, unless the machinery of government allows military and civilian perspectives to mix in the formulation of policy. "The challenge in democratic government is to exercise civilian authority while satisfying the legitimate needs of the military in its pursuit of national security" (Kohn 1997). Constitutional courts can be the translators of each actor's preferences into constitutional discourse that is understandable by both and compatible with democracy. Moreover, they can also be helpful in transforming actors' preferences, not only through the constitutionally, rights-based, rationales in their decisions, but also by making both actors study and learn about each other.[30]

In the following chapters, I empirically assess whether, when the conditions of independence, access, and ample powers of constitutional review are present, constitutional courts are more likely to function as third-party mediators in internal security crises and the uncertainty-driven conflicts between armed forces and civilian governments that these crises generate.

30 Judicial decisions where the military are required to change their curriculum and include human rights, e.g., are common. These decisions can have consequences in changing the military's attitudes because military education is one of the areas of military autonomy that is defended most aggressively. As Pion-Berlin puts it, the military tends to want exclusive control over the socialization of its recruits: "proper indoctrination assures a greater sprit de corps among the rank and file. Educational lessons are reinforced by the close, disciplinary, and conformist nature of the military institution. The armed forces would rather enforce this cloistered learning environment than to expose its soldiers to the unpredictable and divisive influences of civil society and civilian universities" (Pion-Berlin 1992, 86).

3

Constitutional Jurisprudence on Military Autonomy in Colombia, 1958–2013

> A nosotros nos importan un carajo la constitución y las leyes porque estamos fuera de ellas.
>
> (We don't give a shit about the constitution or the laws because we are outside of them.)
>
> Jorge Briceño, *El Mono Jojoy*, former leader of the FARC

This chapter analyzes constitutional jurisprudence on military autonomy in two recent periods of Colombian history: the first starting in 1958, the year when the brief military government of General Rojas Pinilla ended and civilians resumed power thanks to the pact known as the National Front, until 1990; and the second from 1991, the year when the current constitution was enacted, until 2013. Specifically, I analyze quantitatively and qualitatively the decisions made by the supreme court during the first period, and those made by the constitutional court in the second, in two types of cases: cases that reach the constitutional organ challenging a previous decision made by a military authority (e.g., a military court, prosecutor, officer, or military administrative agency) and cases that reach the constitutional organ on the scope of military jurisdiction.

Taking advantage of the fact that the constitutional court enjoys higher levels of independence, access, and powers of judicial review than the supreme court, I assess whether the constitutional court's jurisprudence is closer to the ideal of third-party mediator in conflict resolution than the supreme court's jurisprudence. To quickly preview the conclusion of the chapter, the answer is a clear "yes." In what follows, I first provide an overview of constitutional jurisprudence on military autonomy in the whole period analyzed in the chapter. Then, I analyze in detail each of the two subperiods, focusing on the political context and civilian-military relations, the characteristics of the constitutional organ during the period, and its jurisprudence on military autonomy.

Long-Term Jurisprudential Patterns on Military Autonomy in Colombia, 1958–2013

The Colombian Constitution of 1886 was in force for more than a hundred years, until 1991, when it was replaced by the current constitution. During this long period the country enjoyed a limited but stable democracy that mostly revolved, in political terms, around two parties: the Conservatives and the Liberals (Bejarano and Pizarro 2005). With the exception of a brief military government from 1954 to 1958, Colombia has not suffered military coups or intervention,[1] but this does not mean that the armed forces are a marginal actor. On the contrary, a complex mix of challenges of internal security spanning more than six decades to this date (2015) has mostly been faced by the armed forces and using military strategies. In exchange for their services, and for loyalty to the successive civilian governments since 1958, the armed forces received ample discretion for dealing with the internal security crises. This mostly meant increased military autonomy, not only in terms of the planning and execution of missions, but also regarding the administration of the armed forces and military justice in particular (cf. Andrade Becerra 2012, 150).[2]

The degree of military autonomy, and the tense bargain between civilian governments and the armed forces, has changed in the period since the enactment of the Constitution of 1991, but the armed forces still are a key actor involved in consequential decisions for Colombian politics and society. Some of these decisions, of course, were challenged before the courts of law and some reached the constitutional organ. What did the constitutional organ do when specific cases on military autonomy reached the court?

Figure 3.1 shows decisions by the supreme court (1958–91) and by the constitutional court (1991–2013) on military autonomy.[3] The

1 This pattern of civil-military relations is similar to that found in Mexico, but contrasts with the case of Peru. See Chapter 6 for a systematic comparison of the three countries.

2 This exchange between civilians and the military is often referred to as the "Lleras doctrine," after the speech by President Alberto Lleras in 1958 saying that it was a bad idea that the armed forces participate in politics, but that an equally bad idea is that politicians intervene in military matters. In Mexico there was a similar "civilian-military pact" in which loyalty to the civilian government was exchanged for military autonomy; see Chapter 5.

3 The database consists of 334 constitutional decisions on military autonomy for the period 1958–2013, of which 259 were made by the supreme court during the period 1958–91 and 75 by the constitutional court (1992–2013). The type of cases decided during the period are also varied: 40 correspond to cases of automatic review of constitutionality, 81 to public actions of constitutionality, 112 to cassation decisions made by the supreme court (1958–91),

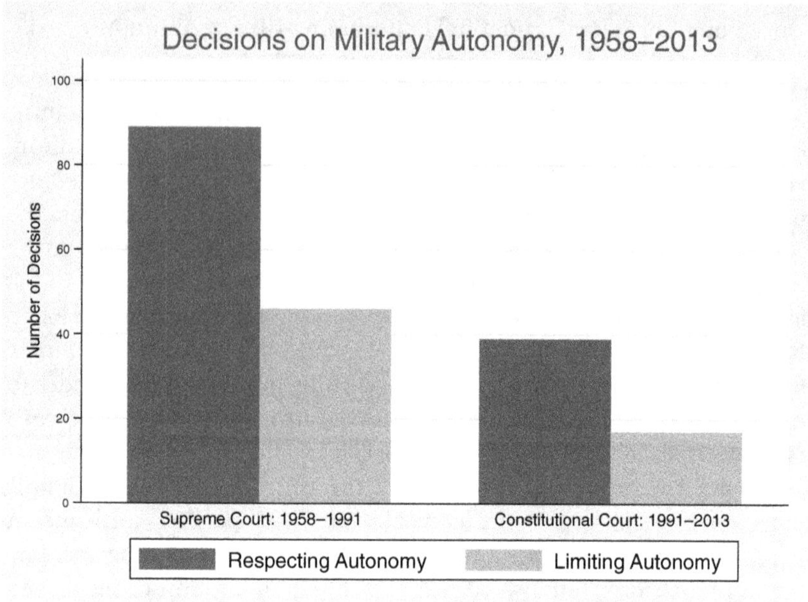

Figure 3.1. The constitutional organ can reject or amend a previous decision made by a military authority, which is coded as "limiting autonomy," or rather uphold it, which is coded as "respecting autonomy." The figure shows raw numbers. The percentages are as follows: in the first period 66 percent of the decisions "respect autonomy" and 34 percent "limit autonomy"; in the second period the figures are 70 percent and 30 percent, respectively.

constitutional organ can reject or amend a previous decision made by a military authority, which I code as "limiting autonomy," or rather uphold it, which I consider to be "respecting autonomy." The most relevant finding

82 to decisions on conflicts of jurisdiction made by the supreme court (1958–91), and 10 to *tutelas* made by the constitutional court (1992–2013). With the help of Camilo Castillo, we systematically and thoroughly searched all the *Gacetas Judiciales* (1958–91) and the webpage of the constitutional court (1992–2013) for all cases on military autonomy. If there are cases not included in this database, we believe they wouldn't alter the tendencies shown in Figures 3.1 and 3.2. The full list of cases can be found at http://www.investigadores.cide.edu/julio.rios/. Notice that the database does not include cases on military autonomy decided by the Colombian Supreme Court, the judicial council, or the *consejo de estado*, the highest administrative court, after 1991 (the year in which the Colombian Constitutional Court was created). The main reason is that since 1991 all the high courts mentioned are required to follow the doctrine established by the constitutional court, and when they do not, the constitutional court can review those decisions. In the last section of the chapter I actually consider whether the high courts followed the constitutional court's precedents as a way to gauge compliance and the effects of constitutional court's jurisprudence.

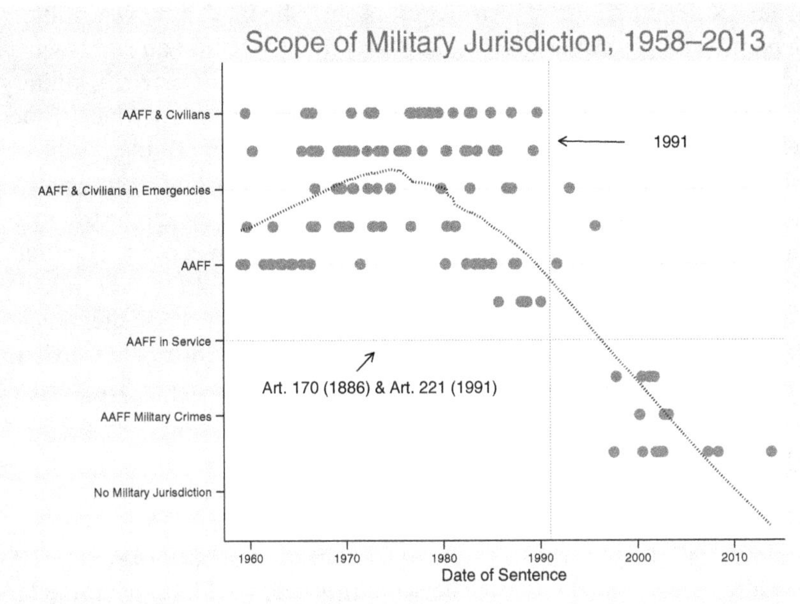

Figure 3.2. Decisions by the supreme court (1958–91) and by the constitutional court (1991–2013) on the scope of the military jurisdiction, which essentially are the courts' answer to the question: Who can be judged in military courts, and under what circumstances? The dotted curved line displays a locally weighted regression on the data (lowess in STATA). The dotted horizontal line at "AAFF in Service" represents the answer to the question on the scope of military jurisdiction by the Constitution of 1868 and the Constitution of 1991.

in Figure 3.1 is that in both periods the number of decisions "respecting autonomy" is considerably greater than those "limiting autonomy." The supreme and the constitutional courts have, on average, let the decisions made by military authorities stand.

Let's zoom in on a specific aspect of military autonomy. Figure 3.2 shows decisions by the supreme court (1958–91) and by the constitutional court (1991–2013) on the scope of the military jurisdiction, which essentially are the courts' answer to the question: Who can be judged in military courts, and under what circumstances?[4] I code judicial answers within twelve categories ordered from the narrowest to the widest: (0) nobody

[4] This question establishes the "constitutional scenario," a factual question in which the interests of actors clash and whose answer requires an interpretation of the constitution (López Medina 2009, 154).

ever, that is, the military jurisdiction is abolished; (1) not even military personnel when crimes against humanity and gross human rights violations are involved; (2) only military personnel, only when strictly military crimes are involved; (3, 4, 5) only military personnel, only when crimes were committed during service construed in a narrow, regular, or broad way respectively; (6) only military personnel, under any circumstance; (7) not only military but also police officers, under some circumstances;[5] (8, 9) military personnel and civilians, only during emergency situations construed in a narrow or broad way, respectively; and (10, 11) military personnel and civilians, under circumstances broader than emergencies narrowly and broadly construed, respectively.[6] The horizontal axis in Figure 3.2 displays the date in which the decision was made. The vertical axis displays the categories on the scope of military jurisdiction in a scale from the narrowest to the widest scope, 0 to 11.

Figure 3.2 also includes the constitution's response to the question of military jurisdiction that is the horizontal line situated at "AAFF in Service." Specifically, the Colombian Constitution of 1886 in Article 170 literally states: "Article 170.- Crimes committed by military personnel in active service and related to such service, will be heard in military tribunals according to the prescriptions of the criminal military code." In the Constitution of 1991 the new Article 221 is the same as Article 170 of the 1886 Constitution, and this is why the horizontal line remains at the same level after 1991. An important difference, however, is that the new Article 213 states that "in no case can civilians be investigated or judged in the military jurisdiction" (an addition that reflects a jurisprudential change that took place in 1987). In terms of the scale this does not change the basic narrower constitutional answer to the legal question on the scope of military jurisdiction. In other words, the first determinant

[5] This is a category exclusive for Colombia used for cases in which the constitutional organ decided that police personnel belong to the military jurisdiction.

[6] While the extreme situations are theoretical possibilities that do not take place as such in reality, there are actual cases that are close to them. For example, on one end, Chile under the military regime expanded the scope of military jurisdiction to include many ordinary crimes (Bovino 1998). On the other end, there are cases such as Costa Rica where the army was abolished, and also cases like France, Germany, or Argentina that have done away with the military jurisdiction within their borders and accepted it only in cases of war abroad or aboard military ships (Pedroza de la Llave 2011). Notice that in the intermediate categories in which only military personnel can appear before military courts the difference is that in (2) only military crimes such as cowardice, insubordination, or treason are admitted in military courts; in (3–5) only service-related crimes are admitted, thus limiting not the type of crimes but the circumstance under which they take place; and in (6) any type of crime, as long as it was committed by a member of the armed forces, is admitted in military courts.

to constitutional interpretation of the scope of military jurisdiction, and of any other topic indeed, namely the constitution, has in general terms remained constant for more than one hundred years.

As shown in Figure 3.2, however, constitutional jurisprudence on military jurisdiction has changed, suggesting that something other than the (constitutional) law is behind the jurisprudential movements.[7] The general pattern in Figure 3.2 is clear: in the period from 1958 to the end of the 1980s, the Colombian Supreme Court held a consistently wide constitutional interpretation of military jurisdiction, wider than what the constitution stipulated, basically holding that both military personnel and civilians could be investigated and tried in military courts under emergency situations. However, from the end of the 1980s (specifically 1987), but more clearly since 1991, to the present the constitutional court has gradually but drastically moved toward a narrower interpretation of the scope of the military jurisdiction.

The Supreme Court, 1958–1991

Political Context and Civil-Military Relations

Since the enactment of the 1886 Constitution and until about 1930, successive Conservative governments dominated Colombia. From 1930 and until 1946, successive Liberal governments ruled the country. In 1946 the Conservative Mariano Ospina Pérez won the elections but faced a congress dominated by the Liberal Party that was divided between moderates and "radicals" that supported the popular leader Jorge Eliécer Gaitán. The conflicts and tensions between the two main political groups started at the local level and went all the way up to the elite, and they escalated when Gaitán was assassinated on the main street of Bogotá in 1948. An undeclared civil war ensued that lasted until the second half of the 1950s (called *La Violencia*).[8] President Ospina, facing impeachment impulsed by

[7] Other articles changed in the Constitution of 1991 that may impact how the judges interpret the scope of military jurisdiction. For instance, Article 93 explicitly incorporates the international human rights law, and Article 214 restricts the possibility of suspending basic rights and liberties. However, notice that it takes a sophisticated kind of judge – the kind of judge I think is consistent with the mediator role – to use those other articles and a "systemic" interpretation of the constitution in order to decide cases that fall squarely within the scope Articles 213 and 221 that directly delimit the scope of military jurisdiction.

[8] During *La Violencia* the conflict between Liberals and Conservatives increasingly politicized the armed forces that became directly involved (more the police than the army, air force, or navy) in pillages, massacres, and other crimes (Andrade Becerra 2012, 150).

congressional Liberals, decided to declare a state of emergency in the whole country (November 9, 1949), suspending congress and the local governments indefinitely (Perdomo 2012, 85).[9] The declaration of a state of emergency became the institutionally preferred option used by Colombian governments to deal with threats, up until after the new Constitution of 1991 was enacted and this practice began to wane. In fact, of the forty-two years between 1949 and 1991 Colombia spent thirty-five (83 percent of that time) under a "state of exception" (Uprimny 2006).

The period of *La Violencia* was ended by the brief military government (1953–7) led by General Gustavo Rojas Pinilla. His government was in turn ended by other generals who intervened and formed the Military Junta that facilitated a pact between the two main political parties, which crystallized in a series of constitutional reforms enacted on December 1, 1957. In political terms, these reforms sealed the so-called National Front (*Frente Nacional*) of 1958–74: a pact for Conservatives and Liberals to alternate in the presidency and to share all positions of power equally for sixteen years.[10] The political stability induced by the *National Front* lasted for a decade and a half, with the armed forces as a kind of guarantor, a loyal implicit partner of the pact between successive civilian governments. This role came with enlarged military autonomy, conceived as necessary to preserve order and stability: less than thirty days before leaving power (on August 7, 1958), the Military Junta published a reformed Code of Military Justice establishing that "political crimes" against the State belonged to the military jurisdiction whether or not they were committed under a state of emergency (Perdomo 2012, 89–90).[11]

The *Frente Nacional* was solid at the level of party and economic elites but it left wide portions of Colombian society underrepresented (Bejarano and Pizarro 2005). The forgotten grassroots level was prey to a dynamic of an increasingly complex spiral of violence that has been developing for decades. The Colombian "restricted democracy" incubated an internal security crisis that to this date (2015) is not yet completely resolved and includes guerrillas, such as the Revolutionary Armed Forces of Colombia (*Fuerzas Armadas Revolucionarias de Colombia*, FARC) and the National

[9] The government also stated in the decree that a three-fourths supermajority of supreme court magistrates was required to declare a state of emergency unconstitutional.

[10] Originally, the pact was going to last for twelve years but in 1959 it was expanded for four more years.

[11] This broadened the scope of the military jurisdiction from the last reform, in 1950 under the government of conservative President Laureano Gómez, when "political crimes" committed under states of emergency were sent to the military jurisdiction. The Military Junta also packed the supreme court before leaving power (see details in the following text).

Liberation Army (*Ejército de Liberación Nacional*); illegal drug processing and trafficking; and the paramilitary phenomenon (see Gutiérrez Sanín 2007). From the end of the National Front (1974) and throughout the 1980s, the country's situation became extremely difficult with the government's declaration of a "war against drugs," the closed nature of the Colombian political system, and the power of the drug cartels that produced a spiral of violence and narco-terrorism.

To deal with such complex internal security challenges, Colombian presidents constantly declared a "state of exception," which not only implied the delegation of legislative powers to the executive but also limited the scope of civil rights and expanded the military jurisdiction. The "tool" of the declaration of emergency came in handy in the context of the Cold War when the concept of threat was broad (and politically biased). For instance, Table 3.1 reproduces the declarations of a state of emergency of the presidents of the National Front, their duration, and the crimes that were transferred to the military jurisdiction. Two things are noteworthy. First, the reasons from declaring a state of exception are not always a clear challenge to internal security, but rather they include regular social protests such as demonstrations by student or labor movements. Second, the list and the type of crimes sent to the military jurisdiction is long and ambiguous amounting to its considerable broadening (Perdomo 2012).[12]

The tension between democracy and violence "deepened dramatically" in Colombia in the years after the National Front ended (Gutiérrez Sanín and Ramírez Rueda 2004, 229). The violence exerted by guerrilla groups, drug traffickers, and paramilitaries reached unprecedented levels. Not only did the number of massacres against the rural population and the selective assassination of leaders of social movements and unions increased, but also that of highly visible attacks in Bogotá and the major cities. The violent takeover of the Justice Palace by the guerrilla group M-19[13] was

[12] The 1980 report of Amnesty International is eloquent on the militarization of justice in Colombia during the period of the *Frente Nacional*: "From 1966 to 1973, military tribunals in Colombia produced more than 3,800 guilty verdicts in 1500 Military Courts.... Massive arrests and torture have been common.... Frequently, the motives that drive the verdicts in these courts are related to being part of the political opposition, union movements, or subversive groups against the state" (cited in Perdomo 2012, 101).

[13] The M-19 guerrilla group was created in response to the alleged electoral fraud that took place on April 19, 1970. That year the candidates were General Rojas Pinilla, who led a party called the ANAPO (*Alianza Nacional Popular*) that he had created in 1961, and the Conservative Candidate Misael Pastrana. This election was the last of the National Front pact, which implied that it was the turn of the Conservative Party to govern. Followers of General Rojas Pinilla denounced a fraud, and some radicalized and created the M-19.

Table 3.1. *Emergencies and expansion of military justice, by president (1962–74)*

Government	Decree of state of exception and reason	Period	Crimes transferred to military criminal justice
Guillermo León Valencia (1962–6)	Decree 1137 of 1963. State of exception declared in Puerto Wilches, Lebrija, and San Vicente due to civic strikes because of solidarity with the workers of the oil zone.	Since May 23, 1963 to May 30, 1963.	None
	Decree 1288 of 1965. State of exception declared throughout the country due to the students' movement that came from Medellin against the U.S. invasion of Santo Domingo.	Since May 21, 1965 to December 16, 1968.	Against the existence and security of the state; against the constitutional regime and national security; conspiracy; fires and other crimes involving criminal offenses; kidnapping, extortion; antisocial behaviors related to the factory and trade or transfer of arms, ammunition, or explosives. Damage to works, facilities, or elements for public service communications, electricity or power, facilities or elements of roads, railways, ports, airports, water supply or used for the production, refining, and transmission of oil. Placement of explosives or flammable items. Theft crimes against banking institutions or savings banks.

Carlo Lleras Restrepo (1966–70)	Decree 1957 of 1969: State of partial exception declared in "Valle del Cauca" due to the kidnapping of the son of the Consul of Switzerland.	Since October 9, 1969 to April 21, 1970.	Kidnapping; extortion; conspiracy; robberies, theft exceeding the amount of 10,000 pesos; antisocial related to the factory, freight and trade or transfer of arms, ammunition or explosives. Crimes related to previous Decree 1661 of 1969.
	Decree 590 of 1970. State of total exception due to demonstrations promoted by the Alianza Nacional Popular (ANAPO) against the electoral results of 1970.	Since April 21, 1970 to May 15, 1970.	Against the existence and security of the State; constitutional order and internal security; conspiracy; fires and other crimes involving public danger; kidnapping, extortion; robbery against banking institutions; and antisocial behavior related to the factory and trade or transfer of arms, ammunition or explosives. (Decree 593 of 1970)
			Instigation to commit crimes and criminal defense. (Decree 636 of 1970)
			Crimes committed against members of the armed forces or national police in performance of their duties, or against any of the belongings of these organisms. (Decree 637 of 1970)
	Decree 1128 of 1970. State of total exception. A "hostile environment" due to the demonstrations promoted by the ANAPO is given as the reason.	Since July 19, 1970 to November 13, 1970.	Against the existence and security of the State; the constitutional order and internal security; conspiracy; fires and other crimes involving public danger; kidnapping, extortion; robbery against banks or savings and related to the above crimes. It also hears criminal offenses affecting the security and public tranquility and heritage. (Decree 1133 of 1970)

(*continued*)

Table 3.1 (*cont.*)

Government	Decree of state of exception and reason	Period	Crimes transferred to military criminal justice
Misael Pastrana (1970–4)	Decree 250 of 1971. State of total exception due to students' movement in "Valle del Cauca," the strike of working people and promoted by Union de Trabajadores Colmbianos (UTC) and the Confederación Sindical de Trabajadores (CST) and the agrarian movement's invasion of land guided by the Asociación Nacional de Usuarios Campesinos (ANUC).	Since February 26, 1971 to December 29, 1973.	Against the existence and security of the State; the constitutional order and internal security; conspiracy; fires and other crimes involving public danger; kidnapping, extortion; robbery against banks or savings institutions and related to the above crimes. It also hears criminal offenses affecting security and public tranquility and heritage. (Decree 254 of 1971) Offenses referred to in Article 276, 308, and 428 of the Penal Code, in the latter case when the material constituting the object of the same things, real or personal property of a company dedicated to providing a public service or who are in the service thereof. (Decree 1518 of 1971) Crimes against the security of the armed forces and against the administration; homicide and personal injury committed against members of the armed forces and civilians who are in the service, throwing objects capable of causing damage, shooting guns at vehicles with people, taking over, hijacking or diverting an aircraft from its route; the carrying of firearms or ammunition without permission of authorities. (Decree 1989 of 191)

Source: Perdomo (2012).

only one of several salient tragedies that took place in Colombia during the 1980s, which included the assassination of the minister of justice, the *procurador general*, the owner of a leading national newspaper, four presidential candidates, and several terrorist attacks on public buildings.

Post–National-Front governments continued declaring states of emergency to deal with internal security crisis, and using the increased powers of executive decree to legislate in many areas of political and social life. At the start of the government of Julio César Turbay Ayala (1978–82), the publication of Decree 1923/19878 actually increased the autonomy of the armed forces for dealing with public order. The strategy backfired because the levels of coercion and repression also increased, and presidents Belisario Betancur (1982–6) and Virgilio Barco (1986–90) tried to limit the autonomy of the armed forces (Andrade Becerra 2012, 151). However, in 1984 President Betancur declared a state of emergency in the whole territory after the assassination by drug dealers of Minister of Justice Rodrigo Lara Bonilla, and from that year until 1991 a total of 225 executive decrees were issued, a great proportion of which increased the discretion of the criminal justice system, the armed forces, and the military jurisdiction for dealing with the internal security crisis (Ariza, Cammaert, and Iturralde 1997, 8).

The Supreme Court: Independence, Access, and Powers

The reforms of 1958 that sealed the National Front (*Frente Nacional*) of 1958–74 included important reforms to the justice system: the reforms transformed the appointment of supreme court judges from a method where a congressional majority selected one of three candidates proposed by the executive, to a self-appointment, or *co-optation*, method. To justify the co-optation method, in the message from the Military Junta to congress on its inauguration day one can read: "breaking the links between the supreme court and the council of state with the congress contributes to giving more respect to judicial decisions … destroying suspicions of political pressures on the judges" (cited in Perdomo 2012, 85).[14]

Interestingly, however, the military had already ensured that the preferences of the judges would not be overly opposed to those of the armed forces. Specifically, between 1957 and 1961 the membership of the supreme court

[14] Some critics suggest that the military decided to remove the elected branches from the appointment process because they wanted to prevent a possible trial against them (Uprimny 2006).

was completely changed three times (in 1957, 1958, and 1959). While the first set of judges appointed by Rojas Pinilla was removed, the final composition of the court reflected a bargain between the Military Junta and the Liberal and Conservative parties because the court was also included in the "parity" agreement of the National Front.[15] Moreover, the Military Junta also created a new Military Code of Justice in 1958 just before leaving power, which was in place until 1988. Thus, whereas the newly appointed supreme court enjoyed good levels of de jure independence,[16] the politically biased appointment of the judges assured that their preferences were close to the conservatives and to the military. Moreover, these judges were going to decide cases related to the armed forces using the Military Code of Justice also created by the Military Junta.[17]

The Colombian Supreme Court during this period was in charge of automatically reviewing the constitutionality of the declarations of state of siege (as had been the case since 1910). In 1968, a constitutional chamber within the supreme court was created and this chamber was granted the additional power to review the constitutionality of the decrees passed during a state of emergency. The supreme court also had original jurisdiction on the public action of constitutionality (also since 1910), which is an abstract instrument of constitutional review that can be filed by any citizen (cf. Constitution of 1886 Article 214). Finally, the supreme court also heard individual constitutional complaints but only through appeals. Therefore, the supreme court had moderate powers of judicial review and it was also moderately accessible.[18]

[15] When General Rojas Pinilla left power, the whole membership of the supreme court that he had appointed resigned after two months. The Military Junta then appointed a whole new court. But in 1959, President Lleras again reshuffled the whole supreme court, this time appointing judges following the spirit of the *Frente Nacional* pact, in particular pleasing the conservative faction led by Laureano Gómez (Castillo Sánchez 2015).

[16] In my de jure index of judicial independence, the Colombian Supreme Court receives a value of 4 (out of 6) (Ríos-Figueroa 2011).

[17] During the military government led by General Rojas Pinilla (1954–57) the military justice was completely autonomous and self-contained. The superior military court decided everything that had to do with the armed forces, even cases that had no relation to the service. This court even decided the conflicts of jurisdiction between ordinary and military courts, which used to be decided by the supreme court. In January 1958 the supreme military court was derogated by the Military Junta and thus the supreme court regained the power to resolve conflicts of jurisdiction and also the power of casation on military courts' decisions (Castillo Sánchez 2015).

[18] In addition to the abstract instruments for review in its original jurisdiction, the supreme court also resolved, in cassation, the disagreements between lower courts. The supreme court, however, did not have *certiorari* power. Also, from 1949 and until 1957 there was

The co-optation method of appointment, combined with the negotiated selection of the first set of judges, made the limited de facto independence of the supreme court to be stable and sticky. The method of self-appointment, or *co-optation*, was combined with the power to the supreme court to appoint and remove lower court judges in order to create a justice system that with time acquired independence from the political parties represented in the elected branches. But it also created a corporatist institution and a rigid jurisprudence (Uprimny 2006). For quite a long time, this institutional design produced a supreme court that could be labeled a "faithful servant of the regime" (cf. Brinks 2011). In other words, the court had a certain degree of independence and powers, and it did use them, but conservatively to preserve the basic agreement that supported the regime.[19] The supreme court's jurisprudence on military autonomy and military jurisdiction is a good example of this. It was not until the end of the 1980s when the supreme court produced a shift in a decades-long jurisprudence on these key areas.

Constitutional Jurisprudence on Military Autonomy

From 1958 and until 1991, the supreme court automatically reviewed the constitutionality of the declaration of states of exception, and from 1968 the decrees issued under them, but very rarely restricted the government.[20] The supreme court considered the declarations of states of emergency a political question beyond the reach of judicial review. In fact, the court limited itself to checking whether such declarations were procedurally correct, that is, whether the signature of the president and the ministers was in place. But the court did not discuss, for instance, whether the declaration of emergency was necessary or whether the decrees were directly related to the problem that triggered the declaration of the emergency (Ariza, Cammaert, and Iturralde 1997; García Villegas and Uprimny 2005).

a supermajority requirement on declarations of unconstitutionality. In my de jure index of judicial review powers (that includes access), the Colombian Supreme Court receives a value of 4 (out of 8) (Ríos-Figueroa 2011).

19 A telling proof of this characteristic of the supreme court was the annulment of the constitutional reforms to the justice system and the territorial governance undertaken by the government of Adolfo López Michelsen (1974–8). The supreme court argued that congress could not delegate constituent powers (see Cepeda Ulloa 2008; Pozas-Loyo and Ríos-Figueroa 2011). This precedent became relevant in 1991, when the supreme court declared the call for a constituent assembly constitutional in a closely divided decision.

20 In 1960 a constitutional amendment had established that congress, by majority vote of any of its chambers, could request the supreme court review the constitutionality of emergency decrees.

Regarding military jurisdiction, the supreme court consistently upheld that military personnel and civilians could be judged by military tribunals during emergencies (see Ariza 1999; Barreto Rozo 2011; Cabarcas Maciá 2011).[21] The militarization of justice can be said to start in 1945 with a decision by the supreme court to uphold the constitutionality of the presidential decrees that allowed for the expedite creation of war tribunals to process military officers and civilians suspected of having participated in attempted *coup d'état* against then-president Alfonso López Pumarejo (Barreto Rozo 2011, 36–8). The decision of June 12, 1945 (MP Aníbal Cardozo Gaitán)[22] allowed the civilians involved in the coup attempt to be tried in military courts on the grounds of the celerity required by the circumstances and the gravity of the offenses. Notice that this interpretation implied a considerably wider scope of military jurisdiction than that established by Article 170 of the 1886 Constitution.

The Colombian Supreme Court during the National Front and Post-National Front governments, and essentially until 1987, basically upheld that 1945 criterion that both civilians and military personnel could be judged in military tribunals under emergency situations. In some later decisions, the court repeats that the justification for this expansive interpretation is the celerity with which military courts need to proceed in times of emergency.[23] As late as 1984, after President Betancur declared a state of emergency in the whole territory after the assassination of Minister of Justice Rodrigo Lara Bonilla, a divided supreme court upheld the constitutionality of the decrees establishing that civilian or military suspects of drug trafficking were to be investigated and tried by military prosecutors and judges (Ariza, Cammaert, and Iturralde 1997, 58–9).[24] Thus, for quite

[21] For example, see Corte Suprema de Justicia. Sentencia del 30 de octubre de 1969, MP Luis Sarmiento Buitrago; Corte Suprema de Justicia. Sentencia del 6 de noviembre de 1969, MP José Gabriel de la Vega; Corte Suprema de Justicia. Sentencia del 5 de abril de 1973, MP José Gabriel de la Vega; Corte Suprema de Justicia. Sentencia del 23 de septiembre de 1973, MP Luis Sarmiento Buitrago; Corte Suprema de Justicia. Sentencia del 10 de julio de 1975, MP Eustorgio Sarria; Corte Suprema de Justicia. Sentencia del 31 de julio de 1975, MP Eustorgio Sarria; Sala Plena. Corte Suprema de Justicia. Sentencia del 27 de enero 1977, MP Luis Sarmiento Buitrago; Corte Suprema de Justicia. Sentencia del 30 de octubre de 1978, MP Luis Carlos Sachica.

[22] MP stands for "Magistrado Ponente," i.e., the judge who produced the opinion that was discussed within the court and becomes the basis for the final decision.

[23] Corte Suprema de Justicia. Sentencia del 13 de agosto de 1970, MP Luis Sarmiento Buitrago; Corte Suprema de Justicia. Sentencia del 2 de diciembre de 1976, MP Luis Sarmiento Buitrago.

[24] Corte Suprema de Justicia. Sentencias Nos. 57, 58, 59, 60 del 3 de julio de 1984, MP Alfonso Patiño Rosselli; Corte Suprema de Justicia. Sentencia No. 68 del 5 de julio de 1984, MP Alfonso Patiño Rosselli.

a long time, the government enlarged the military jurisdiction through decrees passed under emergency situations, and the supreme court developed a jurisprudence of a merely procedural judicial review of the declaration of states of emergency and no review of the decrees passed under it.[25] In a nutshell, the supreme court developed a political-question doctrine and marginalized itself during this long and difficult period of sieged democracy.

An important jurisprudential change took place in 1987 when the supreme court issued a historical decision stating that "the judging of civilians by military personnel is more than a simple transfer of competencies, it actually amounts to a substantial alteration of the equilibrium of powers and a radical change in the idea of administration of justice."[26] This reasoning was later upheld by the court in a series of decisions.[27] One of the motivations of the historical jurisprudential change in 1987 was the death of several members of the supreme court and the council of state in November of 1985 during the assault on the *Palacio de Justicia* perpetrated by the M-19 guerrilla group (Barreto Rozo 2011, 63). The military handled the response to the assault very poorly and many members of the judiciary, and part of the public opinion, considered that the military did not hold the life of the judges in high regard.

Conclusion: The Supreme Court as an Arbitrator

In terms of the theory developed in this book, during the period analyzed thus far the supreme court behaved more as an arbitrator than as a

[25] The first dissenting opinions in my sample of cases related to military jurisdiction appear in 1982, and on the judicial control of states of emergency further back in 1974 when magistrate Sarmiento Buitrago used arguments that will be cited by the constitutional court in 1993 (Ariza, Cammaert, and Iturralde 1997, 42). In 1984 the so-called *faceless justice* (*justicia sin rostro*) was launched (anonymous judges who held secret sessions in drug-related cases in order to protect them from retaliation). It is possible that the launching of *justicia sin rostro*, which reduced considerably the rights of criminal due process of the defendants, was related to the increasing pressure to restrict military justice. I thank Yahayra Bernal for this appreciation.

[26] Sala Plena. Corte Suprema de Justicia. Sentencia 20 del 5 de marzo de 1987, MP Jesús Vallejo Mejía. The decision also states that: "Military tribunals are competent to judge crimes committed by military officers in active service and related to such service. And it bears repeating that there is no explicit constitutional Article or clause within Article 121 that assigns the capacity to judge civilians to military tribunals."

[27] Corte Suprema de Justicia. Sentencia del 20 de agosto de 1987, MP Jesús Vallejo Mejía; Corte Suprema de Justicia. Sentencia del 15 de diciembre de 1988, MP Jesús Vallejo Mejía; Corte Suprema de Justicia. Sentencia del No. 30 del 17 de marzo de 1988, MP Jairo Duque Pérez.

third-party mediator. In other words, the supreme court merely adjudicated responsibilities between both actors but did not engage in creative and forward-looking jurisprudence. The limited de facto independence of the supreme court, generated by the co-optation method of appointment coupled with the appointment of a first set of judges with preferences close to the military and the Conservative Party, combined with moderate levels of access and judicial review powers are important determinants of this pattern.

With time de facto judicial independence increased, as did the negative consequences of a high degree of military autonomy. But the powers of judicial review of the court, and especially access to mechanisms of constitutional review (the court was publicly reachable but only for actions of constitutionality, a mechanism that requires relatively high levels of juridical knowledge to successfully argue for the unconstitutionality of a statute or a decree), were still moderate and so was the supreme court's capacity to provide relevant information to incentivize cooperation. The supreme court made decisions in the 1970s arguing that civilians working for the armed forces do not belong to the military jurisdiction. Moreover, during the second half of the 1970s and the first half of the 1980s key dissenting opinions were published saying that civilians should never be tried in military courts. And, most relevant, the decisions starting in 1987 established this last point jurisprudentially. Though important, as later recognized by the constitutional court, these decisions are not thoroughly argued and do not exhibit the features of informative, mediator-like jurisprudence.

The Constitutional Court, 1991–2013

Political Context and Civil-Military Relations

In the difficult political context of the second half of the 1980s, Colombian presidents Virgilio Barco (1986–90) and his successor César Gaviria (1990–4) managed to convene the constituent assembly that produced the Constitution of 1991.[28] This time a divided supreme court did not

[28] The procedure to convene the constituent assembly was both complex and interesting. Success was not at all assured because attempts to replace the 1886 Constitution had been stopped in the past. To convene the assembly, presidents Barco and Gaviria managed to strike deals with a wide array of political actors, including demobilized guerrilla groups, mobilized students, judicial elites, and leaders and militants of the Liberal and Conservative parties. The assembly represented all the relevant actors in Colombian society and politics, which contributed to generating a sense of a new political beginning (see Cepeda Espinosa 2008; Nielson and Shugart 1999).

intervene negatively. According to Cepeda Ulloa, two facts were of influence: "the serious public order situation generated by narco-terrorism and the pressure of public opinion and, without a doubt, President Gaviria's (1990–1994) skilled handling of the situation" (Cepeda Ulloa 2008, 196). The Constitution of 1991 is a transformative document that opened the political arena to previously marginalized actors (most notably the M-19 guerrilla), created a complex machinery of checks and balances, and in general terms brought the government and the state closer to citizens.

However, the internal security crisis was still there. Other actors such as the long-standing guerrilla FARC did not participate in the transformation of 1991, and their links to drug trafficking increased. Paramilitary forces also grew stronger during this decade, deepening a process of "erosion of the state" (Bejarano and Pizarro 2005, 254). Colombian democracy was again challenged. This time, successive presidents took different measures to increase civilian control over the armed forces, straining civil-military relations (Andrade Becerra 2012, 152). Such measures limited military autonomy, granting to the executive, legislative, or judicial branches the power to decide administrative and disciplinary issues (such as salaries or pensions or the investigation of regular crimes committed by military officers). President Gaviria also transformed the former Ministry of War into a Ministry of Defense and appointed a civilian minister for the first time since the National Front started.[29]

President Ernesto Samper (1994–8), who governed in the midst of accusations of having used drug money in his campaign, attenuated the impulse to increase civilian control over the armed forces (cf. Cabrera Ortiz 2005, 72–80). During his administration the internal security situation did not ameliorate, and he conceded to the armed forces discretion in dealing with guerrilla and paramilitary attacks in some parts of the country.[30] In 1997 the Mapiripán massacre took place, attracting the spotlight to the performance of the armed forces and their relation to paramilitary forces. In particular, between July 15 and July 20, 1997 members of the paramilitary group *Autodefensas Unidas de Colombia* took civilian hostages, tortured and killed more than twenty persons, and then dumped

[29] President Gaviria also conceded, in Decree 1810–1992, that members of the armed forces assumed the functions of the investigative police in crimes related to regional jurisdiction in places with no prosecutors (Ariza 1999, 20–1). The constitutional court, in decision C-034 1993 (analyzed in the following text), assessed the constitutionality of this decree.

[30] The so-called *Special Public Order Zones* (Cabrera Ortiz 2005, 82–3). The constitutional court, in C-295 1996 MP Hernando Herrera Vergara, also reviewed this decree creating the special order zones.

their remains into a river. The legal trajectory of this case is complex, and it involves decisions by the Colombian Supreme Court, the constitutional court (SU-1184 2001, MP Eduardo Montealegre Lynett, discussed in the following text), and the Inter American Court of Human Rights (*Caso Masacre de Mapiripán v. Colombia*, September 15, 2005).

President Andrés Pastrana (1998–2002) started peace negotiations with the FARC as soon as he assumed office. The talks not only failed but also created tensions with the armed forces due to Pastrana's decision to create a "distension zone" for the FARC free from armed forces.[31] More long-lasting were Pastrana's efforts to technify and professionalize the armed forces (the *Plan Colombia*), a process that was consolidated by President Álvaro Uribe (2002–6 and 2006–10). Uribe, a landowner whose father had been killed by the FARC and who had been accused of links with the Medellín Cartel and paramilitary groups, declared a frontal war against drug cartels and guerrilla movements.[32] His administration succeeded in strengthening the Colombian armed forces, weakening the cartels, and cornering the guerrillas. Based on this strategy, his government also implemented a controversial demobilization of paramilitary groups with the so-called Law of Peace and Justice (see García-Godos and Lid 2010). In a nutshell, Uribe championed his so called Democratic Security Policy.[33]

Álvaro Uribe moved fast and directly against the guerrillas and the drug cartels. Four days after he assumed office, he declared a state of interior commotion (a new figure in the 1991 Constitution) and produced a number of decrees (and a constitutional reform) enabling the armed forces to assume control in certain rehabilitation zones, performing judicial police functions in cases of terrorism (Revenga Sánchez and Girón Reguera

[31] The FARC took advantage of the military-free zone to regroup, rearm, and recover politically and financially. Also at the beginning of Pastrana's administration (December 13, 1998), the Santo Domingo massacre took place: going after FARC *guerrilleros*, Colombian Air Force planes bombed a set of houses on the outskirts of a village. Among the dead there were women and children. The legal trajectory of this case is also complex involving decision of the constitutional court (T-932 2002, MP Jaime Araujo Rentería; discussed in the following text) and the Inter American Court of Human Rights (*Caso Masacre de Santo Domingo v. Colombia*, August 19, 2013).

[32] See Uribe's profile, "A President on a Horse," by Marco Palacios in *Revista Semana*, http://www.semana.com/opinion/articulo/un-presidente-de-caballo/53476-3. Last accessed December 1, 2015.

[33] Interestingly, Uribe took the name from a constitutional court decision (C-251 2002, MP Eduardo Montealegre and Clara Inés Vargas) in which the Law of Security and Defense (promulgated at the end of Pastrana's administration) was reviewed (and parts of it declared unconstitutional, such as the idea of a National Power). Interview with Manuel José Cepeda, January 20, 2014.

2004, 29–32). The "frontal-war" strategy succeeded, but sooner rather than later the high number of human rights violations in which the armed forces were involved made headlines. Perhaps the most famous scandal is that of the "false positives" that erupted in 2008.[34] In part as a reaction to the mounting human rights violations, in 2006 Defense Minister Camilo Ospina made an administrative agreement to send most cases of deaths in combat to be investigated and tried in the ordinary jurisdiction.

Members of the armed forces have heavily criticized Ospina's agreement.[35] It is noteworthy that the constitutional court had already decided that whenever there was a doubt as to whether a case should go to military or ordinary jurisdiction, the latter should be favored.[36] But Ospina's agreement went further and implied almost automatically that the ordinary jurisdiction was competent whenever there was a death in combat. The (over)reach of this agreement has been part of the negotiations between the armed forces and civilian governments since then, and especially under the administration of President Juan Manuel Santos (2010–14 and 2014–18), who was defense minister under former president Uribe. In particular, in 2012 a constitutional reform of military justice in essence inverted the terms of Ospina's agreement favoring military jurisdiction. However, as will be discussed in the following text, this reform was declared unconstitutional by the constitutional court in 2013.

The Constitutional Court: Independence, Access, Powers

The Colombian Constitution of 1991 radically transformed the justice system and, in particular, the constitutional jurisdiction. First, an autonomous constitutional court with nine members enjoying an eight-year tenure was created. Each one of three different organs (the council of the state, the supreme court, and the executive) appoints three constitutional judges, subject to the approval of the senate majority. In addition to the public action of constitutionality and the automatic review of declaration of states of emergency and emergency decrees, the powers

34 "False positives" are innocent victims in military operations against guerrilla and drug-trafficking groups that are deliberately misreported as members of such groups. Close to 3,500 military officers are reported to be involved in this practice. See Colombia Reports, February 18, 2012, http://colombiareports.com/colombia-news/news/22286-colombia-withdraws-controversial-military-justice-proposal.html. Last accessed December 1, 2015.

35 Interview with Colonel (R) William Peña, January 27, 2014; and with Lieutenant Colonel Fabio Araque, President of the Superior Military Criminal Tribunal, January 28, 2014.

36 See C-358 1997, MP Eduardo Cifuentes Muñoz; SU-1184 2001 MP Eduardo Montealegre; T-932 2002, MP Jaime Araujo Rentería.

of constitutional review of the newly created court were expanded considerably with the creation of the *tutela*. This is an instrument for the protection of rights that is widely and easily accessible to the citizens who, almost immediately, began using the courts to defend their rights. The *tutela* can be filed with any judge in Colombia; it is free and there is no need for a lawyer or even the need to write down a suit: an illiterate citizen can dictate to the judge why he thinks that a public authority has violated one of his or her rights. The judge is then obliged to submit his or her decision to the constitutional court, which in turn has the discretionary power to select for revision only those *tutela* decisions it considers relevant.[37]

Colombian constitutional judges enjoy institutional incentives for asserting their preferences on many occasions, and for receiving great quantities of information on how actors operate under actual rules. In a nutshell, since 1991 the Colombian Constitutional Court is independent, accessible, and powerful enough to behave as a third-party mediator.[38] It is important to note that since 1991 the governing party does not have a majority in the legislative branch of government, the country has enjoyed relatively high levels of stability in economic terms, and the Colombian Constitutional Court enjoys relatively high levels of public support (Rodríguez-Raga 2011; Wilson 2009). In other words, Colombia since 1991 operates under favorable sociopolitical conditions, making the institutional incentives that impact on the independence, access, and powers of constitutional judges more likely to be more effective.

[37] Every single *tutela* decided by any Colombian judge goes to the constitutional court (after a second judge reviews the decision of the first judge who hears the case). *Tutelas* can also be filed against judicial decisions when procedural rights were violated, or when the substance contradicts the constitution according to the petitioner. The constitutional court after receiving literally hundreds of thousands of *tutelas*, only reviews the ones it considers relevant and transcendent. This explains why in my database there are only ten *tutelas*. These were the most important for the court on the topic of the book and through them it has made a huge impact. In numbers, from 1991 to 2013 a total of 4,200,357 *tutelas* reached the constitutional court; of those, the court selected to review 16,406 (Valderrama 2015, 79).

[38] This increment can be observed in the de jure indexes of judicial independence and judicial powers (that include access). Regarding independence there is no change vis-à-vis the supreme court in the previous period (value of 4 out of 6). Regarding powers there is an increase from 4 to 5 (out of 8) (Ríos-Figueroa 2011). While the difference in the de jure index of judicial review powers between the supreme and the constitutional courts appear low, as I will show, the high accessibility of the *tutela*, and the more discretion granted to the constitutional court proved to have a powerful transformative force on the court's jurisprudence.

The extraordinary conditions under which the Constitution of 1991 was created (see Negretto 2013, ch. 6), and the fact that the constitutional judges interpret a new constitution to which they are linked by birth, so to speak, imbued the first judges with a sense of mission regarding the letter and the spirit of the constitution as a way to deal with the complex causes that put Colombia in a critical situation (Nunes 2010). But this does not mean that judges' attitudinal profiles are similar, actually they have been quite diverse. Table 3.2 shows the composition of the constitutional court under each president from 1990 to 2014 that includes a measure of ideology based on a survey of a sample of forty-three public law professors at universities around the country, as well as former and current court clerks, who were asked to provide an ideological score (on a left-to-right 1-to-10 scale) for each of the justices who has been sworn in from 1992 to 2006 (Rodríguez-Raga 2011, 171–5). It is noteworthy that all presidents have faced a quite ideologically diverse court; if anything, a center-right ideology is what predominates slightly.

In part because of this ideological diversity, the constitutional court has actually behaved differently across issue areas: it is prudent regarding the government, very proactive in social and economic rights, and more cautious regarding social minorities such as the LGBT community (Rodríguez-Raga 2011; Valderrama 2015). In sum, whereas the internal security crisis that partly determined the creation of the Constitution of 1991 also partly determined the sense of mission of the constitutional judges, the effect of this variable is not unidirectional across political actors (who appoint judges) and judges' ideology. This is reflected in constitutional jurisprudence that is differentiated across issue areas.

Constitutional Jurisprudence on Military Autonomy

Despite the challenging political context of the 1990s, it did not take long for the recently created constitutional court to start interpreting the new constitution creatively. As early as 1992 the court marked a new standard regarding the declaration of "states of exception," and what the executive can do under them, going beyond a mere revision of procedural requirements. In open contrast to previous jurisprudence, the constitutional judges adopted a series of decisions establishing a three-prong test: whether the events invoked by the executive actually required the temporary suspension of certain constitutional features; whether the measures adopted by the executive are proportionate to the dangers specified in the declaration; and also whether the executive decrees issued during

Table 3.2. *Composition of Colombian Constitutional Court, by president (1990–2014)*

President César Gavira, Liberal Party (1990–4)			
Magistrate	Ideology score (Nominated by)	Magistrate	Ideology score (Nominated by)
1. Angarita Baron Ciro	N.A. (President)	Gavira Díaz Carlos (1993)	2.186 (Council of State)
2. Arango Mejía Jorge	6.625 (Supreme Court)		
3. Barrera Carbonell Antonio	5.923 (Council of State)		
4. Cifuentes Muñoz Eduardo	4.762 (President)		
5. Hernández Galindo José Gregorio	6.628 (Supreme Court)		
6. Martínez Caballero Alejandro	3.262 (President)		
7. Morón Díaz Fabio	5.691 (Supreme Court)		
8. Rodríguez Simón	N.A. (Council of State)	Herrera Vergara Hernando (1993)	6.737 (President)
9. Sanín Greiffenstein Jaime	President	Naranjo Mesa Vladimiro (1993)	7.784 (Council of State)

President Ernesto Samper, Liberal Party (1994–8)			
Magistrate	Ideology (Nominated by)	Magistrate	Ideology (Nominated by)
1. Arango Mejía Jorge	6.625 (Supreme Court)		
2. Barrera Carbonell Antonio	5.923 (Council of State)		

President Ernesto Samper, Liberal Party (1994–8)			
Magistrate	Ideology (Nominated by)	Magistrate	Ideology (Nominated by)
3. Cifuentes Muñoz Eduardo	4.762 (President)		
4. Gavira Díaz Carlos	2.186 (Council of State)		
5. Hernández Galindo José Gregorio	6.628 (Supreme Court)		
6. Herrera Vergara Hernando	6.737 (President)		
7. Martínez Caballero Alejandro	3.262 (President)		
8. Morón Díaz Fabio	5.691 (Supreme Court)		
9. Naranjo Mesa Vladimiro	7.784 (Council of State)		

President Andrés Pastrana, Conservative Party (1998–2002)			
Magistrate	Ideology (Nominated by)	Magistrate	Ideology (Nominated by)
1. Barrera Carbonell Antonio	5.923 (Council of State)	Cepeda Espinosa Manuel José (2001)	5.488 (President)
2. Beltrán Sierra Alfredo	3.619 (Supreme Court)		
3. Cifuentes Muñoz Eduardo	4.762 (President)	Córdoba Triviño Jaime	4.976 (Supreme Court)
4. Gavira Díaz Carlos	2.186 (Council of State)	Montealegre Lynett Luis Eduardo (2001)	6.119 (Council of State)

(*continued*)

Table 3.2 (*cont.*)

President Andrés Pastrana, Conservative Party (1998–2002)			
Magistrate	Ideology (Nominated by)	Magistrate	Ideology (Nominated by)
5. Hernández Galindo José Gregorio	6.628 (Supreme Court)	Escobar Gil Rodrigo (2001)	7.465 (Council of State)
6. Herrera Vergara Hernando	6.737 (President)	Tafur Galavis Álvaro (1999)	7.093 (President)
7. Martínez Caballero Alejandro	3.262 (President)	Araújo Rentería Jaime (2001)	3.256 (Council of State)
8. Morón Díaz Fabio	5.691 (Supreme Court)		
9. Naranjo Mesa Vladimiro	7.784 (Council of State)	Vargas Hernández Clara Inés (2001)	5.837 (President)

President Álvaro Uribe 1, Primero Colombia (2002–6)			
Magistrate	Ideology (Nominated by)	Magistrate	Ideology (Nominated by)
1. Araújo Rentería Jaime	3.256 (Council of State)		
2. Beltrán Sierra Alfredo	3.619 (Supreme Court)		
3. Cepeda Espinosa Manuel José	5.488 (President)		
4. Córdoba Triviño Jaime	4.976 (Supreme Court)		
5. Escobar Gil Rodrigo	7.465 (Council of State)		
6. Montealegre Lynett Luis Eduardo	6.119 (Council of State)		
7. Sierra Porto Humberto	5.762 (Council of State)		

President Álvaro Uribe 1, Primero Colombia (2002–6)			
Magistrate	Ideology (Nominated by)	Magistrate	Ideology (Nominated by)
8. Tafur Galavis Álvaro	7.093 (President)		
9. Vargas Hernández Clara Inés	5.837 (President)		

President Álvaro Uribe 2, Primero Colombia (2006–10)			
Magistrate	Ideology (Nominated by)	Magistrate	Ideology (Nominated by)
1. Araújo Rentería Jaime	3.256 (Council of State)	Henao Pérez Juan Carlos (2009)	N.A. (Council of State)
2. Cepeda Espinosa Manuel José	5.488 (President)	Calle Correa María Victoria (2009)	N.A. (President)
3. Córdoba Triviño Jaime	4.976 (Supreme Court)	Pretelt Chaljub Jorge Ignacio (2009)	N.A. (Supreme Court)
4. Escobar Gil Rodrigo	7.465 (Council of State)		
5. Palacio Jorge Iván	N.A. (Supreme Court)		
6. Pinilla Nilson	7.476 (Supreme Court)		
7. Sierra Porto Humberto Antonio	5.762 (Council of State)		
8. Tafur Galavis Álvaro	7.093 (President)	González Cuervo Mauricio (2007)	N.A. (President)
9. Vargas Hernández Clara Inés	5.837 (President)	Vargas Silva Luis Ernesto (2009)	N.A. (President)

(continued)

Table 3.2 (*cont.*)

President Juan Manuel Santos, Partido de la U (2010–14)			
Magistrate	Ideology (Nominated by)	Magistrate	Ideology (Nominated by)
1. Calle Correa María Victoria	N.A. (President)		
2. González Cuervo Mauricio	N.A. (President)		
3. Guerrero Pérez Luis Guillermo	N.A. (President)		
4. Vargas Silva Luis Ernesto	N.A. (Supreme Court)		
5. Sierra Porto Humberto Antonio	5.762 (Council of State)	Mendoza Martelo Gabriel Eduardo (2012)	N.A. (Council of State)
6. Palacio Jorge Iván	N.A. (Supreme Court)		
7. Pretelet Chaljub Jorge Ignacio	N.A. (President)		
8. Rojas Ríos Alberto	N.A. (Council of State)		
9. Pinilla Nilson	7.476 (Supreme Court)	Ortiz Delgado Gloria Stella	N.A. (Supreme Court)

Note: The table shows the composition of the constitutional court for each presidential period. Next to the name of the magistrate, there is a measure of ideology (left-to-right, 1-to-10 scale) and, in parentheses, the organ that nominated the judge. The measure of ideology is based on a survey of experts (Rodríguez-Raga 2011, 171–5). Specifically, a sample of forty-three public law professors at universities around the country, as well as former and current court clerks, were asked to provide an ideological score for each of the justices who were sworn in from 1992 to 2006.

the emergency but not directly connected to it should be unconstitutional (see Ariza, Cammaert, and Iturralde 1997; Uprimny 2003).[39]

Interestingly, in its first decision on the topic of states of emergency (C-004 1992, MP Eduardo Cifuentes Muñoz) the court upheld the state of emergency. However, in that same decision the court announced in its reasoning the restrictions on the executive's discretion to call a state of emergency and on the scope and extent of the measures that could be taken under it. In this way, the court began to delineate what would be acceptable under the new constitution for both the government and the armed forces. When new cases on states of emergency arrived to the court (from 1995 to 2002), it continued establishing the proper bounds of the states of emergency, limiting both actors and trying to conciliate their views. This gradual and "strategic [juris]prudence" (Rodríguez-Raga 2011) is one way in which the court reduces the uncertainty over the bounds of exceptions and extraordinary circumstances allowed by the constitution. The court announces a way forward giving time for the actors to adapt and prepare for what is coming. At the same time, by conceding the outcome in the first cases (accepting the constitutionality of the first declarations of a state of emergency in this case) the court avoids shaming the actors or producing outright noncompliance, recognizing that a change of this magnitude takes time to adapt to.

The constitutional court's jurisprudence on military autonomy also started sooner rather than later. In 1993, the court announced its new ideas about military autonomy. That year, the court reviewed an executive decree that allowed the armed forces to assume the investigative function of the police and the prosecutors (C-034 de 1993, MP Eduardo Cifuentes Muñoz). The court upheld the constitutionality of the decree but in order to maintain the spirit of the new Article 213, which precludes civilians from being tried in military tribunals, argued that members of the armed forces could be involved in the management of the investigative units but not in the actual investigation. The court also included in its decision clear argumentation of the very exceptional nature of this case, prudently announcing what the government could expect in similar cases in the future. In other words, in this decision the court considers the decree constitutional,

[39] The effect of this change in interpretation was quite dramatic: from 1992 to 2002, from a total of twelve declarations of state of exception, three were declared unconstitutional, and four partially unconstitutional. Because of this Colombia was in a state of exception less than 20 percent (rather than 80 percent) of the time (Uprimny 2006).

contingent on certain requirements for its application, again reducing the uncertainty of the actors about what the range of acceptable solutions to the question of military autonomy is under the new constitution.

The key decision (*sentencia hito*) on the scope of the military jurisdiction came in 1997 (C-358 1997, MP Eduardo Cifuentes Muñoz). In essence, the court argued that in order for a case to belong to the military jurisdiction three conditions had to be met: a subjective condition according to which only members of the armed forces can be tried in military courts; a functional condition according to which there must be a proximate and direct relation between a crime and the military service or mission under which it was committed; and an additional requirement that the link between crime and service is severed in cases of grave violations of human rights. This decision therefore implies a substantial reduction in the scope of the military jurisdiction vis-á-vis the jurisprudence of the period 1958–91. The court, however, again announced in previous decisions the some aspects of what became after this case the new doctrine on the scope of the military jurisdiction. Specifically, the court had already announced that severe violations to human rights do not belong under any circumstance to the military jurisdiction (Auto 012 1994, MP Jorge Arango; C-399 1995, MP Alejandro Martínez Caballero; and C-017 1996 MP Alejandro Martínez Caballero).

The scope of military jurisdiction was even further reduced. In a series of decisions that build on C-358 1997 (MP Eduardo Cifuentes Muñoz) the court started to carefully distinguish what it meant by a "direct relation between a crime and a military service." For instance, the court argued that not all activities performed by members of the armed forces can be considered "related to service," but only those that are directly tied to the function and goals that the constitution establishes for the armed forces (e.g., C-878 de 2000, MP Alfredo Beltrán Sierra). The court also carefully and gradually justified the exclusion of grave human rights violations from the military jurisdiction. The court's argument proceeds in nicely tied logical steps: the ultimate mission of the armed forces is to defend the country and its constitution, which is grounded upon universal principles and human rights, and therefore violations of human rights by military officers, even if they take place under a specific service, sever the link between the armed forces and their ultimate mission (e.g., SU-1184 de 2001, MP Eduardo Montealegre).[40]

[40] In SU-1184 2001, the constitutional court went even further, arguing that not only grave violations of human rights belong to the ordinary jurisdiction but also that armed forces' omission to act, which lead to such grave violations, also belong to ordinary courts. This

The constitutional court, therefore, gradually established a quite restricted scope of military jurisdiction.[41] The court did this despite the critical conditions of internal security of the 1990s and 2000s. But simply limiting the armed forces in the challenging and complex political context of Colombia could, arguably, have limited the efficacy of the military and exacerbated the tensions with the civilian government. In fact, the perception of the armed forces in the first half of the 1990s was that the government was using the court as "a shield" diverting responsibility for limiting the military's autonomy.[42] Moreover, during the 1990s the activity of the paramilitary groups increased and there is some evidence that this could be linked to the limitation of the armed forces that, explicitly or not, supported the paramilitary groups in doing the dirty work.[43]

But the constitutional court has done much more regarding the armed forces than drastically limiting the scope of the military jurisdiction, albeit gradually and with careful argumentation. The constitutional court has also consistently respected the autonomy and, perhaps more importantly, the specificity of the armed forces. The court has actually transformed the preferences of both the armed forces and the civil government regarding the internal conflict in Colombia, and the way to deal with it. As we shall see, the court has done this through creative and forward-looking jurisprudence.

Regarding military autonomy and the specificity of the armed forces, in some mundane but nevertheless highly consequential issues the constitutional court has argued that the special nature of the job of the armed forces justifies a different treatment for them, reducing in this way uncertainty over clashing constitutional principles. For instance, the court has consistently sustained that despite the principle of equal treatment of the constitution, members of the armed forces have a right to a special pension and retirement system because they put their lives in danger in order

decision refers to the Mapiripán massacre, and General Uscátegui was held responsible for not having stopped the killings perpetrated by the paramilitaries. The armed forces have considered this decision an overreach and have heavily criticized it. Moreover, because some of the alleged victims have turned out to be alive, the armed forces consider that this case is part of a "legal war" against them (interview with Dr. Edgar Saavedra Rojas, General Uscátegui's defense attorney, January 31, 2014).

41 In this way, the Colombian Constitutional Court avoided producing decisions that were too restrictive/expansive too fast or that can either humiliate the civilian government or the military. According to Barany (2012), this is what occurred in Argentina, where derogation of the military jurisdiction was carried out with considerable experience.

42 Interview with Yahayra Bernal on January 26, 2014.

43 Interview with César Rodríguez Garavito and Mauricio García Villegas, January 28, 2014. See essays in Boaventura de Sousa and García Villegas (2001).

to protect the rest of the citizens (e.g., C-461 1995, MP Eduardo Cifuentes Muñoz; C-432 2004, MP Rodrigo Escobar Gil). The court has also maintained itself essentially aloof in cases in which career management decisions (e.g., promotions and retirements) are being challenged (e.g., T-1140 2004, MP Manuel José Cepeda; C-819 2005, MP Marco Gerardo Monroy Cabra). In these decisions, the constitutional court has added that all matters related to the planning, organization, and implementation of a specific mission or strategy are not judicially revisable.

The court has also reduced uncertainty around the balancing of liberty and duties regarding military service. In particular, based on the specificity of the armed forces and the country's circumstances of security, the court has upheld the mandatory character of the military service (e.g., T-218 2010, MP Gabriel Eduardo Mendoza Martelo) and has declared the measures taken to round up draft evaders constitutional (C-879 2011, MP Humberto Sierra Porto). The court has also reduced the uncertainty over the legal consequences for actions of police and military officers in service. Specifically, in a series of decisions the court has distinguished between the police (a "reactive and passive" force) and the military ("an active force of attack") and specified the type of actions that are allowed for each type of force (e.g., C-358 1997, MP Eduardo Cifuentes Muñoz; SU-1184 2001, MP Eduardo Montealegre). Moreover, the court has argued that when police officers are called on to play the role of the army then they should be investigated and tried within the military jurisdiction (e.g., C-444 1995, MP Carlos Gaviria Díaz). Consistent with the preceding lines of argumentation, the court has reversed decisions of the judicial council and sent some cases that fall under the proper domain of the armed forces to the military jurisdiction (e.g., T-1001 2001, MP Rodrigo Escobar Gil; T-932 2002, MP Jaime Araujo Rentería).[44]

The jurisprudence of the constitutional court on military autonomy and the scope of the military jurisdiction has made an impact on other high courts. For some years, the decisions by the constitutional court were resisted, and some actually ignored, by the superior tribunal of military

[44] Decision T-932 2002, MP Jaime Araujo Rentería, is related to the Santo Domingo massacre, which has been highly consequential, in particular for the air force. Since then the air force has deepened its commitment to educating its members in law, human rights, and international humanitarian law. The air force distinguishes itself in this regard from the navy and the army, which partly explains why most of the members of the military tribunal and prosecutorial military office come from its ranks (interview with Yahayra Bernal, January 26, 2014; and with Colonel Rentería, prosecutor before the military tribunal, January 28, 2014).

criminal justice and by the judicial council, the organ that since 1991 has been in charge of deciding conflicts of competence between the civil and military jurisdictions.[45] However, for different reasons, among which is the persuasiveness of the court's argumentation, as time passed the criteria established by the court was progressively adopted not only by the judicial council, but also by the highest military court that has even voluntarily sent some cases to the civil jurisdiction (Ariza 1999; Cabarcas Maciá 2011). The council of state (*consejo de estado*), a court that makes decisions on administrative matters, has also progressively included the jurisprudence of the constitutional court in its decisions. And the armed forces have come to accept, for instance, that cases that involve grave violations of human rights never belong to the military jurisdiction.[46]

More interesting is the impact that the constitutional court's jurisprudence on the proper legal framework applicable to Colombia's situation has had on the preferences of the armed forces and the civil government. Specifically, the court's understanding and application of the International Humanitarian Law (IHL), the law of war, has been highly consequential. The Constitution of 1991 recognized the importance of IHL but only during states of emergency, which we have seen that the constitutional court strongly limited. However, in a crucial decision (*sentencia hito*) the court argued that the IHL was applicable whenever there is an "situation of internal armed-conflict" in the country and, more importantly, that it is not up to the government but to the judges to check whether the criteria for declaring such a situation are present (C-225 1995, MP Alejandro Martínez Caballero).[47]

45 Before 1991, the criminal chamber of the supreme court was in charge of deciding conflicts of jurisdiction.

46 Interviews with Lieutenant Colonel Fabio Araque (January 28, 2014) and with Manuel José Cepeda (January 31, 2014). Neil Oswaldo Rodríguez, prosecutor before the military tribunal, adds that this recognition can already be found in the Military Code of Justice of 1998, and even more explicitly in the current Military Code of Justice of 2010 (interview January 29, 2014).

47 These criteria are present in common Article 3 of the Geneva Conventions, in Protocol II, and in international jurisprudence. Interestingly, the Colombian Supreme Court, which is the highest court in criminal matters, and thus the one in charge of applying the IHL to specific cases, has resisted making such applicability checks because that is an inherently political consideration. Communication with Yahayra Bernal, July 26, 2014. In Peru, the Constitutional Tribunal made a very similar argument regarding the applicability of the IHL (see Chapter 4). Chapter 6 is devoted entirely to the question on whether and how the Colombian, Peruvian, and Mexican constitutional organs regulate the use of force. It includes a more detailed discussion of the IHL and the interesting jurisprudential line on this issue produced by the Colombian Constitutional Court.

The legal consequences of such a declaration are huge: if a "situation of internal armed-conflict" is not officially declared and the armed forces kill someone, the criminal code is used and it presupposes that this death can be a homicide. But if there is an officially declared "situation of internal armed-conflict," then the IHL is used and this death could be just that: a death in combat.[48] In the words of the court: "the death in combat of a member of an insurgent group by the armed forces is not a homicide and thus is not punishable" (C-177 2001, MP Fabio Morón Díaz). The question is, then, who can officially declare an internal armed conflict. As mentioned, the court had argued that this was within the province of the courts, not the government. For years, the Colombian government resisted declaring an internal conflict because that meant "legitimizing" the guerrilla groups by giving them a legal status as recognized combatants. An official declaration of internal conflict also implies less discretion for the state because of, for instance, increases in international supervision such as the presence of the International Red Cross.

The court has built upon a series of decisions exactly how IHL should be used as the legal framework for investigating and judging the participation of the armed forces in an internal conflict (e.g., C-456 1997, MPs Jorge Arango Mejía y Eduardo Cifuentes Muños; C-991 2000, MP Álvaro Tafur Galvis; C-251 2002, MPs Eduardo Montealegre y Clara Inés Vargas; C-1076 2002, MP Clara Inés Vargas; C-004 2003, MP Eduardo Montealegre; C-979 2005, MP Jaime Córdoba Triviño).[49] In essence, one could argue, the constitutional court responded to the concerns of the armed forces with the IHL. Specifically, members of the armed forces wondered what their rights and their legal framework were once the court had considerably limited the scope of the military jurisdiction. The constitutional court, acknowledging the complex situation, creatively responded that in situations of combat the appropriate legal framework is the IHL with the rights for the military officers and limitations of the use of force that it implies.

The jurisprudence of constitutional court on the use and application of the IHL in Colombia has transformed the perceptions and the preferences of both the armed forces and the civilian government. At first, neither actor welcomed the court's initiative: the government because the court took away from it the capacity to declare whether there is an

[48] Of course, there can be violations to IHL whenever, e.g., the principle of proportionality or the principle of necessity in the use of force is violated.

[49] Communication with Nerea Aparicio, international lawyer and former member of the General Secretariat of the Inter American Commission of Human Rights, June 23, 2014. A discussion on this jurisprudential line can be found in Chapter 6.

"internal armed conflict"; the armed forces because they thought the court was "tying their hands" and "undermining their efficacy," simultaneously granting the status of belligerent actor to the "subversives."[50] But then both actors gradually learned that the IHL could be effective for dealing with the internal armed conflict that Colombia actually has. Within the armed forces the acceptance of IHL started in the air force.[51] One of the things that the armed forces learned is that embracing the IHL and the constitutional bounds gives them weapons to win the battle for legitimacy (Jaime Córdoba Triviño, former member of the constitutional court, put it this way). In contrast, remember the epigraph of this chapter: the *Mono Jojoy*, former leader of the FARC, declared: "We don't give a shit for the constitution or for the laws because we are outside them" (interview published in *Revista Semana*, January 10, 1999).[52]

Successive civil governments have also accepted the arguments of the court regarding the IHL, and therefore have recognized the need to give special rules for the engagement of the armed forces in internal security missions. This does not mean that civil military relations are no longer tense, or that all key issues regarding military autonomy have been solved. But the constitutional court has been a key and constructive actor regarding this sensitive issue for Colombian politics and society. Perhaps the strongest impact of the jurisprudence of the constitutional court has been felt during the last couple of years during which a constitutional amendment on the scope of military jurisdiction has been debated. Specifically, in 2012 there were negotiations to create a new legislative framework for military justice in Colombia: they took place under the shadow of years of creative, serious, and forward-looking constitutional jurisprudence of the constitutional court.

[50] Interview with Lieutenant Colonel, Fabio Araque, January 28, 2014; with Neil Oswaldo Rodríguez Morales, prosecutor before the military tribunal, January 29, 2014; and with Jaime Córdoba Triviño, January 28, 2014. Rodrigo Uprimny noted that the original idea of the court expanding the applicability of the IHL in Colombia (in decision C-225 1995, MP Alejandro Martínez Caballero that was written while he was a magistrate in the court) was to limit the military, to "place rules on the armed conflict." Interview January 30, 2014.

[51] Lieutenant Colonel Fabio Araque, president of the superior criminal military tribunal, said that the court started understanding the situation when it wrote "a death in combat is not a homicide" (in decision C-177 2001, MP Fabio Morón Díaz). "I like those words," he said. Interview January 28, 2014.

[52] Interestingly, a fuller embrace of IHL by the armed forces came under President Uribe's administration, specifically with the Law of Peace and Justice, and because of the scandals of violations of human rights and the "false positives." Interview with Manuel José Cepeda and with Rodrigo Uprimny (January 28 and January 30, 2014, respectively).

The armed forces pushed for a reform to military jurisdiction in order to both deal with scandals such as the "false positives" and to provide legal security to the military men that participate in affairs of internal security. One of the demands of the armed forces was to revert Ospina's deal (made under President Uribe's jurisdiction) and to give priority to the military jurisdiction whenever a violation of IHL takes place. To deal with this demand, and to find an agreement acceptable to all the parties and institutions involved, the government created a High Commission formed by experts, both civilian and military. Two of the civilian members of the commission were the very former constitutional judges who drafted some of the most important decisions limiting the military jurisdiction (Manuel José Cepeda and Jaime Córdoba Triviño).

Some of the innovative proposals generated by the High Commission and the negotiation between the armed forces and the civilian government are noteworthy. For instance, both actors agreed that the IHL is the legal framework to be applied in the Colombian situation, and that violations to IHL should be investigated and tried in the military justice system. But both actors also agreed upon a list of crimes that do not belong under any circumstance to military jurisdiction (informed by constitutional jurisprudence) and they also agreed that difficult cases should be heard in a committee with ordinary and military judges that would decide to which jurisdiction the case belongs.[53] As former constitutional judge and member of the Commission, Manuel José Cepeda, put it "these proposals reflect a bargain between the Armed Forces and the civilian authorities that creatively balances the clashing aims of protecting human rights by limiting military jurisdiction and providing legal security and procedural rights to the members of the armed forces that participate in risky and dangerous missions."[54]

Conclusion: The Constitutional Court as a Mediator

The institutional change in 1991 that altered the incentives on the independence, access, and powers of constitutional judges was consequential. A more accessible and powerful constitutional court has produced mediator-like jurisprudence on military autonomy, and thus helped to build bridges between the armed forces and the civilian governments.

[53] See *Revista Semana*, May 22, 2012, http://www.semana.com/politica/senado-no-amplia-fuero-militar-para-combatir-bacrim/177573-3.aspx. Last accessed December 1, 2015.

[54] *El Espectador*, February 25, 2012, http://www.eltiempo.com/justicia/ARTICULO-WEB-NEW_NOTA_INTERIOR-11221141.html. Last accessed February 28, 2016.

Through careful and prudent jurisprudence the court has reduced the uncertainty about the legal consequences of the actions of both actors, the bounds to exceptions allowed by the constitution, and clashing constitutional principles. This contributed to closing the gap between the civil government's and the military's preferences on the appropriate level of military autonomy, as shown in the jurisprudence on the specificity of the armed forces and the scope of military jurisdiction. The constitutional court did this by weighing in and mixing both actors' points of view, promoting deliberation between them – and through mutual understanding.

Conflicts between the armed forces and the civilian governments will still take place in Colombia. However, the constitutional court has been, and will likely continue to be, a key actor shaping this relationship. The constitutional reform on military jurisdiction was passed at the end of 2012. During 2013 the constitutional court declared it unconstitutional, in a 4–5 vote, arguing that there were violations to the process for reforming the constitution. The substantive discussion involves whether a violation of the IHL should go primarily to the military or to the ordinary jurisdiction. One side argues that if it is a violation of IHL then it must have happened under an internal armed conflict, and therefore, it is a matter of war and belongs to the military jurisdiction. The other side argues that a violation of the principles of IHL is a fundamental matter for the state, which is a constitutional democracy, and therefore this violation should be reviewed first by the ordinary (and not the exceptional) jurisdiction. The peace talks with the FARC (2014–15) have also taken place under the shadow of the informative jurisprudence created by the constitutional court. In any case, the fact that civilian-military relations and the peace talks in Colombia are taking place in these terms is proof of the impact of the constitutional court and how it has helped Colombian political actors navigate the troubled waters of internal security crises.

4

Constitutional Jurisprudence on Military Autonomy in Peru, 1979–2013

> Nueve sentencias del tribunal constitucional interpuestas por 64 ONGs casi desaparecen la justicia militar.... Pero con una sola sentencia logramos revertir las nueve en contra y hasta nos devolvieron facultades.
>
> (Nine decisions by the constitutional tribunal filed by 64 NGOs almost destroyed military justice.... But with one decision we managed to revert those previous nine decisions and to even get back some prerogatives.)
>
> Contra Admiral CJ (R) Carlos Mesa Angosto, former president of the Superior Military Tribunal (*El Correo*, December 25, 2012)

This chapter analyzes constitutional jurisprudence on military autonomy in two recent periods of Peruvian history: the first starting in 1979, the year when the constitution was enacted following ten years of military rule, until 1992; and the second from 1993, the year when the current constitution was enacted, until 2013.[1] Specifically, I quantitatively and qualitatively analyze the decisions made by the tribunal of constitutional guarantees during the first period, and in the second those made by the constitutional tribunal in cases that challenge a previous decision made by a military authority (e.g., a military court, prosecutor, officer, or military administrative agency), and in cases that reach the constitutional organ on the scope of the military jurisdiction.

Taking advantage of the fact that the constitutional tribunal enjoys lower levels of independence, but higher levels of access, and powers of judicial review than the tribunal of constitutional guarantees, I explore whether the constitutional tribunal's behavior is closer to the ideal of

[1] The period from April 5, 1992 to October 31, 1993 is the a-constitutional period between Alberto Fujimori's so-called self-coup and the ratification in referendum of the current constitution. Some authors argue that this interim period finished when a new congress was elected, in November 1992 (Tanaka 2005, 263). After that, the period from 1992 to 2001, the year when Fujimori left Peru, cannot be considered as fully democratic. Despite the fact that the theory proposed in this book applies to democracies, I include this period in the analysis because it is interesting as a contrast and also in order to not lose historical continuity in the narrative.

third-party mediator in conflict resolution than the behavior of the tribunal of constitutional guarantees. To quickly preview the conclusion of the chapter: the answer is that the jurisprudence of the two courts is clearly different, but not to the extent that the constitutional tribunal can be considered an actual mediator. The main reason is that the constitutional tribunal lacks independence, which is a necessary condition for producing mediator-like jurisprudence. In the chapter, this lack of independence is nicely reflected in inconsistent jurisprudence produced by the constitutional tribunal and summarized by Contra Admiral Mesa Angosto in the epigraph.

In what follows, I first provide an overview of constitutional jurisprudence in the whole period analyzed in the chapter, and then I devote one section to each of the two subperiods analyzed in detail, focusing on the political context and civil-military relations, the characteristics of the constitutional organ during the period, and the constitutional jurisprudence on military autonomy produced by it.

Long-Term Jurisprudential Patterns on Military Autonomy in Peru, 1979–2013

The armed forces as an organization are a key actor in the twentieth century history of Peru. The military constantly intervened in politics since 1912 and until 1980. During this period, only one freely elected president completed his term without a coup (Palmer 1980, 10). Moreover, military officers held power in Peru from 1930 to 1939, 1948 to 1956, 1962 to 1963, and finally during the *desarrollista* military regime between 1968 and 1980. This history of military interventions, and the peculiar Peruvian pattern of civilian-military relations, produced by the end of the 1970s legitimate armed forces that in general terms enjoyed the respect of the wider society (Palmer 1980, 93). However, the Peruvian armed forces got used to very high levels of autonomy, which was sometimes unduly used to cover up some ordinary crimes committed by military officers that had nothing to do with their specialized mission (Alegría Varona 2003, 50). What did the constitutional organ do when specific cases on military autonomy reached the court?

Figure 4.1 shows decisions by the constitutional tribunal (1997–2013) on military autonomy.[2] The constitutional organ can reject or amend a

[2] The complete database consists of 554 decisions, the bulk of them from 1997 to 2013, of which 10 are actions of unconstitutionality, 435 habeas corpus, and 109 *amparos*. With the help of Jimena Salazar, we systematically and thoroughly searched the webpage and the archives of the constitutional tribunal (1997–2013) for all cases on military jurisdiction. If there are cases not included in this database, we believe they would not alter the tendencies shown in Figures 4.1

previous decision made by a military authority, which I code as "limiting autonomy," or rather uphold it, which I consider as "respecting autonomy." Figure 4.1 shows that in almost all years since 1997 there are more decisions respecting the autonomy of the military. The years in which there are more decisions limiting military autonomy are 2002 and most notably 2003. These are the first two years of the presidency of Alejandro Toledo (2001–6), when his government had publicly stated that it was necessary to make the armed forces, and in particular the system of military justice, fully comply with democratic standards (Salazar Villalobos 2006, 341). However, this commitment faded away in subsequent years and, interestingly, the number of decisions respecting military autonomy again outnumbered those limiting it from 2004 onward.

Let's zoom in on a specific aspect of military autonomy: Figure 4.2 shows decisions by the Tribunal of Constitutional Guarantees (1979–92) and by the Constitutional Tribunal (1993–2013) on the scope of the military jurisdiction, which essentially is the court's answer to the question: Who can be judged in military courts, and under what circumstances?[3] I code judicial answers within eleven categories ordered from the narrowest to the widest: (0) nobody ever, that is, the military jurisdiction is abolished; (1) not even military personnel when crimes against humanity and gross human rights violations are involved; (2) only military personnel, only when strictly military crimes are involved; (3, 4, 5) only military personnel, only when crimes were committed during service construed in a narrow, regular, or broad way respectively; (6) only military personnel, under any circumstance; (7, 8) military personnel and civilians, only during emergency situations construed in a narrow or broad way, respectively; and (9, 10) military personnel and civilians, under circumstances broader than emergencies, narrowly and broadly construed, respectively. The horizontal axis in Figure 4.2 displays the date in which the decision was made. The vertical axis displays the categories on the scope of military jurisdiction on a scale from the narrowest to the widest scope, 0 to 10.

and 4.2. The full list of cases can be found at http://www.investigadores.cide.edu/julio.rios/. In Figure 4.1 only decisions from 1997 to 2013 are displayed. Decisions prior to 1997 made by the tribunal of constitutional guarantees are coded based on secondary literature (described in detail in the following text). The actual decisions produced by the tribunal of constitutional guarantees are hard to access. During Fujimori's self-coup in 1992 part of the archives were destroyed by the armed forces that were looking for files from the 1980s and, specifically, on Vladimiro Montesinos (interview with David Lovatón, June 23, 2012).

[3] As in the previous chapter, this question establishes the "constitutional scenario," a factual question where the interests of actors clash and whose answer requires an interpretation of the Constitution (López Medina 2009, 154).

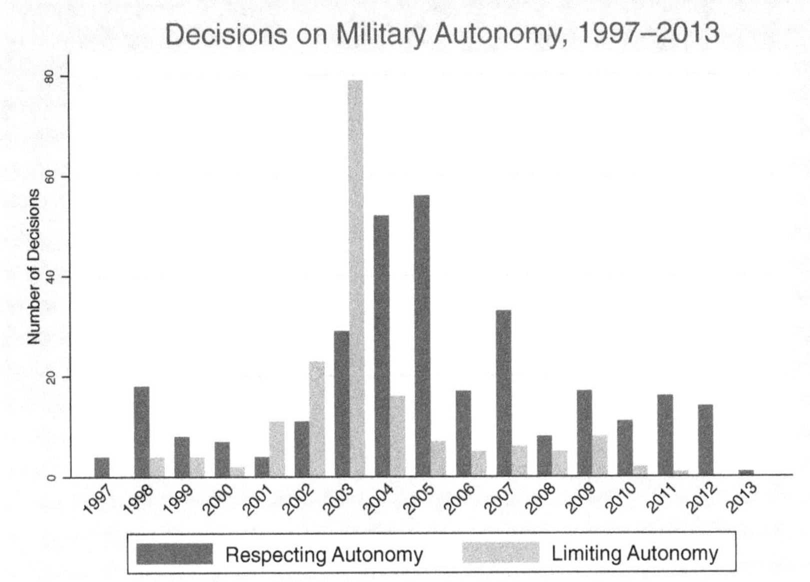

Figure 4.1. The constitutional tribunal can reject or amend a previous decision made by a military authority, which is coded as "limiting autonomy," or rather uphold it, which is coded as "respecting autonomy." The figure shows raw numbers; the percentages of decisions "respecting"/"limiting" autonomy" per year are the following. 1997: 100/0; 1998: 82/18; 1999: 67/33; 2000: 78/22; 2001: 27/73; 2002: 32/68; 2003: 27/63; 2004: 76/24; 2005: 89/11; 2006: 77/23; 2007: 85/15; 2008: 62/38; 2009: 68/32; 2010: 85/15; 2011: 94/6; 2012: 100/0; 2013: 100/0.

Figure 4.2 also includes the constitution's response to the question on the scope of military jurisdiction, which are the horizontal lines situated at "AAFF in Service" (Constitution of 1980) and the horizontal line situated at "AAFF & Civilians in Emergencies" (Constitution of 1993). Specifically, in the 1979 Constitution we find the explicit scope of the military jurisdiction in Article 282 that says: "members of the Armed and of the Police Forces in cases related to military crimes [*delitos de función*] will be subject to a special military jurisdiction and to the Code of Military Justice, but this is not applicable to civilians except in the cases mentioned in Art. 235."[4] This is quite

[4] The conditions in Article 235 are high treason (*traición a la patria*) and external war. In the previous Peruvian constitutions of the twentieth century we find broader definitions. For instance, in the Constitution of 1920, that lasted for a little more than a decade until it was replaced in 1933, Article 156 stated that "the military justice will not be able to, under

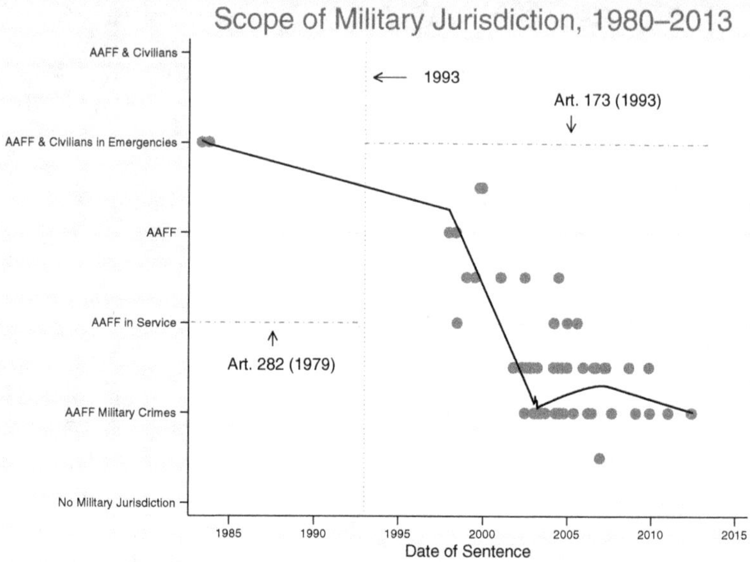

Figure 4.2. Decisions by the *tribunal de garantías constitucionales* (1980–92) and by the tribunal *constitucional* (1993–2013) on the scope of the military jurisdiction, which essentially is the courts' answer to the question: Who can be judged in military courts, and under what circumstances? The solid line displays a locally weighted regression on the data (lowess in STATA). The dotted horizontal lines at "AAFF in Service" and at "AAFF & Civilians in Emergencies" represent the answer to the question on the scope of military jurisdiction by the Constitution of 1979 and the Constitution of 1993, respectively.

a narrow scope of the military jurisdiction, and thus the horizontal line at "AAFF in Service" in Figure 4.2 (cf. Eto Cruz, Landa Arroyo, and Palomino Manchego 1997, 376). In contrast, the current 1993 Constitution defines a broader scope:

> Article 173.- In the case of military crimes [*delitos de función*], the members of the Armed Forces and of the National Police are subjected to a

any circumstance, extend its jurisdiction to persons that are not actively in the service of the Army [or Police Forces], except in the case of National War" (in 1927 there was an amendment to include what is in brackets). The 1933 Constitution, which was in force for almost five decades until 1979, is interestingly silent with respect to the scope of the military jurisdiction because in Article 229 it says that this matter is to be found in the ordinary legislation.

> special military jurisdiction and to the Code of Military Justice. This is not applicable to civilians, except in cases of treason to the fatherland and of terrorism that are determined by law. The appeals referred to by Art. 141 are only applicable in cases of the death sentence.[5]

Thus, in Figure 4.2 the 1993 Constitution's answer to the scope of military jurisdiction is at "AAFF & Civilians in Emergencies."

Figure 4.2 shows that the jurisprudence from 1979 to 1993 is not only sporadic but also supportive of a scope of military jurisdiction broader than what the 1979 Constitution actually stated.[6] In contrast, from 1993 to 2013 (actually from 1996 when the constitutional tribunal was formally established), but clearly after 2002, the jurisprudence sets a scope of the military jurisdiction substantially narrower than what the 1993 Constitution establishes. The period from 2002 to 2013 deserves special attention not only because there is a great deal of constitutional litigation that touches on the armed forces but also because the jurisprudence on the scope of the military jurisdiction follows a kind of zigzag pattern: first a series of decisions limiting the scope of the military jurisdiction, and then around 2006 a series of decisions expanding it. What explains these jurisprudential patterns? Has the organ in charge of defending the constitution in Peru behaved as a third-party mediator in civilian-military relations?

The Tribunal of Constitutional Guarantees, 1979–1992

Political Context and Civilian-Military Relations

The constituent assembly that crafted the 1979 Constitution was popularly elected and multilateral: there was no political party with a majority that allowed it to make decisions by itself. Even though the assembly worked while the military was still in government, the armed forces did not exert undue influence on the negotiations (Eguiguren Praeli 1990, 28–30).[7] However, days before General Francisco Morales Bermúdez handed power over to president elect Fernando Belaúnde Terry in 1980, the military government passed a series of decrees that enhanced the autonomy

[5] Article 141 states that the supreme court can hear appeals to cases in military jurisdiction with some limitations explicit in Article 173 (i.e., only in death sentences).

[6] Secondary literature and personal interviews with experts on the period (including magistrates) support this assertion, as will be clear in the next section of this chapter.

[7] Some authors argue that the 1979 Constitution actually ends a decades-long difficult relationship between the Aprista Party (APRA – after Popular Revolutionary American Alliance) and the armed forces (see García Belaúnde 1990; Palmer 1980).

and the capacities of the armed forces (Rubio Correa 1990, 254–5). The decrees included a new Military Code of Justice with a longer and vaguer list of typified crimes to be heard in military courts, thus establishing a considerably wider scope of military jurisdiction than what the constitution established (Salazar Villalobos 2006, 315).[8] Such a high degree of military autonomy proved to be consequential when President Belaúnde (1980–5) decided to call on the armed forces to face the challenges posed by the Shining Path, a radical faction of the Peruvian Communist Party that started a guerilla war against the state the very same year that Belaúnde assumed office (Alegría Varona 2003).

During the period when the 1979 Constitution was in force, Peruvian citizens first elected president Belaúnde (1980–5) from the right-of-center party *Acción Popular*, then in 1985 they elected Alan García (1985–90) from the left-of-center APRA, and then in 1990 they elected Alberto Fujimori a political outsider who founded the ad hoc party *Cambio 90*. In other words, alternation in power and democracy in Peru during the decade of 1980s was firmly established (Tanaka 2005). However, this democracy faced remarkable challenges in the economic and internal security arenas. On the economic front, Peru shared with countries like Argentina or Brazil or Bolivia the painful consequences of the exhaustion of the state-based development model prevalent in the 1960s and 1970s, such as extremely high levels of inflation and meager economic growth (Tanaka 2005, 266). As Martin Tanaka argues, part of Fujimori's popularity and success in the first two years of his administration is due to the control of inflation and the startup of an economic recovery.

In addition to the economic hardships, Peruvian internal security entered into a critical period in the 1980s. The Shining Path emerged from a split within an already divided Peruvian Communist Party. This radical group refused to participate in the elections for the constituent assembly in 1978 and actually started its fight against the Peruvian state boycotting some voting booths in the general elections of 1980. By October 1980 the Shining Path had already produced 166 terrorist attacks, mostly in the province of Ayacucho and its surroundings (Toche Medrano 2008, 210–11). However, it was not until one year later when President Belaúnde declared the first state of emergency in Ayacucho to deal with the problem: that

[8] Broadening the scope of the military jurisdiction in the Code of Military Justice while keeping a narrower scope in the constitution is not an uncommon practice. The Code of Military Justice enacted in Mexico in 1933 also included a long list of ordinary crimes (see Chapter 5), and something similar happened in Guatemala (Kyle and Reiter 2013, 387), and in Colombia in 1958 (see Chapter 3).

province will remain in a state of emergency for the following ten years. Sooner rather than later other provinces joined Ayacucho and by 1988 the Peruvian population living under emergency conditions reached 43 percent (Eguiguren Praeli 1989, 267).

President Belaúnde intensified the military strategy at the end of 1982, creating the figure of "Political-Military Commands" through which the military took control of the areas declared under a state of emergency, establishing military courts.[9] The purely military strategy was not effective and violence escalated during that decade. The armed forces were internally divided and dealing with the burden of its failed development project implemented during the last military regime (1968–80). But this time the armed forces also faced a better organized and farsighted enemy than those other radical guerrilla groups that it had successfully defeated in the recent past, such as the *Ejército de Liberación Nacional* in 1962 and the *Movimiento de Izquierda Revolucionaria* in 1965 (Toche Medrano 2008, 292).

The internal conflict in Peru escalated considerably. The Truth and Reconciliation Commission, established in 2001, estimated that the total number of deaths during those years was close to seventy thousand. Moreover, the commission's report reveals some grave cases of disproportional and careless use of force by the military as early as 1984 and 1985 (cited in Salazar Villalobos 2006, 316–17). These and other cases that involved military officers were systematically channeled to the military justice system for their investigation and trial.[10] When someone challenged the competence of the military jurisdiction to decide those cases, the organ in charge of solving conflicts of jurisdiction (i.e., the supreme court) decided systematically in favor of the military jurisdiction based on what can be called a personal-identity criteria, in essence establishing that if there are military officers involved in the case then the case belongs

[9] The protracted response to the Shining Path challenge, according to Bonilla, is explained by the fear that President Belaúnde had that the army would not only defeat the terrorist group but also his government as in 1968, when the military staged a coup to depose him (Bonilla 2006, 127).

[10] The final report can be found at http://www.cverdad.org.pe/. Last accessed December 2, 2015. The report states that: "during the period from 1980 until 1992, the ordinary judges practically sent all cases that reached them to the military jurisdiction and, when they did not, after a conflict of competence a superior court usually did rule in favor of the military jurisdiction. Only a handful of cases where police officers were involved … were sent to ordinary courts. At the same time, highly salient cases were decided in favor of the military jurisdiction. This pattern was extended after the cases of Accomarca and Parco-Pomatambo and Cayara, in which the military officers involved were acquitted by military tribunals."

to the military justice.[11] The government went further, widening the scope of military jurisdiction in Law 24150 (June 1985), which regulates states of emergency and the Political-Military Commands, stating that crimes committed by military personnel and policemen in zones declared under emergency were by definition military crimes (*delitos de función*) and thus belonged to the military jurisdiction (Lovatón Palacios 2007, 34).

The strengthening of military justice and its broad scope came in handy in dealing with a handful of salient and complex cases that took place in 1986, under the administration of President Alan García (1985–90), such as the executions in *Accomarca* and *El Frontón* that were processed and tried in the military justice system (Salazar Villalobos 2006, 320). These cases were polemic, as there was public discussion regarding whether they belonged to the military jurisdiction, and they still occupy a place in public discussion. The supreme court again decided in favor of the military jurisdiction in the *Accomarca* case, while in other cases such as *El Frontón* the military jurisdiction was not even challenged.[12]

The pattern of strengthening military autonomy and broadening the military jurisdiction[13] continued during the first two years of the Fujimori government (1990–2). In fact, President Alberto Fujimori even expanded the scope of military jurisdiction in Decree 171-90-PCM (December 21, 1990), stating that military and police officers in emergency zones are in activity 24/7 and covered in all their activities by the Code of Military Justice. Moreover, President Fujimori obtained powers from congress to pass a series of "pacification laws," and used them to produce 126 legislative decrees that understood pacification as the total military defeat of terrorists and drug trafficking. President Fujimori gave more powers not only to the armed forces and the military commands in emergency zones

[11] For example, case Exp. 5–85 on *Alvaro Artaza Adrianzén* in which the supreme court decided in favor of the military jurisdiction based on, essentially, the personal-identity criteria (San Martín 2006, 171).

[12] On June 18–19, 1986 there was a mutiny in three prisons, one of them *El Frontón* that is on an island in front of the coast of Lima, and the prisoners took hostages. Then president Alan García asked the armed forces to control the situation. The Navy bombed *El Frontón* for hours and the bulk of the prisoners were killed. The case was transferred to the military jurisdiction and all the officers were cleared of responsibility. The case then would go the IACHR that found that at least two of the dead prisoners had not participated in the mutiny and were innocent (case *Durand y Ugarte v. Perú*, decided on August 16, 2000). This case still haunts Alan García until this day (December 2015).

[13] President García, in his address to the nation in 1989, even suggested a curious interpretation of the constitution that would allow all civilians between eighteen and fifty years old to be tried in military courts because "they are members of the army reserves" (Eto Cruz, Landa Arroyo, and Palomino Manchego 1997, 376).

but also in other parts of the country not declared under emergency, and he lowered the standards on human rights protection (Abad Yupanqui and Garcés Peralta 1993, 112–13). A couple more salient cases during this period, the extralegal executions in *Barrios Altos* (1991) and *La Cantuta* (1992) (Salazar Villalobos 2006, 325),[14] were also investigated and tried in the military justice system.

In sum, civil-military relations in Peru during the period from 1980 to 1992 were influenced by the mode of transition to democracy and by the severe internal security crisis (Agüero 2001). Successive Peruvian governments chose to deal with internal security problems basically using a strictly military strategy. Part of this strategy depended on the entrenchment of military autonomy and the broadening of the military justice system that were used as tools to serve the armed forces in their mission. One of the consequences was an escalation of violence that took a heavy toll by the end of the period. Thousands of people from the civilian population, the armed forces, and the guerrilla groups saw their lives and many of their rights affected. The Peruvian constitution could arguably have been a more useful guide for the state to deal with this internal security challenge. As we will see, the tribunal of constitutional guarantees essentially remained silent and implicitly legitimated the government's and the armed forces' performance during this period.

The Tribunal of Constitutional Guarantees: Independence, Access, Powers

The tribunal of constitutional guarantees was created in the Constitution of 1979 as the "organ in charge of protecting the constitution" (Article 296). It had nine members, three designated by the legislative branch, three by the president, and three by the supreme court (Article 296), for a six-year period with the possibility of being reelected once (Article 297).[15] The tribunal of constitutional guarantees had the power of judicial review in

[14] These two cases also eventually reached the IACHR, which decided against Peru. *Caso La Cantuta v. Perú. Fondo*, decided on November 29, 2006; *Caso Barrios Altos v. Perú*, decided on March 14, 2001.

[15] Article 297 specifies that a third of the members of the tribunal of constitutional guarantees should be renewed every two years. In September 1982 the rules for the election of the constitutional judges designated by congress were approved by this organ, establishing that judges would be elected by a majority vote in both chambers of congress. As Dargent puts it, "in practice, this gave a party with a simple majority the power to name all of the congress's representatives in the court" (Dargent 2009, 261).

appeals of *amparo* and habeas corpus cases,[16] and also had original jurisdiction in abstract review cases of actions of constitutionality. According to the organic law of the tribunal of constitutional guarantees the votes of six out of nine judges were required to declare a law or act or government unconstitutional (Article 8 Organic Law). Access to the tribunal of constitutional guarantees was severely restricted because, on the one hand, only political actors had legal standing to file constitutional actions (the president, the supreme court, the attorney general, sixty deputies, twenty senators) or fifty thousand citizens whose signatures had to be validated by the electoral court (Article 299). On the other hand, whereas legal standing on *amparos* and habeas corpus was in theory open to every citizen, the tribunal of constitutional guarantees heard these cases only if a party in the case decided to make a final appeal after all the previous legal steps had been made. Moreover, the tribunal of constitutional guarantees was physically located in Arequipa whereas the supreme court (the last court to file an appeal before it could go the tribunal of constitutional guarantees) was in Lima (Article 304). In a nutshell, based on its institutional design, the tribunal of constitutional guarantees had middle levels of independence, low levels of powers judicial review, and very low levels of accessibility (see Dargent 2009).[17]

The expectations explicit in the institutional design of the tribunal of constitutional guarantees actually were met in practice. The tribunal of constitutional guarantees was installed on November 19, 1982, and it was shut down on April 5, 1992, the day that Alberto Fujimori staged his "self-coup." During that decade, the tribunal of constitutional guarantees was a marginal actor in Peruvian politics and society, notwithstanding the fact that Peruvian democracy suffered several critical challenges. Specifically, in ten years a total of only twenty-five constitutionality actions were filed: thirteen by the senators, six by the deputies, three by the attorney general, two by at least fifty-thousand citizens, and one by the supreme court. None of the presidents in that decade, Fernando Belaúnde Terry, Alan García, or Alberto Fujimori filed a single action of constitutionality (Landa Arroyo 2007, 116). To give a sense of the irrelevance of the tribunal

[16] Article 295 reads: "The action or omission by any state or government actor that damages personal liberty can be challenged with an habeas corpus. Amparo, in turn, is useful for protecting all other rights recognized in the Constitution that may be violated by any state or government actor."

[17] The de jure indexes of independence and judicial review powers (that includes access) of the Tribunal of Constitutional Guarantees are four (out of six) and two (out of eight), respectively (Ríos-Figueroa 2011).

of constitutional guarantees, consider that from 1980 to 1993 a total of 5,229 legal norms were enacted (2,200 statutes enacted by congress, 767 legislative decrees by the executive, and 2,262 urgency decrees by the executive). That is, only twenty-five out of 5,229 norms were challenged. Moreover, of those twenty-five cases that reached the tribunal of constitutional guarantees only fifteen were actually decided, and only in five the tribunal found at least one part of the law or decree unconstitutional (Landa Arroyo 2007, 116, 159–61).

The tribunal of constitutional guarantees worked under conditions of political pluralism, which is considered favorable for the effective exercise of judges' independence. Thus, this cannot be part of the explanation for its poor performance. It seems that the appointment mechanism and the short length of tenure did produce judges whose preferences were close to the government's (Dargent 2009, 263). Moreover, the isolation of the tribunal of constitutional guarantees (i.e., its low degree of accessibility) meant that it was hard for cases to reach its doorstep. And when they did arrive the tribunal sent a signal of despair to potential future users: several habeas corpus cases were dismissed even though there were some that involved *prima facie* violations of rights (Eguiguren Praeli 1990, 63). In sum, as former magistrate Manuel Aguirre Roca asserts, the politicized appointment process, the scare powers of judicial review, and the difficulty in accessing the tribunal of constitutional guarantees explain to a large extent the reasons for its overall political irrelevance (Aguirre Roca 1991). Let us look in more detail at the tribunal's jurisprudence on military autonomy.

Tribunal of Constitutional Guarantees' Constitutional Jurisprudence on Military Autonomy

Of the fifteen actions of constitutionality decided by the tribunal of constitutional guarantees, only two were filed against norms that allegedly affected individual security and basic procedural rights. These two actions were filed by a minority of senators from the APRA party against Legislative Decree 46, in which president Belaúnde typified in an ambiguous way the crimes of terrorism, apology of terrorism, and contempt of law (*desacato*) (Landa Arroyo 2007, 116–26). In both cases, the judges of the tribunal of constitutional guarantees were short of the six votes required to declare the decree unconstitutional (the tribunal on September 21, 1984 published a nonbinding opinion). It is worth noting that the armed phase of the Shining Path had begun in May 1980 and the first decree broadening the definition of the crimes of terrorism and apology of terrorism was published in October 1981. In this context, the silence of the tribunal of constitutional guarantees may be interpreted as a legitimation of the government's approach to fighting back the Shining Path. The debates were intense and some judges, such as Aguirre Roca, wrote individual votes criticizing the tribunal of constitutional guarantees for acting like "a court of first instance and not as a constitutional tribunal." However, a majority of judges with a very limited idea of the role of the tribunal of constitutional guarantees blocked the debate, forcing it to publish a nonbinding opinion on the case without any legal validity (Landa Arroyo 2007, 165).

The tribunal of constitutional guarantees also decided *amparo* and habeas corpus cases on appeal. Both types of cases are designed to protect individual rights from violations by state and government actors. In this area, which is an exercise of concrete judicial review, the performance of the tribunal was also marginal and limited. The bulk of habeas corpus, according to Eguiguren, was filed in order to challenge arbitrary detentions (almost 70 percent). But judges at the tribunal, when deciding these cases, automatically applied the criterion that each detention made by the police was valid as long as it did not exceed twenty-four hours, as established in Article 20 of the Constitution, "without questioning the motivations for the detention or what happened during those 24 hours" (Eguiguren Praeli 1990, 49). Remember that the tribunal of constitutional guarantees got habeas corpus cases in a last appeal, generally after three previous judicial authorities had denied granting the habeas. The next to last appeal was filed before the Supreme Court, located in Lima, so a citizen had to travel from Lima to Arequipa in order to reach the tribunal of constitutional guarantees. What did the tribunal do with the habeas that despite all the obstacles were successfully filed by citizens challenging an arbitrary detention or another violation of an individual liberty? In the ten years that the tribunal was working, it received eighty-three habeas corpus: only eight were granted (9.6 percent), and in other eight cases it produced nonbinding opinions. In other words, in sixty-seven cases (80.7 percent) the tribunal of constitutional guarantees upheld the denial of the habeas corpus made previously by the supreme court (Landa Arroyo 2007, 162–3).

In fact, from the very beginning after its creation the tribunal of constitutional guarantees established criteria that discouraged citizens from actually approaching it. For instance, in a case filed by *Juana Huaracha* the tribunal decided that "during a state of emergency the police can detain a person for more than 24 hours without presenting her before a judge and without a judicial warrant justifying the detention" (Eguiguren Praeli 1990,

63).[18] The tribunal of constitutional guarantees used similar reasoning in the habeas corpus presented by *Ángela Horna* in favor of *Alcibíades Díaz*, validating the argument that the court cannot look into the causes that motivated a detention as long as it does not exceed the twenty-four-hour limit (and it did not take place during a state of emergency) (Eguiguren Praeli 1990, 63).[19]

Conclusion: The Tribunal of Constitutional Guarantees as an Arbitrator

In terms of the theory advanced in this book, the tribunal of constitutional guarantees behaved more as an arbitrator than as a mediator. The tribunal of constitutional guarantees rejected the petitions of habeas corpus because "they did not provide evidence of the violation, or threat of violations, of basic human rights." As explained by Landa Arroyo (2007, 166–7), the tribunal's line of argumentation proceeded as follows: "the function of habeas corpus is to defend constitutional rights, if there is no evidence of rights violations (or evidence of likelihood that they might occur) then it follows that the case should be rejected" (see also Aguirre Roca 1991). Notice how limited this reasoning is because "in contrast to ordinary proceedings where supporting evidence is necessary, this is not the case in habeas corpus especially if they are filed in a context of violence and social crisis where the constitutional judge can reasonably assume that the rights of the individuals are in danger" (Landa Arroyo 2007, 67). In other words, Peru was under a critical security situation, but this fact did not have any impact on the reasoning of the tribunal of constitutional guarantees as a constitutional organ in charge of protecting the constitution and its principles and rights. Instead, the tribunal decided these cases as if it was a first instance court, an arbitrator looking at the past written record, simply adjudicating responsibility on a single case as if it was an isolated instance, and demanding unreasonable proof in a critical situation.[20]

[18] There was a dissenting vote by magistrate Aguirre Roca who, although not clearly, arguably was in favor of stricter judicial control (Eguiguren Praeli 1990, 63).

[19] The supreme court, the organ in charge of deciding conflicts of competence, also systematically favored the military jurisdiction. For instance, on April 10, 1985 the supreme court sent a case to the military jurisdiction based on the personal-identity criteria (Exp. 5–85 case of Alvaro Artaza Adrianzén) (cited in San Martín 2006, 171–2). San Martín mentions that the particular vote in this case did argue that the military jurisdiction should be limited to military officers who commit strictly military crimes.

[20] The report of the Truth and Reconciliation Commission argues something similar regarding the tribunal of constitutional guarantees' performance: "The abdication of the

Interestingly, during this period there were jurisprudential assessments of the situation in Peru regarding military autonomy that markedly differ from those of the tribunal of constitutional guarantees. They came from the Inter American Court of Human Rights (IACHR). For instance, in *Castillo Petruzzi v. Peru* (May 30, 1999) and in *Durand y Ugarte v. Peru* (August 16, 2000), the IACHR essentially argued that the military justice system did not meet the requirements of independence and impartiality; that the system of military justice was not the place to investigate and try cases of human rights violations; and that civilians should not be tried in military courts. In some instances, the intervention of the IACHR had rapid consequences. For instance, after the decision in the so-called Barrios Altos case the superior council of military justice nullified its decision, and opened the door to an investigation and eventual trial in the ordinary judiciary (Salazar Villalobos 2006, 343). These decisions by the IACHR would be more important for the constitutional tribunal, as we will see now.

The Constitutional Tribunal, 1993–2013

Political Context and Civil-Military Relations

The presidential elections of 1990 took place in a context of an economic and an internal security crisis, and the peculiarities of that election favored the election of a political outsider who created an ad hoc political party (Tanaka 2005). Alberto Fujimori, however, faced a majority of opposition in congress. To respond to the economic crisis, the new government managed to build some alliances with center-right forces in congress and started an ambitious process of market reform. This prompted left-wing and centrist parties to file actions of constitutionality against a number of the reforms. Interestingly, the previously submissive tribunal of constitutional guarantees began to exercise its authority: during 1991 and until March 1992 a tribunal composed mainly of judges elected by the defeated parties in the 1990 election declared four pieces of legislation concerning economic matters partially unconstitutional (Dargent 2009, 264). As Dargent explains, the Fujimori government perceived these decisions as a threat to the process of economic liberalization.

tribunal from its role of guarantor of basic rights was based on a shaky interpretation of the constitution according to which anything was acceptable under states of emergency, despite the norms included in international law and the opinion of the international legal community."

But more importantly, in retrospect, was Fujimori's ability to portray the judiciary and the congress as the main obstacles for making more progress in this area (and in others, such as ironically the combat of corruption). As Conaghan puts it, the Fujimori regime exploited some questionable judicial decisions to blame "politicians" and the "traditional political parties" (Conaghan 2005, 32). In particular, a supreme court decision of February 1992 that dismissed the corruption charges against former president Alan García was opposed by 60 percent of those polled. Moreover, Fujimori touted a series of unpopular judicial decisions that released convicted and suspected terrorists from jail, and a ruling that found insufficient evidence to support a slew of criminal charges against Abimael Guzmán, the leader of *Sendero Luminso*.[21] Interestingly, in the politically charged atmosphere of the first two years of the Fujimori government, "among government institutions, only the executive branch and the armed forces scored approval ratings above 50%" (Conaghan 2005, 32).

The political stalemate between the executive and congress intensified until President Fujimori decided, on April 5 1992, to shut down congress and other political institutions including the tribunal of constitutional guarantees. The so-called self-coup received the support of the armed forces, an institution that worked closely with the government from the very outset of the administration. Vladimiro Montesinos, a former military officer who had been expelled amidst accusations of organized crime, was Fujimori's key advisor who carefully knitted and created an alliance with top military officials. Right after the presidential election Fujimori took up an unusual residence stay in an exclusive military facility on the advice of Montesinos (Conaghan 2005, 25). Once Fujimori assumed office, his first cabinet included five military officers (Roberts 2006).

Moreover, there is some evidence that President Fujimori was planning the coup with General Nicolás de Bari Hermoza Ríos, the head of the *Comando Conjunto* of the armed forces, and national security advisor Vladimiro Montesinos. According to Conaghan, Montesinos later said that the coup "was a response to congress' derogation of a series of counterterrorism and counter drug-trafficking measures decreed by

[21] The attorney general stated that "in the last 11 years [from 1980 to 1991] out of 4395 terrorists captured only 10% (497) were sentenced, while the rest were set free, 2584 because the accusation was rejected on procedural grounds, 890 for lack of evidence, and 421 for lack of basis enough for an oral trial." According to the *Procurador* "no more than 20% can be considered innocent, and thus the sentences are really benevolent." In this context, on March 2, 1992 the *sala penal* of the supreme court released Abimael Guzmán (Abad Yupanqui and Garcés Peralta 1993, 132).

Fujimori in November 1991. Hermoza testified that his involvement in the coup meetings began in early February after congress passed Law 25379, a measure aimed at reducing the president's ability to use decree laws to govern" (Conaghan 2005, 31). In sum, the support of the armed forces to both Fujimori's constitutional government that started on 1990, and to the a-constitutional Fujimori government that started on April 5 1992, "was open, institutional and programmatic" (Alegría 2003, 61).

Right after the coup, Fujimori once again expanded the military jurisdiction giving more autonomy and discretion to the armed forces. Specifically, on May 1992 Decree Law 25475 (May 6, 1992) established the crime of "treason to the fatherland" and created the figure of faceless judges (*jueces sin rostro*) to decide on those cases. A couple of months later, a new Decree Law 25659 (August 13, 1992) stated in its Article 4 that "crimes of treason and terrorism would be investigated and tried in the military jurisdiction." That this legislation was clearly contradictory with the wording of the 1979 Constitution (Eto Cruz et al. 1997, 381) of course did not matter much for the Fujimori government, which quite soon managed to make some improvements on the internal security front including the capture of Abimael Guzmán, leader of the Shining Path (on September 12, 1992).

On November 1992 a new congress was elected, and this congress produced a new constitution, which was approved in a referendum in October 1993. In 1995 Alberto Fujimori was reelected president with 64 percent of the vote. The relationship of the government with the armed forces remained close and actually was strengthened. Even before being reelected, Fujimori managed to get the congress/constituent assembly to back a provision giving the executive complete control over promotions in the armed forces, thus eliminating any congressional oversight of the process. In the years ahead, this provision effectively allowed Vladimiro Montesinos to control the top echelon of the armed forces by promoting officers loyal to him (Conaghan 2005, 57–8).[22]

The close alliance between the government and the armed forces again implied high levels of military autonomy and a broad scope of military jurisdiction. For instance, in the salient cases of *La Cantuta* and *Barrios Altos* that were reopened in 1994 and 1995, the government used its influence

[22] A particularly shameful witness of Montesino's control of the armed forces was the "Submission Act" in which the president's advisor managed to make more than a hundred top military officials sign a document explicitly exchanging support for the regime for immunity in case of abuses. Interview with David Lovatón, July 1, 2014.

in the supreme court and in congress to protect the military officers involved in human rights violations and either send the cases back to the military jurisdiction or simply pardon them.[23] When a judge decided that one of the pardons was unconstitutional, the army responded with a tank parade in Lima. After the show of force, congress passed Law 26479, which is a blanket amnesty to all military and police personnel implicated in human rights abuses during the course of Peru's war against counterinsurgency since the 1980s. The law included an article stipulating that it could not be judicially reviewed (cf. Conaghan 2005, 74–5, 105–7).

Fujimorism took on an increasingly authoritarian character after 1996, when the president began the maneuvers that led to his reelection in 2000. In those years, the government intervened every institution that opposed the president's reelection plans: the electoral board, the constitutional tribunal, the attorney general's office, the *defensoría del pueblo*, and the judicial council (Tanaka 2005, 278). The pressure started cracking the system. Regarding the armed forces and the military justice, the brave reports by the *Defensoría del Pueblo* that started appearing that year are noteworthy. Specifically, the now famous *Informe #6* basically argued that the broad scope of the military jurisdiction was unconstitutional and asked for a thorough reform of the military justice system.

In the supreme court, whereas a series of cases were sent to the military jurisdiction, others were decided in the opposite direction. For instance, cases of simple murder committed during an antisubversives' operation in a zone declared under emergency were sent to military courts; cases that involved injured civilians were sent to military courts when the injuries were the product of a military crime; and even nonmilitary crimes not committed during a state of emergency were also sent to military courts because both parties belonged to the armed forces.[24] But other cases involving the liberty of

[23] On February 11, 1994 the supreme court decided the conflict of jurisdiction regarding the *La Cantuta* case (Exp. 07-94), which involved the kidnapping and killing of one professor and nine students from a university nicknamed *La Cantuta* (on July 18, 1992) by a special group from the armed forces called *Colina*. The court argued that the case belonged to the military jurisdiction because soldiers were "following orders," without limiting the type or content of orders, and also mentioning that Lima at that time was under emergency (San Martín 2006, 171). The case was scandalous. When a majority of judges appeared to lean in favor of the ordinary jurisdiction, the rules for supreme court decisions on jurisdiction conflicts (four votes necessary) were overruled by a legislative decree that was then applied retroactively to the case in order to force a decision in favor of the military jurisdiction.

[24] Competencia 17–97, case of Marco Quispe Yucra, December 12, 1997. Cited in San Martín y Mendoza 2008, 83. Competencia 1983–97, case of Marco Dávila Robles, January 29, 1998. Cited in San Martín 2006, 173. Competencia 7–98, case of José Jaime Coronel and others, July 23, 1998. Cited in San Martín (2006, 174).

civilians and public administration officials, or civilians as passive actors in a crime, were sent to ordinary courts.[25]

Fujimori was reelected in 2000, but the toll on his popularity and his ruling coalition was high. Ultimately, after a series of corruption scandals Fujimori resigned in November 2000, and Valentín Paniagua, elected interim president by Congress, began a transition government. Alejandro Toledo won the elections and assumed office on July 28, 2001 for a period of five years. Paniagua's transition government set the agenda of reforms, including the reform of the armed forces. During the first years of Toledo's administration, an executive commission explicitly mentioned the urgency of adapting the military and the military justice system to democratic standards (cited in Salazar Villalobos 2006, 341).

However, this impulse lost traction and indeed was reversed by Executive Decree 009-2004 (July 14, 2004), which says that all actions of members of the armed forces executing Law 28222 (a law allowing the participation of the armed forces in cases of terrorism and acts that altered the public order) are to be considered actions under service and, thus, belong to the military jurisdiction (Salazar Villalobos 2006, 341). But, as we will see, with democratic conditions back in place, the constitutional tribunal did have a say on these matters. A fascinating legal battle over the scope of the military jurisdiction and the autonomy of military justice started then and continues until this date (December 2015).

The Constitutional Tribunal: Independence, Access, Powers

The Constitution of 1993 includes in its Article 201 the constitutional tribunal as the "organ in charge of protecting the constitution." The constitutional tribunal is composed of seven members elected by a two-thirds majority of the members of congress for a period of five years without the possibility of immediate reelection (Article 201). The constitutional tribunal decides, in its original jurisdiction docket, conflicts of competence and actions of constitutionality, and in its appellate jurisdiction, habeas corpus, *amparo*, habeas data, and actions of compliance (Article 202). Access to the constitutional tribunal is, compared to the

[25] Competencia 20–98, case of Luis Zara Llanos, October 20, 1998. Cited in San Martín 2006, 173. Competencia 26–98, case of Encarnación Suyón Sánchez, November 27, 1998. Cited in San Martín 2006, 173. Competencia 11–98, case of Carlos Álvarez Bobadilla and others, July 23, 1999. Cited in San Martín (2006, 173).

tribunal of constitutional guarantees, easier.[26] Legal standing in actions of constitutionality is restricted to political actors such as the president, the attorney general, the *defensor del pueblo*, 25 percent of members of congress, regional presidents and local mayors (in matters of their competence). Non-political collective actors such as five thousand citizens whose signatures have to be validated by the electoral court, 1 percent of the habitants of a certain municipality against ordinances by their municipal government, and professional associations (in matters of their competence) can also file actions of constitutionality (Article 203). Article 4 of the organic law of the constitutional tribunal requires a supermajority of six votes, out of seven, for the tribunal to declare a norm unconstitutional.[27] In addition, in contrast to its predecessor the tribunal of constitutional guarantees, the constitutional tribunal is located in the capital of the country, Lima. In a nutshell, based on its institutional design the constitutional tribunal has lower levels of independence, but higher levels of powers of judicial review and greater access than the tribunal of constitutional guarantees (see Dargent 2009, 254).[28]

The constitutional tribunal was not properly installed until June 1996, because there was a protracted negotiation process to appoint the first set of judges. As soon as it started working, the constitutional tribunal received the politically difficult case regarding whether Fujimori's attempt at reelection in 2000 was constitutional. On January 1997 the constitutional tribunal circulated an opinion arguing that it was not (see details in Conaghan 2005, 126–32). Quite soon after that, on May 29, 1997, the three judges who were for the unconstitutionality of Fujimori's reelection were removed through impeachment, which meant that from that moment on the constitutional tribunal continued functioning with only four members whose preferences were close to the president's. Interestingly, four judges was the minimum required by law for the constitutional tribunal to continue working and decide all types of cases except actions of

[26] However, access to the constitutional tribunal is not that easy when compared, e.g., to the Colombian Constitutional Court. See Chapter 3 on Colombia, and Chapter 6 for a systematic comparison across both countries.

[27] On October 20, 2002 this article was modified, making the requirement five votes out of seven, to declare a norm unconstitutional.

[28] The de jure indexes of independence and powers of judicial review (that includes access) of the tribunal of constitutional guarantees are one (out of six) and three (out of eight), respectively (Ríos-Figueroa 2011). While the differences in the de jure indexes between the tribunal of constitutional guarantees and the constitutional tribunal appear low, as I will show, the slightly greater powers of judicial review and access enjoyed by the tribunal of constitutional guarantees were used and used enough to produce quite different jurisprudence.

constitutionality. Fujimori's regime collapsed at the end of the year 2000 and on November of that same year the three impeached judges were reinstalled in the constitutional tribunal. The four judges who were close to Fujimori ended their terms in 2001, and on May 2002 four new judges were elected. According to César Landa Arroyo (2007, 280) this event marks two periods of the constitutional tribunal, "the tribunal in captivity" (1997–2002), and the "tribunal in liberty" (2002–).

The actual composition of the "tribunal in liberty" included some high-caliber and respected magistrates. That time, in the aftermath of the Fujimori regime and in an atmosphere of consensus around needed reforms, the appointment process worked rather well. To attain the required two-thirds vote, the four majoritarian groups in congress arrived at an agreement that allowed each of them to name a magistrate. As Dargent explains, "in order to reach the two-thirds requirement for the candidates' appointment, parties were careful to nominate candidates that were acceptable to all of the political groups." This mechanism produced judges that, even though they could be linked to a particular political group, were individuals with personal prestige as politicians or as lawyers (Dargent 2009, 271). In addition, these four judges joined the three independent magistrates still in the court, which permitted a plural mixture of past and new magistrates. The constitutional tribunal from 2003 to 2008 was indeed quite remarkable in the type and breadth of jurisprudence it produced.

However, the length of tenure of Peruvian judges is quite short (five years), which means that even high-caliber and professional judges face uncomfortable choices regarding the pace and the depth of the jurisprudence they want to produce. Moreover, the short length of judges' tenure coincides with the tenure of their appointers (congressmen), making this an unstable institution and prey to political manipulation. In Table 4.1 it is easy to see that during each president's administration the full membership of the constitutional tribunal is renewed. The remarkable performance of the tribunal from 2003 to 2008, which demonstrated how consequential it can be, paradoxically also partly caused its demise because political actors wanted to influence the composition of such an influential organ. In a nutshell, the judicalization of Peruvian politics led to the politicization of the judiciary, which was successful because the right institutional incentives and political conditions for the independent working of judicial institutions were not in place (cf. Ferejohn 2002).

A case in point is the appointment process of four new constitutional judges in 2007–8, which was not transparent and was far from the way in which the election took place in 2002. This time, the process involved

Table 4.1. *Composition of Peruvian Constitutional Tribunal, by president (2000–2014)*

Interim President Valentín Paniagua, Acción Popular (2000–1)
President Alejandro Toledo, Perú Posible (2001–6)

Magistrate	Chosen by congress of president	Magistrate	Chosen by congress of president	Magistrate	Chosen by congress of president
1. Delia Revoredo*	Fujimori			Javier Alva Orlandini (2004)	Toledo
2. Manuel Aguirre Roca*	Fujimori			César Landa (2004)	Toledo
3. Guillermo Rey Terry*	Fujimori			Juan Vergara (2004)	Toledo
4. Ricardo Nugent	Fujimori	Juan Bautista Bardelli (2002)	Toledo		
5. José García Marcelo	Fujimori	Victor García Toma (2002)	Fujimori	Víctor García Toma (2004)	Toledo
6. Luis Díaz Valverde	Fujimori	Magdiel González (2002)	Fujimori	Magdiel González (2004)	Toledo
7. Francisco Acosta	Fujimori	Javier Alva (2002)	Fujimori		

President Alan García, Partido Aprista Peruano (2006–11)

Magistrate	Chosen by congress of president	Magistrate	Chosen by congress of president	Magistrate	Ideology
1. César Landa	Toledo			Óscar Urviola	García
2. Juan Vergara	Toledo				
3. Javier Alva Orlandini	Toledo	Gerardo Eto Cruz (2007)	García		
4. Juan Bautista Bardelli	Toledo	Ernesto Álvarez (2007)	García		
5. Víctor García Toma	Toledo	Ricardo Beaumont (2007)	García		
6. Magdiel González	Toledo	Fernando Calle (2007)	García		
7. Carlos Mesía	García				

(continued)

Table 4.1 (*cont.*)

President Ollanta Humana, Partido Nacionalista Gana Perú (2011–16)			
Magistrate	Chosen by congress of president	Magistrate	Chosen by congress of president
1. Óscar Urviola	García		
2. Gerardo Eto Cruz	García	Ernesto Blume (2014)	Humala
3. Ernesto Álvarez	García	Carlos Ramos (2014)	Humala
4. Ricardo Beaumont	García	Manuel Miranda (2014)	Humala
5. Fernando Calle	García	Marianella Ledesma (2014)	Humala
6. Carlos Mesía	García	José Luis Sardón (2014)	Humala
7. Juan Vergara	García	Eloy Espinosa (2014)	Humala

Note: The table shows the composition of the constitutional tribunal by presidential period. Next to the name of the magistrate, there is the congress that appointed the judge (in Peru the appointment is made by a two-thirds congressional super majority). According to Ponce and Tiede (2014) a good proxy for the judges' "ideology" can be which congress appointed him. The judges with an * (in the period from 2000 to 2004), elected by the Fujimori congress in 1997, were removed for voting against Fujimori's reelection in 2000. After Fujimori resigned, they were reinstated in their positions in November of 2000.

resignations, internal fights, and the loss of collegiality that characterized the tribunal from 2002 to 2007 (Justicia Viva 2008). In fact, a first set of judges already selected by congress was removed after legislators faced strong opposition from nongovernmental organizations (NGOs) and public opinion regarding the characteristics of some of the judges and the lack of transparency in the election process. A new set of four judges had to be appointed and even then some, whose closeness to a political party had been denounced, were elected. In 2013, again, congress had to cancel the appointment of four new judges due to strong criticisms of some of the judges and of the way in which the election was carried out, and the appointment process had to be made again. The changes in composition were felt also in the quality and depth of jurisprudence produced by the constitutional tribunal. As we will see, the jurisprudence on military autonomy is not an exception.

Constitutional Jurisprudence on Military Autonomy

Decisions made by the constitutional tribunal regarding the armed forces do in fact vary across the periods of the "tribunal in captivity" (until 2002) and the "tribunal in liberty" (from 2002). During the first period, the constitutional tribunal basically decided cases of habeas corpus, whereas during the second period it has also decided actions of constitutionality. The constitutional tribunal had already started limiting the scope of military jurisdiction in habeas corpus cases in 1999. For instance, the tribunal clearly established that the Code of Military Justice had to be adjusted to what the constitution states regarding procedures in the military courts.[29] In another decision the tribunal reiterated that active military officers cannot be judges in military tribunals, but upheld that civilians could be judged in military courts for treason and terrorism.[30] By 2001 the constitutional tribunal argued that drug trafficking is not a military crime (*delito de función*) but rather an ordinary crime that has to be tried in ordinary courts (Exp. 008-2001-HC/TC).

Decisions in habeas corpus cases, however, are limited because in them the tribunal does not expand its argumentation in a mediator-like way. In

[29] Exp. 934-1998-HC-TC, case of Valdemar Cabanillas Quispe, January 1999 (cited in San Martín 2006, 161).

[30] Exp. 1131–1999/HC/TC, Asunto Giovanni Cavangnaro Castro, December 1999, cited in San Martín 2006, 159. See also Exp. No. 1154-2002-HC/TC, Asunto Werner Huamaní Tipismana, June 20, 2002 (cited in San Martín 2006, 159).

these cases, the tribunal generally only decided whether or not the habeas corpus should be granted, but did not go deep into the causes of the problem, and did not elaborate on the reasons that led to a particular decision. This is why some decisions on military jurisdiction on habeas corpus appear to contradict previous decisions; the tribunal does not make an effort for consistency or coherence in decisions across cases. In a word, in habeas corpus decisions the constitutional tribunal has produced a case-by-case arbitrator-like jurisprudence. It should be noted that this is not always the case with concrete-review cases that, in a way, force the court to make decisions on a specific case. In Colombia, for instance, after a series of concrete-review decisions on a similar topic, the constitutional court sometimes produces a *sentencia de unificación*, a decision that unifies its jurisprudence and establishes the criteria it has been developing in a series of concrete cases (see Chapter 3).

In abstract review cases, such as the Peruvian action of constitutionality, the tribunal has greater flexibility to expose at length its view on the underlying causes of conflict and its reasons for interpreting the constitution in a specific way. This is evident when we contrast the decisions on *habeas corpus* with a series of *actions* that start on January 2003 (notice the coincidence with the selection of new judges). In Exp. 010-2002-AI/TC (January 3, 2003), the tribunal essentially argues that ordinary crimes should go to ordinary and not military courts and goes to great length to explain that this is based on the principle of "natural judge" that must be observed in order to make certain that cases are not allocated to judges who have, or appear to have, an interest in a case, or who may appear otherwise prejudiced.

Decision 010-2002-AI/TC (January 3, 2003) is also important because the tribunal declared parts of the antiterrorism decree-laws passed during the Fujimori regime[31] unconstitutional, essentially mandating a retrial of all cases of treason and terrorism originally tried by military courts (the huge increase in habeas corpus granted by the constitutional tribunal in 2003 is a direct consequence of this decision, see Figure 4.1). In this decision, the constitutional tribunal produced a so-called interpretative decision, that is, it declared that the law, or some of its challenged parts, is constitutional if it is understood in a certain way. This is an interesting feature that helps the tribunal to preserve a law and to avoid a direct

[31] Specifically, Decree Law 25475 (May 6, 1992) that established the crime of "treason to the fatherland" and Decree Law 25659 (August 13, 1992) that allowed investigation and trial in military courts of civilians accused of treason and terrorism (plus a couple of other decrees and their related norms).

confrontation with those affected by the ruling (Justicia Viva 2008, 8). The tribunal also innovated with the figure of "observatory participants" through which it allowed actors to express their views on the lawsuit, in open sessions.[32]

Notwithstanding these efforts by the constitutional tribunal to jurisprudentially reduce uncertainty about the legal framework and thus the legal consequences of certain actions, the military heavily criticized the decision to retry hundreds of cases because of the difficulty in finding the witnesses and in obtaining evidence in cases that were held under extraordinary circumstances. According to Contra Admiral CJ (R) Carlos Mesa Angosto (former president of the military jurisdiction), a wiser decision would have been to stop any further trial of those crimes in military courts but to accept those that had already been made.[33]

On 2004 the tribunal delivered a couple of key decisions on military autonomy and the scope of military jurisdiction, in actions of constitutionality filed by the *Defensoría del Pueblo*.[34] Specifically, with this topic the tribunal engaged in cases 0017-2003-AI/TC (decided on August 24, 2004) and 0023-2003-AI/TC (decided on June 9, 2004). The actions of constitutionality were filed against the Organic Law of Military Justice, the Military Code of Justice (both decree-laws promulgated in June 1980), and the Law No. 24150 of June 1995 that regulated the participation of so-called Politic-Military Commands and the crimes committed by members of the armed forces under states of emergency. This is a clear example of the tribunal reducing uncertainty over the legal framework: notice that the first two laws were enacted prior to the 1993 Constitution, which raises the question of whether it is possible to assess the constitutionality of laws according to a constitution that did not exist when the laws were promulgated and enforced. To add to the drama, the constitutional tribunal decided these cases at the same time, politically, that the executive

32 Interview with César Landa Arroyo, former constitutional tribunal magistrate, June 27, 2014.

33 Interview June 24, 2014. Interestingly, this action of constitutionality was filed by 5000+ citizens who were mostly former members of the Shining Path (interview with David Lovatón Palacios, June 2, 2014).

34 It is noteworthy that the *Defensoría del Pueblo* is an institution that since 1998 had been both critical and vocal regarding the system of military justice. It is also noteworthy that since 1998 the armed forces had reacted vocally and critically regarding "undue intrusions" in its autonomy (Lovatón Palacios 2007, 10). The *Defensoría del Pueblo* continued criticizing the military justice in its reports No. 64 ("Military Justice in the Transition: Analysis of Reform Projects"), and No. 66 ("Who Decides What? Military vs. Ordinary Justice").

published Decree 009-2004 (on July 14, 2004) that expanded military jurisdiction effectively establishing the "personal-identity criterion."

The tribunal engaged with both the procedural and the substantive questions posed by the actions of constitutionality. First, the constitutional tribunal used a theory of continuity to argue that the "old laws" (i.e., laws promulgated under the previous 1978 Constitution) could be challenged and their constitutionality evaluated according to the 1993 Constitution, otherwise these laws would be granted a privileged status vis-á-vis the "new laws" (case 010-2002-AI/TC of January 3, 2005). Then, the constitutional tribunal entered into the substance of the actions, military autonomy, and in this regard its decisions constitute a breaking point in the Peruvian system of military justice (Lovatón Palacios 2007, 46). With rigorous and systematic argumentation, the constitutional tribunal argued that the scope of military jurisdiction should be restricted even under situations of emergency because it is false that giving more discretion and autonomy to the armed forces under those circumstances necessarily makes them more effective.

Specifically, in case 0017-2003-AI/TC the constitutional tribunal argued that it was unconstitutional that in states of emergency the armed forces took over the roles and functions of civilian authorities because this is tantamount to "establishing a kind of military government" (para. 70). Regarding the scope of military jurisdiction, the constitutional tribunal argued that "the military jurisdiction should not be understood as a personal-identity criteria because it is not the case that each and every crime committed by a member of the armed forces should be heard in military courts simply because it was committed by a member of the armed forces" (para. 129). Also outside of the military jurisdiction are considerations of the place where the crime was committed, "because even in the barracks regular crimes can be committed." With these arguments, the constitutional tribunal effectively reduced the uncertainty about the consequences of certain actions by military officers.

Moreover, the constitutional tribunal argued that only the strictly military crimes (*delitos de función*) belong to the military jurisdiction, and that it is not enough for a conduct to be typified in the military code of justice in order for it to be considered a military crime. In other words, the constitutional tribunal argued for a quite narrow definition of military crime in deciding whether a given conduct does violate a military duty or obligation. For instance, reducing the uncertainty due to the clash between the principles of duties and responsibilities, the court argued that "not to obey orders that imply the violation of fundamental rights of persons, or violations of the constitutional order, does not amount to an infringement of the military code of justice" (paras. 131–3) (see Lovatón Palacios 2007, 46–9). In another decision, 3194-2004-HC/TC, the tribunal clearly established two conditions for the military jurisdiction to apply: first, a personal criterion according to which only members of the armed forces should be sent to the military jurisdiction but; second, not for any crime, but only for the crimes established under a specific criminal type (arguably military crimes) (cf. Salazar Villalobos 2006, 370).

In case 0023-2003-AI/TC (June 9, 2004), the constitutional tribunal limited the autonomy of military justice. In this case, the *Defensoría del Pueblo* challenged several articles of the Military Code of Justice including those in which the procedural rules were established. The constitutional tribunal argued that active members of the armed forces cannot sit as judges in military courts because this violated the principle of judicial independence, given that the military officers in active service are directly appointed by the executive and do not have sufficient guarantees of job stability (cf. Lovatón Palacios 2007, 14). This is important because what the constitutional tribunal is effectively saying is that even in those cases that do belong to the military jurisdiction the military courts should guarantee the minimum rights of due process that the Peruvian Constitution grants to every citizen. As a result, the constitutional tribunal in case 0023-2003-AI/TC invited congress to produce a new Code of Military Justice within the next twelve months, the so-called *vacatio sententiae*, which essentially means that the law just declared unconstitutional should remain operational until a new law is produced. This is an interesting, though not so elegant, feature of the decision that provided a reasonable time for congressional compliance.

The 2004 decisions by the constitutional tribunal restricted the scope of military jurisdiction and military autonomy across the board. The political actors were particularly responsive to one of the many areas that were affected by the tribunal's decisions: the criterion according to which civilians should not be tried in military courts, especially in cases in which grave violations of human rights are involved. For instance, the supreme court did change its decisions regarding conflicts of jurisdiction, essentially sending to ordinary courts cases that it would probably have sent to military courts before.[35] Congressmen and the executive have also

[35] E.g., Contienda de competencia No. 18–2004" (caso de Indalecio Pomatanta, decided November 23, 2004). Contienda de competencia No. 29-04 (caso Chuschi, decided December 14, 2004). Contienda de competencia No. 8-2005 (caso Efraín Aponte, decided July 1, 2005) (cited in Lobatón 2007, 50–2). The supreme court gave the force of jurisprudence to its decision on the Indalecio Pomanta case.

accepted such a criterion. And the armed forces also welcomed the clarification of criteria and the reduction of uncertainty over the bounds of this exceptional jurisdiction because they have not disputed the jurisdiction of some of the cases with those characteristics.[36]

However, other features of the constitutional tribunal's decisions, specifically concerning which crimes should be considered military crimes (*delitos de función*) and what procedural guarantees should be adopted in the military justice system, were contested or simply not complied with. Military officers in the military jurisdiction realized that a silent but steady legal battle should be fought in preparing a proposal for a new Code of Military Justice and in a strong lobby campaign in congress and the executive. The executive and the legislative reacted favorably to the armed force's requests. First, on October 28, 2005 an executive decree was published (024-2005-DE/SG) regulating the intervention of the armed forces in zones not declared under emergency, and expanding the scope of the military jurisdiction through the reestablishment of the "personal-identity criterion." Then, in January 6, 2006 the executive published Executive Decree 961, the new Code of Military Justice that deviates considerably from the guidelines and principles that the constitutional tribunal had established in its decisions. Finally Law 28665, which regulates the organization and functions of the military justice system and was published on January 16, 2006, brought about the regression to the pre–tribunal's decisions status quo in terms of the scope of military justice.

This executive and legislative response has produced an intense debate in Peru regarding the scope of the military jurisdiction, and ultimately military autonomy and civilian-military relations. For starters, then attorney general Adelaida Bolívar filed an action of constitutionality against Law 28665. On April 12, 2006, the *Defensoría del Pueblo* published another report arguing for the unconstitutionality of Law 28665 and Decree 961.[37] Even the judicial council decided not to apply this law until the constitutional tribunal decided on its constitutionality (Salazar Villalobos 2006, 369). Quite rapidly, the constitutional tribunal, in decision Exp. 0004-2006-AI/TC responded to the demand filed by the attorney general arguing that Law 28665 was partly unconstitutional

[36] Interview with Capitán de Navío CJ Carlos M. Schiaffino Chierre, Presidente del Tribunal Superior Militar Policial del Centro, and with Teniente Coronel EP Alejandro Roosevelt Bravo Maxdeo, Sub-Director del Centro de Altos Estudios de Justicia Militar, June 25, 2014.

[37] Report No. 104, "Military Code of Justice, Law 28665 and Decree 961, are Unconstitutional."

(March 29, 2006).[38] In this decision, the tribunal restates that military officers in active service cannot be judges or prosecutors because this violates the principle of independence. The tribunal again gave the legislative power a six-month period to fix the problems with Law 28665. Regarding Decree 961, the constitutional tribunal did not give congress time to create another law; it simply struck down thirty-seven articles of the decree and upheld the rest (Justicia Viva 2010, 4).

But congress again only partially complied with the tribunal's decision. In December 2006 it passed Law 28934 that basically extended the legal force of the law that the constitutional tribunal had just declared unconstitutional. The *Colegio de Abogados de Lambeyeque* challenged this law and, again quite rapidly, the constitutional tribunal decided it was unconstitutional (Exp. 005-2007-PI/TC). In response, congress produced a new Law 29182 insisting that judges and prosecutors in the military jurisdiction can be military officers in active service, which of course was challenged by the *Colegio de Abogados* de Lima that filed a new action of constitutionality against it (Exp. 00001-2009-PI/TC). This time the constitutional tribunal could not decide the new case[39] rapidly because during 2007–8 a political battle (discussed in the following text) was being fought for the appointment of four new judges. This time, the government that was able to place judges with close preferences in the constitutional tribunal won the battle. The newly composed constitutional tribunal on December 4, 2009 then produced a jurisprudential U-turn: in Exp. 00001-2009-PI/TC, the tribunal argued not only that it is constitutional that active military officers serve as judges and prosecutors in the military justice system, but also that military judges and prosecutors be designated by the president of the republic.[40]

After the jurisprudential U-turn, the executive asked congress for legislative powers and on September 2010 published four decrees with yet another new set of law: the Criminal Code of Military Police (Decree 1094), a Law on the Use of Force (Decree 1095), a decree that modified some articles of the Law on the Organization of the Military Justice (Decree 1096

[38] See also 0006-2006-AI/TC, which is an action of unconstitutionality also against Law 28665 filed by the *Colegio de Abogados de Lima.*

[39] But it certainly did not apply the law in habeas corpus cases: 08353-2006-PHC/TC (published April 9, 2007) and 01605-2006-PHC/TC (published January 11, 2008). See Justicia Viva 2010, 15–16.

[40] This implies that the constitutional tribunal considered the existence of a separate military prosecutorial body to be constitutional even though the constitution says nothing about it.

modifying Law 29182),[41] and a decree that regulated the application of procedural law in cases of violations of human rights (Decree 1097). The latter Decree 1097 was openly favorable to potential releases of military officers convicted of human rights violations (such as the members of the *Grupo Colina*, a military special-forces squad that had been involved in cases such as *Barrios Altos* and *La Cantuta*). For this reason, it was severely criticized from numerous fronts (among others by Nobel Prize winner Mario Vargas Llosa in a strongly worded open letter) and it was derogated.

But Decrees 1094, 1095, and 1096 are still in force (December 2015). They are vaguely written so that they can be construed to imply an extension of the scope of the military jurisdiction. Specifically, the Law on the Use of Force (Decree 1095) states that "illicit behavior by military officers during service belong to the military jurisdiction," it also allows the use of force against "hostile groups" that again are vaguely defined. Moreover, the new Code of Military Justice (Decree 1094) increases the list of crimes that belong to the military jurisdiction, and rewrites the definition of some military crimes such as "devastation" or "confiscation" in such an ambiguous way that it actually opens the door to a considerable broadening of the scope of the military jurisdiction (cf. Justicia Viva 2010, 29–38).

How was this jurisprudential U-turn possible? First, as already mentioned, after the constitutional tribunal's decisions of 2003–4, the armed forces (in particular, the military justice) started not only a self-regulation in order to adapt to what they agreed to in the decisions, but also a legal strategy to counteract the measures that they opposed. The self-regulation included the training of several officials in law, human rights, and in particular on International Humanitarian Law (IHL) that has been adopted as the basic legal framework.[42] This self-regulation was considered sufficient by the armed forces that did not look favorable upon the "intromissions" and "sudden and drastic" changes required by the constitutional

[41] This decree includes the direct designation of military judges and prosecutors by the president of the republic (instead of the previous system in which the president selects one from a list of three candidates suggested by the military justice). This method was publicly considered an undue intromission by the government by then president of the Superior Military Tribunal Carlos Mesa Angosto (*El Correo*, January 2, 2013).

[42] In 2007, e.g., after negotiations between the Ministry of Defense and the armed forces (through the Joint Command), the Center of International Humanitarian Law and Human Rights of the Armed Forces was established. It is interesting how members of the Peruvian armed forces perceive the IHL. In an article by Lieutenant Colonel Roosevelt Bravo Maxdeo he considers that the IHL will give an "advantage to the Armed Forces in the fight against the subversives because they will be able to use the arms that the nation has confided to them" (Bravo Maxdeo 2009, 40).

tribunal.[43] The legal strategy included proposals on bills on the code of military justice and other related norms plus lobby efforts on key congressmen and congressional committees.[44]

Second, and politically more important, is the return to power in 2006 of President Alan García, leading a considerably weakened APRA and in the context of a highly volatile political party system, who made alliances with the de facto powers such as business, the Catholic Church, and the armed forces (Vergara 2013, 105–20, 131–6). Regarding the alliance with the armed forces, García's choice of vice president, Vice Admiral Luis Giampietri Rojas, is noteworthy as he was directly involved in the case of *El Frontón* (the forceful suppression of a penal mutiny that involved several deaths in June 1986, during the first administration of Alan García).[45] This alliance explains not only the lack of pressure that García put on congress to comply with constitutional tribunal's decisions, but also the "covert amnesty law" (Decree 1097 discussed previously, that was withdrawn by García after heavy criticism).[46] This alliance was also operative when four vacancies opened in the constitutional tribunal in 2007–8: the obscure process to elect the new judges was heavily questioned, and at least one of the judges was directly linked to

[43] Remember the epigraph of this chapter: Counter Admiral, and former president of the Superior Military Tribunal, Carlos Mesa Angosto declared in a newspaper interview that the Constitutional Tribunal and "some NGOs ... almost destroyed the military justice" but that they "with one decision [Exp. 00001-2009-PI/TC] managed to revert nine previous decisions and to get back some faculties" (*El Correo*, December 25, 2012).

[44] Interview with Capitán de Navío CJ Carlos M. Schiaffino Chierre, Presidente del Tribunal Superior Militar Policial del Centro, and with Teniente Coronel EP Alejandro Roosevelt Bravo Maxdeo, Sub-Director del Centro de Altos Estudios de Justicia Militar, June 25, 2014. See also, e.g., the inauguration address by then president of the Superior Military Tribunal, Contralmirante Carlos Mesa Angosto, of the seminar on "Military Justice: Proposals and Perspectives" (June 15–23, 2004) where he acknowledged the preparation of a bill that was submitted to Congress by the executive. (Memoirs of the seminar on file with the author.)

[45] Critics suspect that the choice of Giampetri as vice president was a preemptive move by García who feared that his own responsibility in the *El Frontón* massacre would be raised and haunt him during his second administration.

[46] In a published interview on February 18, 2006 then president of the Supreme Council of Military Justice, General EP Juan Pablo Ramos Espinoza, declared that "it was healthy to amnesty military officials accused of human rights violations because the Final Report of the Truth and Reconciliation Commission was biased in favor of the victims and some NGOs" (cited in *Desde el Tercer Piso*, June 6, 2007). It should also be mentioned that during García's administration (2006–11), a president who staunchly opposed transitional justice trials and publicly defended the military, many civilian and military officers were sent to prison. Most notably, in April 2009, after nearly seventeen years of legal battles, the supreme court found former president Fujimori responsible for mounting a repressive apparatus that executed the crimes in *La Cantuta*, and other crimes (see González Ocantos 2012).

the armed forces.[47] The election of four judges was cancelled, and four new judges were elected but again some of them were identified as being close to Vice Admiral Giampetri, Vice President of the Republic.[48]

This newly composed constitutional tribunal produced the jurisprudential U-turn on military autonomy and the scope of military jurisdiction. It is noteworthy that the quality of the argumentation in the constitutional tribunal decision (Exp. 00001-2009-PI/TC) is considerably different from previous decisions by the tribunal. For instance, whereas constitutional courts can alter their own jurisprudence, such a decision should be thoroughly justified in legal, theoretical, and practical terms in order to preserve the authority of the tribunal and the coherence and consistency of the law (see López Medina 2009). In this decision, the constitutional tribunal only included practical considerations of dubious argumentative quality, such as "the time has come to make the jurisprudence evolve ... according to the changing social, political, economic, and cultural phenomena" without ever explicating which phenomena they are talking about nor how exactly they affect their interpretation of the constitution (see Justicia Viva 2010, 22). Moreover, the constitutional tribunal also deliberately cited only the fragments of IACHR's jurisprudence that justified its new interpretation of the constitution, distorting their original meaning (the particular vote of magistrate César Landa Arroyo exposed this practice).

As mentioned earlier, the legislation produced after the jurisprudential U-turn was again challenged. At the time of this writing (December 2015), a newly composed (again) constitutional tribunal has partly consolidated the jurisprudential U-turn. The election of new judges during 2013 was again heavily questioned for its lack of transparency. Congressmen were accused of disingenuously distributing seats in the constitutional tribunal among party factions, and the result was the inclusion of some judges that caused a public uproar.[49] The election, again as in 2008, was canceled and after the scandal a new set of judges was finally appointed in May 2014 (see Table 4.1 for final composition). The jurisprudential status quo on

[47] The lawyer Javier Ríos Castillo was elected by a congressional majority to serve in the Constitutional Tribunal on June 2007. But a day before that, he was photographed having lunch with members of the armed forces among which there were former assistants of Vladimiro Montesinos (*Revista Caretas* 2180. May 12, 2011).

[48] This is the case of magistrates Carlos Mesía, Fernando Calle Hayén, and Gerardo Eto Cruz (see Table 4.1 for the changes in composition of the constitutional tribunal).

[49] Among the judges elected was Ronaldo Sousa, partner of the firm that defended former president Fujimori and that also defended General Hermoza Ríos, the same general who plotted the "self-coup" with Fujimori and who was involved in several cases of violations of human rights. Other judges were involved in corruption scandals, such as Victor

the autonomy of the military and the scope of military justice was given, as explained in previous text, by the constitutional tribunal's decision 00001-2009-PI/TC and Decrees 1094, 1095, and 1096. The constitutional tribunal in decision 00022-2011-PI/TC (August 18, 2015) ratified that grave human rights violations belong to the ordinary jurisdiction, limited the military jurisdiction for strictly military crimes (*delitos de función*), but also ambiguously defined and arguably extended the role and participation of the armed forces in internal security crisis.[50]

Decision 00022-2011-PI/TC, which restricts the scope of the military jurisdiction but also potentially increases the participation of the armed forces in internal public security, enters the public debate in a context of increasing calls for the armed forces to deal with illegal mining, drug-trafficking, and even mounting but regular crime in Peru. The current president of the *Fuero Militar Policial*, Gen. Brigadier Juan Pablo Ramos Espinosa, already asked for more funds to strengthen the role of the military jurisdiction in some regions of the country.[51] Moreover, in the way to the presidential election that will take place in April 2016 some potential candidates such as Alan García and Alejandro Toledo are taking advantage of the fact that 78 percent of the people reported being favorable to bringing the armed forces back in the streets to help the police combating crime.[52] The ambiguity of the tribunal's decision in this regard may come in handy not only for the presidential campaign but also for the public security decisions by the next president.

Conclusion: The Constitutional Tribunal as a Mediator?

In contrast to the tribunal of constitutional guarantees, the constitutional tribunal has produced decisions that go to the heart of the problem regarding military autonomy and the scope of military jurisdiction and has provided ample justification for them. Such contrast expands

Mayorga and Cayo Galindo (see "Los anticuchos de los nuevos funcionarios que nombró el Congreso," *Perú 21*, July 17, 2013).

50 Cf. David Lovatón Palacios, "Justicia militar y uso de la fuerza por las FFAA: en pos de la república", in Blog Justicia Viva, http://www.justiciaviva.org.pe/blog/justicia-militar-y-uso-de-la-fuerza-por-las-ffaa-en-pos-de-la-republica/. Last accessed December 7, 2015.

51 "Fuero Militar Policial tendrá mayor presencia en regiones". *El Peruano*, 9 de septiembre de 2015. Available at http://www.elperuano.com.pe/eppo/noticia-fuero-militarpolicial-tendra-mayor-presencia-regiones-32688.aspx. Last accessed December 7, 2015.

52 As reported in César Bazán Seminario, "¿Militares combatir la delincuencia? No, gracias, in Blog Justicia Viva, http://www.justiciaviva.org.pe/blog/militares-combatir-la-delincuencia-no-gracias/. Last accessed December 7, 2015.

to other areas where the tribunal has been able to rule in cases in which political branches or other constitutional bodies had strong interests. The range of cases decided by the constitutional tribunal includes issues concerning freedom of expression, access to information, social and economic rights, the jurisdiction of military courts, municipal matters, pension laws and constitutional reform, among others (Dargent 2009, 273. See also Landa Arroyo 2007; Ponce and Tiede 2014). However, does the constitutional tribunal's jurisprudence on military autonomy amount to what this book defines as mediator-like jurisprudence (see Chapter 2)?

The constitutional tribunal's jurisprudence reduced uncertainty and shows some of the characteristics of mediator-like jurisprudence listed in Chapter 2, such as the "interpretative sentences" and the time to compliance (*vacatio sententiae*) included in some of the more important decisions on military autonomy. Moreover, the constitutional tribunal created the figure of the "observatory participant" that permitted having open hearings with the parts in a case in order to obtain further information on the conflict and on the views of the participants. Through its jurisprudence, the constitutional tribunal has indeed limited the scope of the military jurisdiction (see Figure 4.2) and also basically favored the autonomy of the military justice system in most of its decisions (see Figure 4.1). Notwithstanding the jurisprudential U-turn of 2009-15, there is now a consensus on keeping civilians and cases on gross violations of human rights out of military courts (key issues such as whether, when, and how the armed forces should intervene in internal public security matters as well as some definitional aspects of military crimes, *delitos de función*, and the autonomy and structure of the military justice are still open and presumably will continue to be strongly contested).

However, other features of the mediator-like jurisprudence are not present in the constitutional tribunal's decisions. For instance, because access to the tribunal is limited, it has produced relatively few sentences on the subject in which it explains its reasoning (e.g., actions of constitutionality) and its arguments in decisions on habeas corpus cases are sparse; focused on a specific case; and, with some exceptions, do not reveal whether and to what extent the constitutional tribunal understands military autonomy cases as an ongoing conflict and that it will thus receive more similar cases in the future.[53] Also, whereas the constitutional tribunal created the figure

[53] In contrast, the Colombian Constitutional Court in concrete-review cases has created the figure of "unified decisions" precisely to give coherence to its decisions and to extract from specific cases lessons for future cases (see Chapter 3).

of *vacatio sententiae* in order to give congress time to produce new legislation, the constitutional tribunal failed to include some oversight mechanisms for increasing the likelihood of compliance, such as a road map and a schedule, public roundtables on the topic, or public consultations with the armed forces and congressmen (see, e.g., Botero 2014).

But the biggest obstacle to the constitutional tribunal becoming a full third-party mediator is its limited independence that stems from incentives set forth in the mechanisms of appointment and tenure. Specifically, the method of appointments (two-thirds of the congressmen) incentivizes crude bargaining among parties represented in congress that is not tempered by a second organ with different interests participating in the appointment. Moreover, judges enjoy quite a short tenure (five years, which coincides with the legislative term). The short length of tenure of the constitutional judges, coupled with the partisan bias of judges and the limited accessibility of the tribunal, implies that few cases on a given topic reach the tribunal and that when they do, the judges who want to change the status quo do have to make deep and drastic changes quite rapidly. In other words, judges at the constitutional tribunal do not have the long horizons that allow them to engage in a systematic and continued attempt at transforming the preferences of the actors involved in a conflict. Deep and drastic changes made rapidly do affect the political actors who, then try to influence the composition of the court because they know that current judges will leave relatively soon.

The short horizons of judges also make it more difficult to produce jurisprudence that transforms the preferences of the actors in a conflict, and that helps actors understand each other. A case in point is the IHL. In contrast to the Colombian case, in which in a 1995 decision the constitutional court limited the government by empowering judges to declare an internal conflict (see Chapter 3), the Peruvian Constitutional Tribunal did not take such a step. Even though the IHL had been discussed in the constitutional tribunal since 2003, it argued that it was "not competent to declare that there is a non-international armed conflict" (Exp. 010-2002-AI/TC, p. 102). Members of the military justice system considered that the constitutional tribunal "missed a great opportunity" in that decision.[54] In other words, the constitutional tribunal's jurisprudence has not been fully capable of translating and transforming the military's preferences

[54] Interview with Capitán de Navío CJ Carlos M. Schiaffino Chierre, Presidente del Tribunal Superior Militar Policial del Centro, and with Teniente Coronel EP Alejandro Roosevelt Bravo Maxdeo, Sub-Director del Centro de Altos Estudios de Justicia Militar, June 25, 2014.

into democratically acceptable solutions. The most recent decision on the topic (00022-2011-PI/TC published in August 18, 2015) does incorporate openly references to the IHL, which may indicate a change in that direction. But, again, the short tenure of the tribunal's judges implies that if political actors represented in congress do not want the tribunal going in that direction they will have in three more years (2019) the chance to again completely renew the tribunal's membership perhaps with judges who are closer to their preferences.

In sum, the constitutional tribunal's jurisprudence has come only halfway on the road to becoming a mediator-like jurisprudence. The reason, according to the theory defended in this book, lies in the limited levels of judicial independence and access of the constitutional tribunal. The limited levels of judicial independence make the political context under which judges make decisions a key factor that influences their behavior, much more than the ideology or political leanings of the judges. This is true for the jurisprudence on military jurisdiction but also for the rest of the constitutional tribunal's decisions (Ponce and Tiede 2014). The period 2002–6 was marked by the recent fall of the Fujimori regime, the explicit intentions by social and political actors to make things right, and the pressure of public opinion to actually do so. The constitutional tribunal jurisprudence during that period reflected that context; it was perceived as a "golden window of opportunity" in the words of David Lovatón. As economic growth made politicians cautious, the impetus for reforming institutions such as the armed forces ceded. This new political context was, in turn, reflected in the constitutional tribunal's jurisprudence of the period 2007–13. Based on this pattern, it is unfortunately likely that the current (December 2015) context of increasing social tension, internal insecurity, and the growth of illegal mining and drug-trafficking in some areas of the country, coupled with the callings for the increasing participation of the armed forces to deal with these problems, will also be reflected in the tribunal's jurisprudence.

5

Constitutional Jurisprudence on Military Autonomy in Mexico, 1917–2013

> Los militares de México aportaremos nuestros mejores esfuerzos al servicio de los ciudadanos sin amedrentarnos por juicios injustos, algunos sin duda erróneos, carentes de fundamento, malintencionados y que la institución armada no merece.
>
> (We, the Mexican military officers, will offer our best efforts at the service of citizens without fear of unfair trials, some of them without a doubt wrong, lacking foundation, malicious. The national armed forces do not deserve it.)
>
> General Salvador Cienfuegos Zepeda, Secretary of Defense
> (*La Jornada*, November 11, 2014)

The epigraph is from a speech by the current (December 2015) Mexican secretary of defense in reaction to the decision by the Mexican attorney general to charge seven soldiers with crimes against public service, and three of them with more serious charges of murdering eight of the twenty-two gang and drug traffic suspects and altering the crime scene, in a military intervention in the small town of Tlatlaya on June 30, 2014. The military initially reported that all twenty-two suspects were killed in a shootout. Days after the event, the governor of the State of Mexico, where Tlatlaya is, said that "The Mexican Army showed braveness in Tlatlaya. Unfortunately, one soldier was hurt but the Armed Forces in legitimate defense intervened and shot down the criminals." The state attorney general also confirmed and supported the military's version.

But an anonymous witness later contradicted the official version of events, telling *Esquire* magazine that twenty-one of the suspects, including her teenage daughter, were killed after they had surrendered. In a "bold rebuke for Mexico's powerful military," as the *New York Times* reported it, "the National Commission of Human Rights issued a report confirming that bodies had been moved at the rural warehouse to suggest that everyone was killed in a shootout and that most of the people had surrendered before they were shot and killed" (*New York Times*, October 21, 2014). After considerable national and international pressure, the

Mexican attorney general intervened and charged seven soldiers. General Cienfuego's reaction speaks for itself, but it is puzzling. What "unfair" or "malicious" trials does he have in mind? If anything, as we will see in this chapter, the Mexican armed forces have been treated with great deference by judicial actors. Or is he sending a bold signal to civilian authorities and to the judges that are going to decide on these cases, eventually including the supreme court?

This chapter analyzes constitutional jurisprudence on military autonomy in three periods of Mexican history: the first starting in 1917, the year when the current constitution was enacted, up until 1940, when President Cárdenas' administration ended after building the foundations of what will become the hegemonic party period, which is the second period that covers from 1940 until 1994. The third period starts in 1995, the year when key constitutional reforms reshaped the basic characteristics of the supreme court, until 2013.[1] Specifically, as in the previous two chapters, I quantitatively and qualitatively analyze the decisions made by the supreme court during the three periods in two types of cases: cases that reach the constitutional organ challenging a previous decision made by a military authority (e.g., a military court, prosecutor, officer, or military administrative agency), and cases that reach the constitutional organ on the scope of the military jurisdiction.

Taking advantage of the fact that the supreme court enjoys the same levels of independence but higher levels of access and powers of judicial review in the third period in comparison to the first, I explore whether the court's behavior since 1995 is closer to the ideal of the third-party mediator in conflict resolution. To quickly preview the conclusion of the chapter, the answer is that the supreme court does not behave as a mediator, neither in the first period nor in the third, although this might be changing at the very end of the third period. The main reason is that access to the supreme court remains severely limited. In the chapter, this lack of access is nicely reflected in sporadic and timid jurisprudence on military autonomy produced by the court.

The structure of the chapter is the same of that of the previous two: In the first section, I provide an overview of constitutional jurisprudence

[1] The second period, 1940 to 1993, falls squarely in a classification of hegemonic party regime that is nondemocratic. Despite the fact that the theory proposed in this book applies under democracies, I include this period in the analysis because it is interesting as a contrast and also in order to not lose historical continuity in the narrative.

in the whole period analyzed in the chapter. After that, I devote one section to each of the three subperiods, focusing on the political context and civil-military relations, the characteristics of the constitutional organ during the period, and the constitutional jurisprudence on military autonomy produced by it.

Long-Term Jurisprudential Patterns on Military Autonomy in Mexico, 1917–2013

The long period from 1917 until 2013 has witnessed interesting differences in regime types: a competitive but highly unstable democracy (approximately from 1917 to 1940), a hegemonic party regime (approximately from 1940 to 1994), and a more stable democracy (from 1994 to date).[2] The armed forces have been a key actor in all three periods, but civil-military relations have changed across these. In the first period, many political parties coexisted and competed for power in the aftermath of a civil war that fragmented even the victorious faction. During this period, presidents were mostly military generals, and they had to deal with high levels of competition and factionalism in both political parties and within the armed forces (see Rath 2013, ch. 1).

The second period is marked by the birth, development, and decay of a corporatist political party that became hegemonic and included the armed forces as one of its key limbs. The first civilian president assumed power in 1946 and a so-called civilian-military pact was established: military loyalty and support to the civilian governments in exchange for military autonomy in a wide array of areas (Serrano 1995).[3] As the hegemonic party melted down, democratic political competition emerged by top-down reforms that progressively liberated the steam produced by bottom-up pressures. In this third period, the civilian-military pact has been revised as the armed forces and civilian governments have been protractedly finding new accommodation under a proper democratic framework (Díez 2012). Interestingly, the supreme court's jurisprudence on military autonomy also varies across the three periods.

[2] The peculiarities of the Mexican political system make any choosing of dates to establish periods debatable. The pillars of the second period began to be built in the first, and those of the third in the second. Thus, the historical narrative that follows is not strictly limited by the dates chosen, but overlaps a bit to give a sense of continuity.

[3] This pact is similar to the one established in Colombia after the "Lleras doctrine" (see Chapter 3).

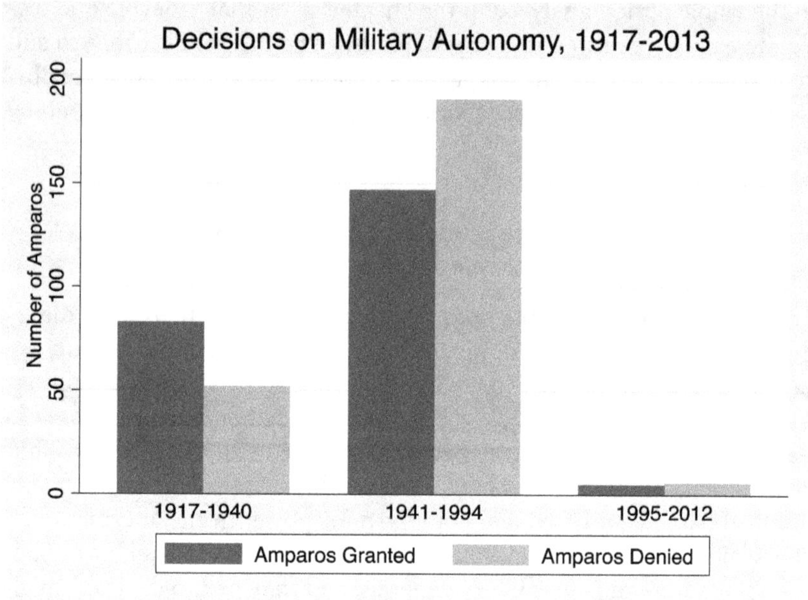

Figure 5.1. The supreme court can reject or amend a previous decision made by a military authority, which is coded as "limiting autonomy," or rather uphold it, which is coded as "respecting autonomy." This figure does not include *tesis* on conflicts of jurisdiction. The figure shows raw numbers; the percentage of "amparos granted"/"amparos denied" in the first, second, and third periods (respectively) are 62 percent/38 percent; 43 percent/57 percent; and 48 percent/52 percent.

Figure 5.1 shows so-called jurisprudential thesis (*tesis de jurisprudencia*)[4] by the supreme court (1917–2013) on military autonomy.[5] The constitutional organ can reject or amend a previous decision made by a military

[4] A *tesis de jurisprudencia* is an authoritative interpretation of the constitution emitted by the Mexican Supreme Court. Jurisprudential *tesis* are short, lawlike paragraphs or sentences, free of the facts of the case. While the ideal *tesis* contains a summary of the main argument made in the decision, the *tesis* are generally simple statements that make it difficult (sometimes impossible) to capture the legal reasoning that led the judges to reach that interpretation. The *tesis* are extracted from decisions on specific cases, and they constitute the relevant and obligatory interpretative guidelines of the constitution, the laws, and even the general principles of the law. This admittedly weird system of jurisprudence has its roots in Mexico´s hybrid legal system, in place since the nineteenth century, which combines features from Anglo-Saxon common law and the European civil law systems (see López Medina 2009, 2011).

[5] The database consists of 680 jurisprudential *tesis*, of which 507 come from *amparos* (individual constitutional complaints), 159 from conflicts of jurisdiction (between the ordinary and the military) that the supreme court resolves, and 14 from cases in which the supreme

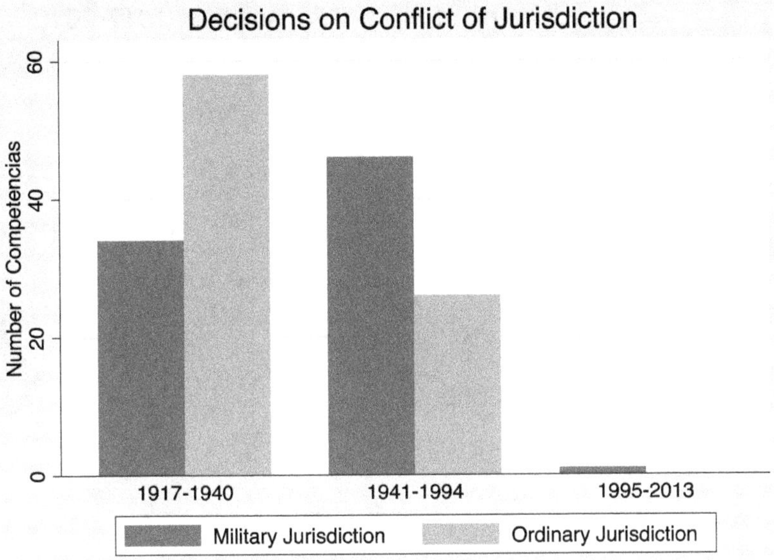

Figure 5.2. The supreme court decides whether a given case should be sent to the military or to the ordinary jurisdiction when such jurisdiction is contested. The total number of so-called *competencias* is 159, of which 79 were sent to the ordinary and 78 to the military jurisdiction. Two cases were sent to both jurisdictions. The figure shows raw numbers, the percentage of cases sent to the military jurisdiction in period one is 37 percent, period two 64 percent, and period three 100 percent; the correspondent percentages sent to the civil jurisdiction are 63 percent, 36 percent, and 0 percent.

authority, which I code as "limiting autonomy," or rather uphold it, which I consider "respecting autonomy." The most interesting finding in Figure 5.1 is that whereas during the limited-democratic period of 1917–40 there are more decisions limiting military autonomy, the opposite is the case during the hegemonic party period (1940–4). Figure 5.2 shows a similar pattern on

court solves conflictive interpretations of the same constitutional article or principle among circuit courts. With the help of Javier Zúñiga Ramiro, we systematically and thoroughly searched the supreme court's database (IUS) for all cases on military autonomy. If there are *tesis* not included in this database, we believe they would not alter the tendencies shown in Figures 5.1 and 5.2. The full list of cases can be found at http://www.investigadores.cide.edu/julio.rios/. Finally, this is a database of *tesis*, not decisions and there is not a one to one relation between them. Moreover, the *tesis* deliberately omit facts and argumentation. Thus the *tesis* are used to establish general jurisdictional patterns, but when necessary the analysis in some parts of the chapter resorts to actual decisions.

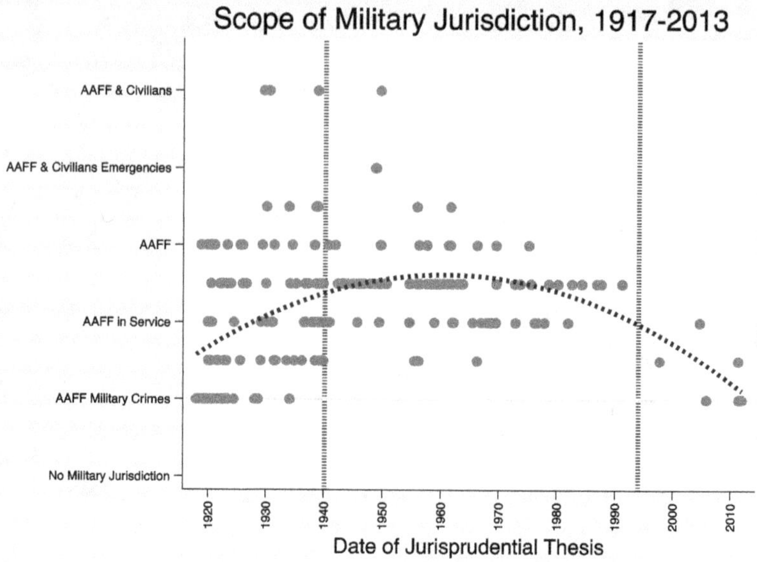

Figure 5.3. Decisions by the Mexican Supreme Court on the scope of military jurisdiction, which essentially are the court's answer to the question: Who can be judged in military courts, and under what circumstances? The curved dotted line displays a locally weighted regression on the data (lowess in STATA). The horizontal dotted line at "AAFF Military Crimes" represents the answer to the question on the scope of military jurisdiction by the Constitution of 1917. The dotted vertical lines at 1940 and 1994 represent the cutoff points of the subperiods analyzed in this chapter.

decisions that involved a competence of jurisdiction: whenever the military jurisdiction was challenged as the appropriate forum for investigation and trial, the supreme court sent more cases to the ordinary jurisdiction in the first period, and more to the military jurisdiction in the hegemonic party period. In other words, in general, the supreme court's decisions follow the political context under which they were made.

Figure 5.3 shows jurisprudential *tesis* by the supreme court (1917–2013) on the scope of the military jurisdiction, which essentially are the courts' answer to the question: Who can be judged in military courts, and under what circumstances?[6] I code judicial answers within eleven categories

[6] This question establishes the "constitutional scenario," a factual question in which the interests of actors clash and whose answer requires an interpretation of the constitution (López Medina 2009, 154).

ordered from the narrowest to the widest: (0) nobody ever, that is, the military jurisdiction is abolished; (1) not even military personnel when crimes against humanity and gross human rights violations are involved; (2) only military personnel, only when strictly military crimes are involved; (3, 4, 5) only military personnel, only when crimes were committed during service construed in a narrow, regular, or broad way respectively; (6) only military personnel, under any circumstance; (7, 8) military personnel and civilians, only during emergency situations construed in a narrow or broad way, respectively; and (9, 10) military personnel and civilians, under circumstances broader than emergencies narrowly and broadly construed, respectively. The horizontal axis in Figure 5.3 displays the date on which the decision was made. The vertical axis displays the categories on the scope of military jurisdiction on a scale from the narrowest to the widest scope, 0 to 10.

Figure 5.3 shows the general trajectory of the supreme court's jurisprudence: from 1920 to roughly 1940, the court more often than not held a narrow scope of military jurisdiction but it progressively expanded its interpretation of Article 13 (see following text); from around 1940 to roughly 2005, the court established a wider scope of military jurisdiction; and from 2005 to 2012, although there are relatively few *tesis* apparently the court is moving toward narrowing the scope of military jurisdiction. Notice the period of 1930 to 1940 when there were widely different interpretations on the proper scope of military jurisdiction that are reflected in inconsistent jurisprudence. Figure 5.3 also includes the constitutional response to the question on military jurisdiction that is the horizontal line situated at "AAFF for military crimes." Article 13 of the Mexican Constitution of 1917 establishes and delimits military jurisdiction. It clearly states that:

> Article 13.- . . . The military jurisdiction will deal with **military crimes** and **offenses to the military discipline. The military tribunals never, and for no reason, will extend their jurisdiction to persons that do not belong to the armed forces.** When a civilian is involved in a military crime or an offense to the military discipline, the case will be decided in the correspondent ordinary court. (Emphasis added)

It is apparent that the scope of the military jurisdiction is defined very narrowly in the constitution. During the debates of the constituent assembly in 1916 some deputies even proposed to eliminate the military jurisdiction altogether (González Oropeza 2006, 190). Article 13 is exactly the same today as it was in 1917, which makes it one of the few relevant articles that have not been changed in the more than five hundred amendments that the Constitution of 1917 has undergone. While Article 13 is quite clear and has remained constant, the supreme court's jurisprudence on the scope of military jurisdiction has fluctuated in important ways. This is one of the reasons why this issue is particularly fruitful for pinning down the extralegal determinants of the supreme court's jurisprudential changes.

The Supreme Court, 1917–1940

Political Context and Civil-Military Relations

After years of armed conflict that started toward the end of 1910, the constitutional congress that convened in Querétaro produced the constitution that since February 5, 1917 is Mexico's fundamental law. Even though the enactment of the constitution signals the victory of one of the three main revolutionary factions, sealed with the appointment of Venustiano Carranza as president under the new rules of the game, the political scene until 1920 was marked by the successive elimination of the revolutionary leaders – Zapata, Villa, and Carranza, who was assassinated in May of that year. The administrations of Generals Álvaro Obregón (December 1, 1920 to December 1, 1924) and Plutarco Elías Calles (1924–1928) are the ones that begin relatively more regular politics after the so-called armed phase of the Mexican revolution.

During the 1920s, however, the multiplicity of political forces continuously threatened to derail the already precarious postrevolutionary regime (Rath 2013, ch. 1). In this context, the main threat to Obregón's administration came from within his own group, with the rebellion of General De La Huerta that was successfully repressed in 1923. This paved the way for the election of Obregón's favorite in 1924, General Plutarco Elías Calles, who presided over a period when other rebellions were crushed, and when the constitution was amended to allow for the reelection of Obregón in 1928. Obregón won the election but was assassinated before assuming office.

To channel the diversity of political forces, and in the shadow of the assassination of the president elect, General Calles pushed for the creation of an umbrella political organization under the name of National Revolutionary Party (PNR, 1929) that would become the main vehicle for politics and governance for the following seventy years (see Garrido 2005). For a few years, Calles successfully became the leader of the party and the "power behind the throne" who effectively selected and controlled successive presidents. But Calles' pick for presidential candidate for the PNR in the elections of 1934, General Lázaro Cárdenas, managed to sideline Calles, forcing him into exile in 1936. During Cárdenas' presidency (1934–40), the PNR (that became the *Partido de la Revolución Mexicana*, PRM in 1936, and then the *Partido Revolucionario Institutional*, PRI in 1946) was transformed and consolidated as a corporatist political machine.

To the extent to which the revolution provided common ground for both civilian and military elites, it contributed indirectly to shaping and circumscribing the role of the armed forces (Serrano 1995, 428). Indeed, Obregón and Calles initiated a series of reforms intended to reduce the size and budget of the armed forces as well as to make them more professional. Both purged the armed forces of rivals, or perceived rivals, by retiring hundreds of generals, eliminating others, and bribing the rest. They cut the budget of the armed forces almost in half. However, Obregón and Calles also made progress in professionalizing the armed forces, creating the Commission of Military Studies (1926) and the Superior School of War (1929) (Díez and Nicholls 2006, 6–8).[7]

The Supreme Court, 1917–1940: Independence, Access, and Powers

According to the 1917 Constitution, supreme court judges were elected by a simple majority of the total members of both houses of congress from a list composed of candidates submitted by state legislatures (one candidate per each legislature) (Article 96), they enjoyed life tenure (i.e., "during good behavior") (Article 94),[8] and could be eventually removed only if a simple majority of the house of deputies initiated an impeachment process (Article 109). The supreme court was at the top of the judicial power, not only in jurisdictional terms through constitutional interpretation and as a court of cassation, but also because it was in charge of the appointment of judges of the lower federal court (Article 97). Regarding the instruments for constitutional review, the Constitution of 1917 included the *amparo suit*, an instrument to protect constitutional rights from government violations with *inter partes* effects, and created the constitutional controversy, an

[7] Important measures to professionalize and discipline the army actually started under Carranza, such as the reopening the Military College, the practice of rotation, the reduction in the number of troops, and the reorganization of the cavalry and infantry corps (Serrano 1995, 428).

[8] Article 94 explicitly mentions that tenure during good behavior applies for those judges appointed after 1923. Those appointed in 1917 had a two-year tenure, and the second cohort had tenure of four years.

instrument to adjudicate conflicts of constitutional competence between branches and levels of government (Article 103 and Articles 105–7).

Therefore, the constitution established quite independent supreme court justices, albeit with limited powers and limited access to decide on the governmental infringement of individual rights as well as to become the arbiters of political conflicts.[9] In the first case, the supreme court did not hear *amparos* as part of its original jurisdiction, but rather on appeal, and it did not have the power to pick and choose what cases to decide. Regarding constitutional controversies, the supreme court shared the role of adjudicator of political conflicts between branches and levels of government with the senate that enjoyed the power to resolve "political questions between branches of state governments" (Article 76).[10] Moreover, access to the supreme court was also quite limited: only political authorities, such as a governor or a state legislature, who believed that their constitutional competencies had been encroached upon, could file a constitutional controversy. In turn, whereas in theory the *amparo* suit could be filed by anyone who had been directly injured by a state authority, in fact enough legal knowledge or money to hire a lawyer was also necessary because the *amparo* had already become a technically complex legal instrument.[11]

The de jure expectations established in the constitutional text were somewhat exceeded in practice, in particular because the supreme court during that period established itself as an independent authority with preferences that diverged from the successive postrevolutionary governments. Specifically, the supreme court in delicate matters such as agrarian or labor reform consistently challenged the programs established by the governments "emanated from the revolution." It was true that the Constitution of 1917 established a quite ambitious social program, but it was equally true that the constitution included principles of property rights and liberal market, and quite often the supreme court decided

[9] The de jure indexes of independence and judicial review powers (that includes access) of the Supreme Court in this period are five (out of six) and two (out of eight), respectively (Ríos-Figueroa 2011).

[10] Notice that the supreme court in that period did not have the power to review the constitutionality of laws or acts in the abstract. In Mexico, this capacity was granted to the supreme court only in 1994 with the creation of the action of constitutionality.

[11] The *amparo* was introduced in the Mexican legal landscape in 1847, and recognized as an individual constitutional complaint instrument in the Constitution of 1857. By 1917 the *amparo* had already existed for four decades and, interestingly, it was widely used despite the authoritarian nature of some of the governments of that period. During those decades, the *amparo* had grown in legal complexity (Pou Giménez 2012).

against the interests of the revolutionary government, upholding property rights and the market forces (James 2006).[12] Something similar happened with military autonomy, as we will see in the following text. However, as I will argue, this jurisprudence was not enough to turn the supreme court into a third-party mediator and, in the end, its challenges to the government were extremely costly: by 1940 the independence of the court had been undermined and it was incorporated into the logic of the hegemonic party regime.

The incorporation of the supreme court into the hegemonic party regime proceeded gradually. In 1928 a constitutional amendment augmented the number of supreme court justices from eleven to sixteen and modified their method of appointment: instead of congressional appointment by a majority vote, the reform gave the president the right to propose a candidate, subject to senate ratification. In 1934 another amendment again increased the number of judges to twenty-one and transformed the original life tenure of justices into a six-year tenure coincident with the presidential administration. By 1940, the goal had been accomplished: the court had been packed, and de jure judges' independence was also curtailed. In a nutshell, the court had been incorporated into the hegemonic party machinery.

Constitutional Jurisprudence on Military Autonomy

What did the supreme court do in cases related to the armed forces? When the armed phase of the Mexican Revolution ended in 1920 and some kind of regular politics started to operate under a vigorous multiparty system, cases on military jurisdiction began to arrive at the Mexican Supreme Court. And the court consistently upheld, in line with Article 13, a quite narrow scope of military jurisdiction. For instance, in a *tesis de jurisprudencia* of 1924, the court argued that "it is not enough that a crime has been committed by a member of the armed forces, because if it does not affect military discipline or the armed forces honor, or it was not committed during military service, it cannot fall under the jurisdiction of military tribunals" (Reg. No. 285360).[13] This strict application of constitutional

12 It has to be noted that the armed forces were divided regarding the extent and scope of some revolutionary goals, such as the agrarian reform program (Tobler 1971).

13 *Reg. No.* is the number with which the jurisprudential thesis cited is registered in the Supreme Court's Jurisprudence Database (IUS). The cited thesis can be accessed simply by writing down the reference number on the supreme court's website: http://sjf.scjn.gob.mx/sjfsist/Paginas/tesis.aspx?Tesis=Tesis (accessed June 2, 2015).

Article 13 was the norm during the period. The court usually does not provide further argumentation than simply restating the literal content of Article 13 (e.g., Reg. No. 811824; Reg. No. 290730).

During those years, the court also clearly stated that civilians should not be tried in military courts. Again, the court more often than not simply restates Article 13 without further argumentation: "military tribunals never, and for no reason, will extend their jurisdiction to persons that do not belong to the armed forces" (Reg. No. 290340). The court again upheld a limited scope of military jurisdiction when facing the difficult case of military officers committing a crime with civilians as accomplices: presumably responding to the litigant's request that the military official should be judged in a military court and the civilian in a civilian court, the court decided that "the same civilian tribunal should decide the case, so that it is not split into two courts" (cited in Cossío 2010, 328).

The supreme court's narrow interpretation of the scope of military jurisdiction, in line with Article 13, was in general upheld until 1933–4. During those years the supreme court also restricted, more often than not, military autonomy mostly in administrative matters. For instance, when an ordinary judge suspended a military court order to detain a soldier, the supreme court upheld the lower court's decision saying nothing more than "military discipline is not damaged simply by suspending a detention order" (Reg. No. 291315).[14] These decisions were not welcomed by members of the government or by members of the armed forces. The governments of those years, led by Generals Obregón and Calles, were trying to discipline the armed forces while getting rid of rivals within them. For this political goal, a broad military jurisdiction comes in handy, in particular if the government has influence over the top echelons of the armed forces and, through them, over the military judges and prosecutors. But the supreme court consistently truncated these efforts upholding the spirit of the constitution regarding a narrow scope of military autonomy and military jurisdiction.

Then the process of undermining the independence of the supreme court was launched, and its effects can be seen in the erratic, yet interesting, jurisprudence on military autonomy during the period 1934–40. In an important thesis of February 12, 1934 (that is atypical because of its relative length, its argumentation, and the fact that was a divided vote of 8–7),

[14] Apparently, the court did not have a preferential treatment for generals either. Tobler tells a story of General Escobar who was accused of not paying for a ranch and lost his case before the supreme court (Tobler 1971, 69).

the supreme court sustained the criteria that when both military personnel and civilians are involved in a crime an ordinary court should decide the case (Reg. No. 279 328; see also Reg. No. 309 807, a thesis of August 30, 1939). But by the end of the period the Court consolidated a striking criterion that had already appeared in 1933: when military officers and civilians are involved in a crime, the former should go to military courts and the latter to civilian courts (e.g., Reg. No. 815 803; Reg. No. 809 416), even though this was contrary to the basic rights of due process (i.e., of equality and unity of justice) and also created significant problems in practice. The court went further in expanding the scope of military jurisdiction when it held that civilians could be considered capable of committing military crimes (Reg. No. 310 173). It should be noted that despite the fact that the supreme court admitted the expansion of military jurisdiction from strictly military to service-related crimes, the Court did establish some limits to what it meant to be "in service" excluding passionate crimes (Reg. No. 309 272) and those committed by drunk officers in a bar fight (Reg. No. 309 881).

To understand the erratic jurisprudence from 1934 to 1940 it is important to remember the political context. As Mónica Serrano puts it, "while it is true that by 1940 the possibility of army officers securing control of the party was averted with the withdrawal of the military sector, it is also clear that between 1920 and 1940s disagreements and differences regarding the selection of party candidates and institutional responsibilities continued to challenge the civilian-military pact" (Serrano 1995, 433). The conflicts of competence between civilian and military courts, and the pressures that both sides exerted on the supreme court, are nicely reflected in the jurisprudence produced during those years. At that time, the supreme court was in transit from being quite independent to becoming a functional institution of the hegemonic party system.

Conclusion: The Supreme Court as an Arbitrator

The political arena in the unstable period that immediately followed the Mexican Revolution was characterized by competition among several groups all led by military *caudillos*. There were no consolidated political parties and the political system had not yet produced a set of political norms for stabilizing expectations. These political conditions enabled the operability of supreme court justices' autonomy granted by the constitution, which was materialized in jurisprudence that upheld the constitutional limits of military jurisdiction. These decisions that created discomfort in the armed forces, and upset the "revolutionary family" in government, were not isolated: similar jurisprudential patterns can be found regarding challenges to the revolutionary labor and agrarian legislations produced by the regime (James 2006).

But the supreme court during this period acted more like an arbitrator than like a mediator. The supreme court's decisions in *tesis* emanating from concrete cases (mostly *amparos*) were severely lacking in argumentation: they literally merely transcribed to the letter Article 13 of the constitution. This is explained in part by institutional design: jurisprudential *tesis* are meant to be short lawlike sentences, void of the facts of the case, to limit as much as possible "judge-made law."[15] But other characteristics of mediator-like jurisprudence are also absent. Most conspicuously is the court's failure to somehow recognize that the interests of the parties in these cases (soldiers or civilians vs. a military authority) will very likely clash again in the future. The court decided each case as if it was the first and the last on this topic, without establishing a rule or guide for foreseeable similar cases. Needless to say, this type of jurisprudence does not reduce uncertainty of any type (and even if there is an identifiable pattern in the jurisprudential *tesis*, there is remarkable variance at any point in time; see Figure 5.3). Other characteristics of mediator-like jurisprudence, such as the attempt by the court to transform the armed forces' preferences with careful argumentation on why military jurisdiction should be limited, or preparing the armed forces for what the jurisprudence is going to be but conceding particular cases, are simply way out of the court's league.

Toward the end of this period the need for an organization capable of coordinating all political-military groups was palpable. To that effect General Calles founded the PNR in 1929. The PNR stabilized and centralized political power: heterogeneity of alliances within the military was no longer tolerated. This did not mean that the civilian government and the armed forces were separated. In this period the military and political power were one and the same. This political transformation had negative consequences for the supreme court, in particular for its independence, as I already anticipated, but that will be explored in further detail now.

[15] Interestingly, there is broad variation even within the *tesis*. Some are better written and argued than others. Therefore, even if the system of *tesis* limits the capacity of the court to act as a mediator, at some points in the court's history and on some topics, the court is clearly developing an argument in a series of *tesis*, revealing that the court understands that there is a conflict underlying the recurrent appearance of certain actors before the court.

The Supreme Court, 1940–1994

Political Context and Civilian-Military Relations

From 1928 to 1934 Plutarco Elías Calles became the *Jefe Máximo de la Revolución*, the leader of the newly founded PNR who pulled the political strings behind the presidential seat. Things changed when General Lázaro Cárdenas, selected by Calles as the PNR candidate to the presidency and elected in 1934, managed to expatriate Calles and expel the *callistas* from his government. During the administration of General Lázaro Cárdenas (1934–40), the party successfully integrated the army, the organized workers, and the organized peasants into its structure and changed its name in 1936 to *Partido de la Revolución Mexicana* (PRM). The PRM gradually became the single most important political machine in the country within which most decisions regarding "who gets what, when, and why" were made. A decade later, in 1946, the party became hegemonic and changed its name to *Partido Revolucionario Institucional* (PRI). That same year the first civilian president, Miguel Alemán, was elected (see Garrido 2005; Serrano 1995).

Cárdenas's incorporation of the organized peasants, workers, and the armed forces into the PRM secured stability for the nascent regime, simultaneously reducing the relative power of the army. Despite the resistance of the armed forces (Serrano 1995, 433), Cárdenas introduced further changes for disciplining and professionalizing them, such as dividing the Ministry of War and Navy into two autonomous defense ministries (the Ministry of Defense, which included the army and the air force, and the Ministry of the Navy), enacting legislation barring serving officers from participating in any political activity, and expanding earlier efforts aimed at the progressive education and training of the forces.[16] By the end of Cárdenas's administration, "the Mexican armed forces had been weakened and brought under the control of the national party" (Díez and Nicholls 2006, 9).

In exchange for loyalty to the PRM, as well as to the revolution and to the "revolutionary family," the armed forces were given an important degree of autonomy in both legal and real terms with regard to the military's internal functioning, training, and promotions, along with a high level of discretion in spending. The exchange of loyalty for autonomy is, in essence, what

[16] At the same time, Cárdenas passed the Law of National Military Service establishing compulsory basic military training for eighteen-year-old males.

scholars refer to as the civilian-military pact (e.g., Díez and Nicholls 2006, 10; Serrano 1995, 433). While the basis of the pact was established under Cárdenas, it was further developed and sustained in successive administrations. A cornerstone of this development was the election of Miguel Alemán (1946–52) as the first civilian president of the PRI era.

Civilian supremacy, however, did not imply that the armed forces lost political influence, but rather that it was channeled through more subtle mechanisms, and often behind the scenes (Ronfeldt 1985). In fact, while the president of the republic has been a civilian since 1946, the president of the PRI was a member of the armed forces until 1964, when Carlos A. Madrazo was elected.[17] Moreover, from 1940 and until 1994 "the presence of at least one military officer serving as a supreme court justice was a constant" (Caballero 2010, 157–8).[18] Military officers have also held several seats in Congress since 1940, always elected under the PRI label (Díez 2008).

The armed forces were a key actor in securing internal political order during the golden years of the PRI regime. Importantly, the armed forces intervened at the behest of civilian authorities and always on a temporary basis. This was the case in 1958 when they were asked to suppress a railroad workers' strike, in 1968 when they intervened to suppress a student movement, and indeed throughout the 1960s and 1970s when they were ordered to put down guerrilla uprisings, especially in the southern state of Guerrero (Díez and Nicholls 2006, 10). The basic exchange of loyalty for autonomy of the civilian-military pact remains to this day (December 2015), but with some important changes produced by both the transition to democracy and by the increase in nontraditional tasks performed by the military since the 1970s and especially since the 1980s (Díez 2008, 2012; Serrano 1995).

The Supreme Court, 1940–1994: Independence, Access, and Powers

The amendments of 1928, 1934, and another one in 1944, changed the appointment and tenure of supreme court judges, and one of their main goals was to subordinate the court to the dynamics of the one-party

[17] The presidents of the PRI during that period were Generals Sánchez Taboada (1946–52); Gabriel Leyva Velázquez (1952–6); Agustín Olachea (1956–8); and Alfonso Corona del Rosal (1958–64). Carlos A. Madrazo (1964–5) was the first civilian president of the PRI.

[18] "The case of Agustín Mercado Alarcón who joined the SCJN in 1944 and was there until 1967 is noteworthy. In 1969 another military officer joined the SCJN, Alberto Jiménez Castro" (Caballero 2010, 159).

system. As mentioned before, in 1928 the number of justices went up from eleven to sixteen and the method of appointing them changed from congressional election by a two-thirds vote to presidential appointment subject to senate ratification. In 1934 the number of judges increased again to twenty-one and tenure was reduced to six years, coincident with the presidential administration. Ten years later, in 1944, life tenure was restored with an interesting caveat: the president of the republic could initiate proceedings to remove a judge who exhibited "bad behavior." When the life tenure was restored, the justices' political role as key players of the hegemonic party regime had already been established so that this increment in de jure independence was no longer a threat to the interests of the party.

I argued that the fragmentation and instability of the political arena during the previous period was one of the conditions that enabled the efficacy of the constitutional incentives that gave judges independence and some powers. During this period, in contrast, as the political fragmentation and instability disappeared giving way to a new highly centralized political reality, the government was able to respond to the independent judicial decisions that threatened its interests. In particular, the three constitutional reforms described in the preceding text were a reaction to the independent supreme court decisions during the 1920s that, according to the government, were delaying the implementation of the revolutionary program (Marván Laborde 2010, 309–11).

The incorporation of the court into the hegemonic party regime was accomplished by reducing its independence and by two other features. First, starting in 1933 and until 1994, an important unwritten political norm was in place: to be part of the supreme court, the justices needed to be affiliated to the hegemonic party (Cabrera Acevedo 1998, 145). Second, the justices' circulation and advancement within the political elite depended upon their loyalty to the system. New presidents had the de facto prerogative to ask the justices to "move on." This was the case even with the restoration of de jure life tenure. From 1944 to 1994 most presidents appointed more than 50 percent of justices during their terms and almost 40 percent of the justices lasted less than five years, coming and going in keeping with the presidential term (see Caballero 2010; Magaloni 2003, 288–9). Justices who left the bench often "moved on" to another institutional post, and the possibility of continuing in the "political circuit" required obedience to the norms of the system (Magaloni 2003).

During this period, the supreme court was also delegated great power over the administration of human and material resources of the whole federal judiciary (Pozas-Loyo and Ríos-Figueroa 2011). External subordination (i.e., vis-à-vis the president and the party) and internal dominance (i.e., vis-à-vis the judiciary) was a typical combo in the operation of the hegemonic party, which is similar to the accommodation with the armed forces. While the heads of the major institutions were required to stand the "stick" of external subordination, they could enjoy the "carrot" of internal domination that gave them great political and economic gains. Losing these gains increased the costs of breaking the system's rules. In addition, the presence of military lawyers in the supreme court, or a high degree of autonomy of the military jurisdiction, helped cement the pact between groups in the autocratic governing coalition (Aguilar and Ríos-Figueroa 2014).

Internal dominance was (and to a great extent still is) a characteristic of the Mexican Supreme Court. Since 1917 the supreme court has had control over the appointment and promotions of lower court judges, which has arguably promoted clientelistic practices. According to former justice Jorge Carpizo, supreme court judges used to take turns filling a vacancy at any level of the judiciary, and the new judge's career was overseen by his "mentor" on the court, so that after some time each justice had his own loyal clientele within the judiciary (Carpizo 2000, 209–12). Also, some supreme court judges protected unprofessional and dishonest judges whom they had mentored, reasoning that public scandals damaged the reputation of the entire judiciary.[19] It is noteworthy that in 1987 a constitutional amendment transferred the power to control the material resources of the judiciary, including not only the budget, but also decisions over the number and jurisdiction of courts to the supreme court. These new capacities added to the already great administrative powers.[20]

Constitutional Jurisprudence on Military Autonomy

The supreme court's jurisprudence on military jurisdiction nicely reflects its loss of independence from the government. The place to start is the Code of Military Justice enacted in 1933, which in its Article 57 not only

[19] The corporatist logic within the judiciary reached its summit in 1993 when a former supreme court judge was convicted on corruption charges in a case in which circuit judges had liberated a defendant charged with the rape and murder of a little girl after their "mentor" on the court asked them to do so in exchange for a sum of money paid by the defendant.

[20] The reform of 1987, however, by limiting even further the jurisdiction of the supreme court to "important cases," also signals the beginning of a new series of reforms aimed at the empowerment of the supreme court as a constitutional tribunal. There was another important reform in 1982 that took away from the president the capacity to initiate a removal procedure of supreme court judges based on "bad behavior."

considerably expanded the list of crimes that can be decided in military courts (including, e.g., fraud, robbery, and assault) (González Oropeza 2006),[21] but also stated that service-related crimes committed by military personnel are to be decided in military courts. Thus, the scope of military jurisdiction defined in Article 57 of the Code of Military Justice is manifestly broader than what Article 13 of the constitution stipulates. What did the Mexican Supreme Court do? After resisting a bit in the erratic jurisprudence from 1934 to 1940, the court interpreted the constitution in such a way that made the code constitutional. In other words, the court adapted the constitution to the code, instead of the other way around.

Regarding military autonomy, there are several examples (actually the majority of *tesis*, as shown in Figure 5.1) where the supreme court upholds what had been done within the armed forces. This included cases in which the court relaxed some rights of due process, for instance, regarding times of appeal or standards of evidence, for cases within the military jurisdiction on the grounds of an ambiguous notion of military honor (e.g., Reg. No. 233985; Reg. No. 235275; Reg. No. 235276; Reg. No. 304493). There is also a thesis where the court defends the due obedience of a soldier even if he or she knows that obeying an order implies committing a crime (Reg. No. 295749).[22] Of course, in the ambiguous nature of the authoritarian electoral regime of the PRI (Schedler 2013), there was room for the supreme court to also limit military autonomy, for instance, reversing a military court decision based exclusively on hearsay provided by an untrustworthy witness (Reg. No. 802453), or a murder conviction made without an autopsy (Reg. No. 302454). The court sometimes also granted an *amparo* against military courts whose composition violated some requirements (Reg. No. 300502), and even granted one when the petitioner argued that his or her right of freedom of expression had been violated (Reg. No. 235466).

Regarding the scope of military jurisdiction from 1940 onward, the Mexican Supreme Court basically upheld a criterion based on the identity

[21] The Military Code of Justice was published on August 31, 1933 by then president Abelardo Rodríguez who made use of extraordinary legislative powers delegated to him by congress. The constitutionality of this executive unilateral publication was challenged in 2011, but the supreme court said its publication had been constitutional (with a dissenting vote by Justice Cossío, see Reg. No. 161045 and Reg. No. 161046). The strategy of including regular crimes in the Code of Military Justice so that they are investigated and tried in military tribunals is also present in Colombia (Chapter 3) and Peru (Chapter 4).

[22] The topic of what constitutes "due obedience" is raised in many *tesis* but the court does not develop a doctrine nor even some rules on the matter (e.g., Reg. No. 233978; Reg. No. 233979; Reg. No. 234162; Reg. No. 234316; Reg. No. 234306; Reg. No. 234305; Reg. No. 235077; Reg. No. 235193; and Reg. No. 235271).

of the person involved in a crime: if the person belongs to the armed forces then the case belongs to military jurisdiction. Some outrageous examples that were sent to military courts include a rape case based on the argument that it was a "crime against military honor" (Reg. No. 235610), a case of a drunk officer "in service" who killed a civilian (Reg. No. 236995), or a case in which a military officer dressed as a civilian and off-duty killed another military officer for reasons unrelated to any kind of military service (Reg. No. 257727). As with military autonomy, the "personal-identity" criterion was sometimes attenuated by sensibly keeping some conducts and situations out of military courts, such as when the officer is on vacation (Reg. No. 235143), or when a military officer killed the referee during a soccer game (Reg. No. 235231). It is noteworthy that the court explicitly invoked the "personal-identity" criterion as late as of 1991 (Reg. No. 206199).

In this electoral authoritarian regime, it is not completely surprising that there are also many *tesis* in which facing apparently identical situations the court reaches opposite conclusions. For instance, sometimes being drunk is enough to consider that the military officer had abandoned his position (Reg. No. 234522) but other times it is not (Reg. No. 245676). Sometimes obedience to a superior officer is due even when the subordinate is off-duty (Reg. No. 312980) but not others (Reg. No. 313404). Sometimes retired officers still enjoy the prerogatives of the military jurisdiction (Reg. No. 315464) but not others (Reg. No. 315245). One possible explanation for these inconsistencies may be that the supreme court decided differently depending on the level and the political connections of the military official in question. For instance, in 1945 there was a case against the governor of Sinaloa, a military officer close to then president Manuel Ávila Camacho, who was accused of murder. The national secretary of defense, none other than former president General Lázaro Cárdenas, who argued that the case should be tried in military courts, filed an *amparo* suit. In the end, the governor was granted the *amparo* and eventually set free (cited in Caballero 2010, 142).

Conclusion: The Supreme Court as a Delegate

The role of the Mexican Supreme Court drastically changed with the emergence of the hegemonic party regime because it brought changes that transformed the judges' incentives. In essence, judges lost their independence and became delegates of those who had power over them. This does not mean that they became mere window dressing. Nonindependent supreme court judges in an authoritarian regime share the broader goal of wanting the *regime* and their own benefits to survive,[23] but they would not necessarily share the interests of a *particular dictator* or a *particular group* within the ruling coalition. This is clear in Mexico where the hegemonic party regime implied that the identity of the autocrat (i.e., president) changed but the authoritarian nature of the regime remained. In a setting like this, a delegate supreme court provides for the ruling coalition a venue for solving conflicts among them, or a venue in which opponents are punished and friends rewarded. In other words, during this authoritarian period the Mexican Supreme Court helped making credible the power sharing deal between the military and the civilian leaders that was the cornerstone of the civil-military pact (Aguilar and Ríos-Figueroa 2014).

The Supreme Court, 1994–2013

Political Context and Civilian-Military Relations

One of the most interesting features of the PRI was its capacity to remain in power for more than seven decades (1929–2000). Through a series of gradual reforms, the PRI successfully adapted to changing conditions, both internal and external, while holding on to power. These reforms touched on every issue of the political and social system. The electoral reforms since 1977 are the paradigmatic example of constant and hard bargaining between the PRI, which did not want to lose much, and opposition forces, which needed to gain enough, that made the PRIísta order possible during seventy-one years. There are three crucial dates in the gradual electoral decline of the PRI: 1988 when the PRI lost the two-thirds majority in the lower house and thus the capacity to unilaterally change the Constitution, 1997 when the PRI lost the majority in the lower house of congress, and 2000 when it lost the presidency.

The changing political circumstances since the 1960s, but especially those of the 1970s and 1980s, had an impact on civilian-military relations. In particular, several crises in Central America in the 1980s, the emergence of drug trafficking as a threat to national security, and the 1994 Chiapas rebellion changed the role of the Mexican military as they acquired responsibilities well beyond acting as guardians of the regime, and of the "revolutionary family." These new responsibilities have been accompanied by a corresponding growth in the size of Mexico's standing army; influence on policy making, especially regarding public security; distortions in the

[23] If they do not, and they behave as if they were independent of the regime, then they risk being undermined, sacked, or worse by the autocrat.

process of promotions; and the development of military industries (Díez and Nicholls 2006, 27; Serrano 1995, 439–42).

The military's involvement in combating drug trafficking has been particularly consequential. This involvement started in the 1970s, but accelerated in the late 1980s under Carlos Salinas's administration (1988–94) when he declared drug trafficking to be an issue of national security, and continued to grow under presidents Zedillo (1994–2000) and Fox (2000–6). Under the administration of Felipe Calderón (2006–12) it acquired tragic proportions. It is possible to trace a parallel increment in the involvement of the armed forces in policy making, in particular regarding public security: since the Zedillo administration, for example, "the Drug Control Planning Center (CENDRO), the Federal Preventive Police (PFP) and the National Institute to Combat Drugs have been headed by military officers, and the Center for National Security and Intelligence—Mexico's intelligence agency—increasingly has been run by the military" (Díez and Nicholls 2006, 33). Perhaps the clearest example of the increased penetration of the armed forces into the civilian branches of government was the appointment in 2000 of Brigadier General Rafael Macedo de la Concha to be attorney general, the first time in Mexico's history that a military officer has ever served in that office.

The increased involvement of the military in the antinarcotics campaign also had a huge cost in terms of violations of human rights, especially under the Calderón administration. From 1999 until 2004 the National Human Rights Commission received 1,069 complaints of abuse perpetrated by the armed forces. In 2008 the number of complaints was 1,231 and during the first six months of 2009 the National Commission of Human Rights received more than two thousand complaints against the army (Díez 2012). The Inter American Court of Human Rights (IACHR) has also decided against Mexico in cases in which the army is involved, most famously in the *Radilla* case.[24] In any event, the involvement of the armed forces in the "war on drugs" as well as in other nontraditional activities has been accompanied not only by increments in the military's size, budget, and influence on policy making, but also by very mild reductions in terms of military autonomy.

The armed forces have continued to operate with significant autonomy and weak legislative oversight, especially in the area of promotions and of the internal allocation of the military budget, both processes in which civilians are not involved despite the prerogatives of both houses of congress to

[24] *Caso Radilla Pacheco v. México*, November 23, 2009.

do so (Díez 2008, 2012). In this regard, it is noteworthy that a restriction of military autonomy, in particular of the scope of military jurisdiction, came from the IACHR in the *Radilla Pacheco* case in 2009, followed by the intervention of the supreme court in 2010 in response to *Radilla* and, especially, with a series of decisions in related cases during the summer of 2012.

The Supreme Court, 1995–2013: Independence, Access, and Powers

The key constitutional reform during this period took place in late 1994 (see Fix-Fierro 2003). In terms of independence, the method of appointment was slightly altered to allow the president to propose three candidates for each vacancy from which two-thirds of the senate has to elect one. Tenure was changed from life to fifteen years. The number of judges was also changed and brought down to eleven. More importantly, the entire supreme court's membership was renewed and the new judges were elected using the new rules and in a context where the PRI did not have the two-thirds majority in the senate to impose its candidates. In sum, in terms of independence, the reform of 1994 not only maintained a high level of de jure independence but also augmented the legitimacy of the court because bargaining in the senate between two parties motivated that competent and respected lawyers were appointed.[25]

The reform also substantially increased the powers of judicial review of the Mexican Supreme Court judges by creating instruments of both concrete and abstract control with the possibility of generating *erga omnes* effects. Access to the court, however, was still limited because legal standing in the two new instruments of constitutional review created or strengthened in the reform (the action of constitutionality and the constitutional controversy, respectively) is limited to political authorities such as political parties, the representatives of the three branches of government, or a legislative minority. Ordinary citizens do not have standing to use these instruments, and this is also true for most autonomous organs such as the National Electoral Institute or the National Institute of Transparency and Information (see Ansolabehere 2010).[26]

Moreover, the other instrument for constitutional review, the *amparo* suit, remained weak mainly because of its limited, *inter partes*, effects, and also due to its de facto inaccessibility for ordinary citizens because of its

[25] The de jure index of independence of the supreme court after the reform is still a five (out of six) (Ríos-Figueroa 2011).

[26] The exception is the CNDH but only since 2006.

technical complexity and high cost (see Pou Giménez 2012). By contrast, since 1987 (but strengthened in 1994) the court enjoys the so-called *facultad de atracción*, the possibility to take from lower courts cases that it deems important in order to decide them. This does not amount to certiorari power, but it does give the court the possibility of going after some cases in order to make a jurisprudential contribution.[27] Finally, the reform of 1994 did not much alter the "internal-dominance" of the supreme court: even though an autonomous judicial council was created so that the supreme court could focus on interpreting the constitution, the court resisted this aspect of the reform and managed to obtain a counterreform in 1999 that restored court's influence over the judicial council to it (Pozas-Loyo and Ríos-Figueroa 2011).[28]

In sum, the transition to democracy and in particular the reform of 1994 brought an end to the court's external subordination but it has still been unable to break its internal dominance. This had, and still has, negative effects on the supreme court's jurisprudence because it takes a great deal of time and energy away from constitutional adjudication, which is its most important (still underdeveloped) task. Not to mention that the clientelistic relations within the judiciary have been more difficult to eradicate and arguably to some extent restored.

The incentives on independence, access, and powers established by the reform of 1994 have operated in a fertile political context for implanting and growing. This context is essentially the gradual melting down of the PRI regime. For starters, the informal practice that required justices to be members of the PRI disappeared. As mentioned, the appointment of most of the new judges in 1995 was the product of consensus between at least two political parties, more often the PRI and the right-leaning PAN (*Partido Acción Nacional*) (Magaloni, Sánchez, and Magar 2011. See Table 5.1 for the court's composition since 1995). The elite circulation system also became ineffective: when the tenure in the supreme court finished, justices could no longer rely on "moving on" to other important political offices.

[27] The de jure index of judicial review powers (that includes access) of the supreme court after the reform is three (out of eight) (Ríos-Figueroa 2011).

[28] The judicial council was originally composed of a majority of judges selected by lottery, a method that effectively took away from the supreme court the control over lower court judges and over the material resources of the judiciary. In 1999, after four years of an interesting battle between the council and the supreme court, a constitutional amendment changed the mechanisms for appointing judicial council members. In essence, the amendment transformed the selection by lot of judges from different levels into a direct designation by the supreme court of judges from the district and circuit courts. This effectively gave the court control over the majority of seats in the council.

Table 5.1. *Composition of the Mexican Supreme Court, by president (1994–2014)*

President Ernesto Zedillo, PRI (1994–2000)	
Magistrate	Senate election by
1. Juventino Castro	PRI-PAN
2. Genaro Góngora	PRI-PAN
3. Sergio Aguirre	PRI-PAN
4. José de Jesús Gudiño	PRI-PAN
5. José Aguinaco	PRI-PAN
6. Guillermo Ortiz	PRI
7. Juan Silva Meza	PRI
8. Olga Sánchez	PRI
9. Humberto Román	PRI
10. Juan Díaz	PRI-PAN
11. Mariano Azuela	PRI-PAN

President Vicente Fox, PAN (2000–6)			
Magistrate	Senate election by	Magistrate	Senate ratification by
1. Juventino Castro	PRI-PAN	José Ramón Cossío (2003)	PRI-PAN-PRD
2. Genaro Góngora	PRI-PAN		
3. Sergio Aguirre	PRI-PAN		
4. José de Jesús Gudiño	PRI-PAN		
5. José Aguinaco	PRI-PAN	Margarita Luna (2003)	PRI-PAN-PRD
6. Guillermo Ortiz	PRI		
7. Juan Silva Meza	PRI		
8. Olga Sánchez	PRI		
9. Humberto Román	PRI	Sergio Valls (2004)	PRI-PAN-PRD
10. Juan Díaz	PRI-PAN	José Franco (2006)	PRI-PAN-PRD
11. Mariano Azuela	PRI-PAN		

(*continued*)

Table 5.1 (*cont.*)

President Felipe Calderón, PAN (2006–12)			
Magistrate	Senate election by	Magistrate	Senate ratification by
1. José Ramón Cossío	PRI-PAN-PRD		
2. Genaro Góngora	PRI-PAN	Arturo Zaldívar (2009)	PRI-PAN-PRD
3. Sergio Aguirre	PRI-PAN	Alberto Pérez Dayán (2012)	PRI-PAN-PRD
4. José de Jesús Gudiño	PRI-PAN	Jorge Pardo Rebolledo (2011)	PRI-PAN-PRD
5. Margarita Luna	PRI-PAN-PRD		
6. Guillermo Ortiz	PRI	Alfredo Gutiérrez Ortiz Mena (2012)	PRI-PAN-PRD
7. Juan Silva Meza	PRI		
8. Olga Sánchez	PRI		
9. Sergio Valls	PRI-PAN-PRD		
10. José Franco	PRI-PAN-PRD		
11. Mariano Azuela	PRI-PAN	Luis María Aguilar (2009)	PRI-PAN-PRD

President Enrique Peña Nieto, PRI (2012–18)	
Magistrate	Senate election by
1. José Ramón Cossío	PRI-PAN-PRD
2. Arturo Zaldívar	PRI-PAN-PRD
3. Alberto Pérez Dayán	PRI-PAN-PRD
4. Jorge Pardo Rebolledo	PRI-PAN-PRD
5. Margarita Luna	PRI-PAN-PRD
6. Alfredo Gutiérrez Ortiz Mena	PRI-PRI-PAN
7. Juan Silva Meza	PRI
8. Olga Sánchez	PRI

President Enrique Peña Nieto, PRI (2012–18)			
Magistrate	Senate election by		
9. Sergio Valls	PRI-PAN-PRD	Eduardo Medina Mora	PRI-PAN
10. José Franco	PRI-PAN-PRD		
11. Luz María Aguilar	PRI-PAN-PRD		

Note: The table shows the composition of the supreme court by presidential period. Next to the name of the magistrate, there is the party or senatorial coalition that voted to ratify the presidential appointee (the president sends the senate three candidates for each vacancy, and the senate elects one by a two-thirds supermajority). Magaloni, Sánchez, and Magar (2011) (from which the data until 2011 are taken; the rest were complemented by the author) argue that this is a proxy measure for "ideology" or political preferences of the judges.

This change arguably has effects on justices who have started to become more concerned about their legacies. Moreover, since 1997 Mexico has lived in a fragmented political context in which the party of the president does not control legislative majorities. This increasing political diversity in the legislative and the executive branches, as well as in local governments, decreased the threat of retaliation to rulings disliked by political actors (Ríos-Figueroa 2007).

Constitutional Jurisprudence on Military Autonomy

Since 1994 and until 2009, despite the judicial reform, the supreme court mostly kept a deferential silence regarding military autonomy. During more than a decade after the reform of 1994, the most important decisions of the Mexican Supreme Court regarding military justice were a handful of *tesis* in which the court imposed some restrictions on what are considered military crimes for military jurisdiction (e.g., Reg. No. 195107; Reg. No. 192786); a few *tesis* respecting the autonomy of the military jurisdiction on procedural matters (e.g., Reg. No. 200451; Reg. No. 200540; Reg. No. 200661; Reg. No. 198706); and a highly consequential 1996 (Action of Unconstitutionality 1/96) decision in which the court upheld the constitutionality of military participation in matters of internal public security (cf. Carbonell 2002; Pedroza de la Llave 2011).

In the action of unconstitutionality 1/96 (that produced *tesis* Reg. No. 192084; Reg. No. 192083; and Reg. No. 192082) the court established four conditions for the participation of the armed forces in internal public security: that a civilian authority ask for help, for a limited time, specifying the functions to be played by the armed forces, and without violating human rights. Whereas the conditions were sensitive and well intended, the internal security crisis overwhelmed them. Cases of human rights violations by the armed forces piled up and increasingly made headlines (remember the figures of complaints filed before the National Commission of Human Rights [CNDH]: more than a thousand only in 2008). Meanwhile, for quite a long time the supreme court remained aloof. The most telling example of this is the "Reynalda Morales" case. The case is named after the woman who filed an *amparo* suit against a lower court that granted jurisdiction to a military tribunal over a case related to her husband's death by military officers (the officers shot to kill when the family did not stop at a military checkpoint in the northern state of Sinaloa). The Mexican Supreme Court dismissed the *amparo*, arguing that Ms. Morales lacked the "juridical interest" in this case required to file an *amparo* suit, because she was not "directly affected" by the members of the armed forces.[29] This was in 2009.

The Reynalda Morales case also marks the beginning of a change regarding the jurisprudence on military autonomy. Justice José Ramón Cossío wrote a dissenting opinion in which he basically argued for the unconstitutionality of Article 57 of the Code of Military Justice and proposed a radical jurisprudential change in military jurisdiction (Cossío 2010). The importance of this dissenting opinion lies in its close resemblance to a recent opinion by the Mexican Supreme Court, where the scope of military jurisdiction is interpreted in very narrow terms (the so-called Radilla Case). Interestingly, on the Radilla Case the Mexican Supreme Court merely issued an opinion agreeing with the arguments of the IACHR that pointed to, among other things, the unconstitutionality of Article 57 of the Code of Military Justice (see Mejía Garza 2011).

During the summer of 2012 the Mexican Supreme Court issued a series of decisions upholding and even extending its holding in the Radilla case, arguing that cases of violations of human rights do not belong in military courts, and started to delimit the type of crimes that can properly be heard in them.[30] To illustrate the spirit of this jurisprudence, let

[29] A similar "deciding without resolving" strategy can be found in a constitutional controversy filed by the Mexico City mayor against the restriction placed by Mexico when ratifying the international treaty on forced disappearances (see Reg. No. 180 652).

[30] The Supreme Court created a webpage on the topic in which it displays all the relevant materials, and holdings, on these recent cases. See http://fueromilitar.scjn.gob.mx/fm_jurisprudencia.htm (accessed December 7, 2015).

me focus on the case of Bonfilio Rubio (AR 133/2012). Bonfilio was killed by members of the armed forces at a military checkpoint in the state of Guerrero in June 2009. The military jurisdiction attracted the case but Bonfilio's relatives, his father and brother, with the assistance of some nongovernmental organizations filed an *amparo* suit arguing that the case should be heard in an ordinary criminal court. The *amparo* was granted, the Ministry of Defense appealed this decision, and the case reached the supreme court.

The first interesting point is that, in contrast to the Reynalda Morales case, the supreme court did not argue that Bonfilio's relatives lacked "juridical interest" and thus did not dismiss the *amparo* (although a couple of justices argued that it should have been dismissed on those procedural grounds). Moreover, the court ruled that Bonfilio's case should be decided by a regular criminal court. But perhaps more importantly, in its decision the court declared parts of Article 57 of the Code of Military Justice unconstitutional, as it had already established in the Radilla opinion but this time in a decision with real jurisprudential value. The Bonfilio case, therefore, closes a long history that started during the 1930s when the supreme court disingenuously interpreted the constitution in light of the Code of Military Justice.[31] This jurisprudential change was clearly influenced by the so-called human rights and the *amparo* reforms.

During April and July of 2011, that is to say in between the Radilla and Bonfilio cases, yet another couple of important constitutional reforms that directly affect the supreme court were approved in Mexico. The first reform transforms the human rights regime in the country. First, it expands the catalogue of justiciable rights: the reform introduces into the constitution the term *human rights* instead of *individual guarantees*, which is not merely a linguistic change because whereas "individual guarantees" were located in the first twenty-nine articles of the constitution, "human rights" can be found anywhere in the constitution or in international treaties.[32] Second, the reform changed Article 1 of the constitution, which now includes that wording that all Mexican citizens enjoy the

[31] In the series of cases on military autonomy that the supreme court decided in the summer of 2012 the focus was violations of rights of civilians. However, the court ignored potential violations of the rights of soldiers either by their superiors or by other soldiers.

[32] The human rights reform also gives new powers to the CNDH. Among the most important are the power to investigate cases of grave violations of human rights and to give the results of investigations to prosecutors; the power of subpoena; the power to call on public security forces; and the capacity to demand detailed explanations from actors that fail to act according to the CNDH's recommendations.

rights established in the constitution and in international treaties ratified by Mexico, and that the interpretation of those rights should always be the most favorable to the person.

While the reform of human rights is important in itself, its potential was considerably augmented by the simultaneous reform of the *amparo* suit: the individual instrument of constitutional complaints that is the main legal tool for the protection of rights in Mexico. This reform expands the accessibility, scope, and applicability of the *amparo*. Contrary to the old *amparo* that was accessible only for someone with a "juridical interest" in a case (someone directly affected by a public authority), the new *amparo* is accessible for anyone with a "legitimate interest," and it will be useful for filing so-called *acciones colectivas*, which are similar to class actions. Contrary to the old *amparo* that was useful only for challenging governmental acts allegedly violating one of the "constitutional guarantees" present in the first twenty-nine articles of the constitution, the new *amparo* will be useful for challenging government acts that violate any human right recognized by the constitution or by international treaties. Last but not least, effects of decisions with the new *amparo* are somewhat more easily generalizable to a set of people beyond the parties in the case.

Conclusion: The Supreme Court as an Arbitrator

The jurisprudence on military autonomy produced by the Mexican Supreme Court since 1994 does not display the characteristics of what I have labeled "mediator-like jurisprudence." The Mexican court does not announce the change of doctrine in advance: it does not innovate with compliance-fostering mechanisms; it has not attempted to transform the preferences of the government or the armed forces regarding military autonomy.[33] Moreover, the supreme court's decisions do not reveal that it understands the cases of military autonomy as part of an ongoing conflict and thus that it will receive more similar cases in the future. In a nutshell, the Mexican Supreme Court in cases of military autonomy has been reactive, not proactive, and it has not helped to consistently reduce the three types of uncertainty that surround civilian-military relations. The court reacted, positively, to the IACHR's decision in the Radilla case, and it has also reacted, again positively, to the reforms of human rights and *amparo* constitutional. This is fine, of course, but the *Theory of Constitutional*

[33] However, the 2012 decisions are clearly better in terms of their reasoning, that is clearly developed, and go into greater depth on the underlying causes of the conflict.

Courts as Mediators require some proactivity, some thinking ahead, some forward-looking jurisprudence.

Notice that the court's aloofness regarding matters of military autonomy has taken place during the most violent decade that Mexico has undergone since the revolution. During this decade, civilian governments and the armed forces have been struggling with how to deal with the internal security crisis. And military autonomy has been an issue in these debates: in the ceremony of its one hundredth anniversary (on August 20, 2013) the Mexican military publicly asked for new legislation that clearly delimits its faculties vis-à-vis the war on drugs; they don't want ambiguous bounds anymore. In other words, the armed forces prefer less, not more autonomy in certain areas. The supreme court has mostly remained marginal in the debate on what is the appropriate legal framework for the intervention of the armed forces under the specific circumstances that Mexico is living in now. True, the court has declared parts of Article 57 of the Code of Military Justice unconstitutional, but that is about it regarding clarification of the legal framework. A telling example is the lack of debate regarding the role of International Humanitarian Law (IHL) in the current situation. Despite the internal security crisis of Mexico during the past decade, whether IHL is an appropriate legal tool is rarely raised.[34]

One of the reasons why the Mexican Supreme Court has not become a mediator is the still quite low level of access to it. It is very hard to take cases to the supreme court. A simple contrast between the number of complaints against the armed forces filed before the CNDH (in the thousands) and the very few cases on this topic that have reached the supreme court tells it all. Another reason may be related to the nature of the institutional change in Mexico that has taken place incrementally through reforms to the Constitution of 1917, instead of through a constitutional replacement like that of 1991 in Colombia or 1993 in Peru. When changes occur through amendments most things remain the same, and they become burdens and decelerators for the things that do change. Regarding the supreme court, I believe that the most conspicuous "decelerator" is its centralized administrative power or "internal dominance." Simply stated: judges in the Mexican Supreme Court devote too much of their time to things other than interpreting the constitution, deliberating, and writing good

[34] Contrast this situation to Colombia, where the constitutional court introduced the IHL (see Chapter 3), and to Peru, where even though the constitutional tribunal refused to use it, the government and the armed forces have used it (see Chapter 4). In Chapter 6, I contrast the constitutional organ's intervention regarding the internal use of force, and use the example of the IHL, across the three countries.

decisions. In contrast, the Colombian Constitutional Court and the Peruvian Constitutional Tribunal are courts situated outside the judiciary with the special and unique mission of interpreting the constitution.

Whether or not these are the reasons behind the supreme court's slow jurisprudential motion, the Court seems to be moving in the right direction. Studies have documented a prudent but consistent change since about 2005 in the jurisprudence of the Mexican Supreme Court, favoring the protection of, for instance, the right to privacy, some rights of criminal due process, and the right to health (e.g., Madrazo and Vela 2011; Magaloni Kerpel and Ibarra Olguín 2008). The court has also more proactively used its faculty of attraction since 2008 (Abad 2014, ch. 2). The recent human rights and *amparo* reforms may accelerate this process. That said, in a recent decision (October 20, 2014) the court argued that soldiers accused of drug trafficking and other federal crimes should be tried in military courts. In other words, by six votes to four, the court limited its own jurisprudence set forth, in among others the Radilla and Bonfilio cases, considering that limits of military law apply only when civilians are involved as victims or accomplices of crimes committed by soldiers, but not in other settings (*Reforma* October 20, 2014). The Tlatlaya case referred to at the beginning of this chapter has not yet arrived to the supreme court (December 2015). It may never, and if it does, the Secretary of Defense, General Cienfuegos, has already signaled the position of the armed forces.

6

Judicial Regulation of the Use of Force in Colombia, Peru, and Mexico

> In this kind of situation, more than facing an enemy, what you are actually doing is trying to re-establish the rule of law. You want to win the battle of governance, you want to show that you are the legitimate authority.... Accordingly, the use of force has to match that goal
>
> Sergio Jaramillo Caro, Vice Minister of Defense in Colombia, 2006–9 (cited in Pfanner, Melzer, and Gibson 2008, 825)

Bringing in the armed forces to face an internal security crisis in democratic countries implies many challenges. Soldiers, who are traditionally trained to fight wars and to engage in conventional combat against another country's armed forces, are called on to fight among fellow citizens against armed groups that do not resemble a regular army. Moreover, the armed forces, which are traditionally conceived of as a proactive force whose aim is to defeat an external enemy in a war, are called upon to perform as both a proactive and a preventive force whose aim is to restore security and the legitimate authority of the state. As the epigraph implies, when dealing with an internal security crisis *how* the armed forces prevail is as important as the fact that they do prevail. In a nutshell, the armed forces have to operate effectively in their internal security missions, but they also have to perform within the bounds of the democratic rule of law.

But it is not evident *prima facie* what the appropriate law governing these uncommon situations is and how balancing the clashing aims of addressing the threat to security while restoring legitimacy and the rule of law should be achieved. This comes down to how the use of force is regulated and who is in charge of doing so. Several questions arise: When the civilian government calls the armed forces in to face an internal security challenge, is the regular criminal law the appropriate framework for regulating the consequences of how lethal force is used? Alternatively, is the traditional law of war – the International Humanitarian Law (IHL) – a more appropriate framework? What are the legal consequences of using each legal framework – for the soldiers, the government, the regular citizens, the victims, and the armed groups challenging the forces of the state? What are the human rights principles that should guide the regulation of the use of force? How should clashing aims, rights, and principles be balanced?

This chapter analyzes whether, why, and how constitutional courts contribute to solving the uncertainties posed by the involvement of the armed forces in an internal security crisis in democracies. It complements the previous chapters by empirically evaluating the *Theory of Constitutional Courts as Mediators*, leveraging a most-similar cases research design in Colombia (since 1991), Peru (since 2002), and Mexico (since 2000). During these years, whereas the Colombian Constitutional Court produced world-renowned jurisprudence reconciling the humanitarian and human rights law in order to regulate the use of force, the Peruvian Constitutional Tribunal and the Mexican Supreme Court lagged considerably behind in this endeavor. At the same time, whereas the three countries display considerable similarities regarding relevant variables that may lead to courts regulating the use of force, only in Colombia do we find an independent constitutional court that also enjoys high levels of access and powers of judicial review.

In what follows, I first analyze the legal uncertainties that are produced when the armed forces intervene in an internal security crisis. Then, I make the case for comparing Colombia, Peru, and Mexico within a framework of the most-similar cases research design, discussing both the dependent and the theoretically relevant independent variables (including the alternative hypotheses that may explain the judicial regulation of the use of force and that are controlled for by design). In this section, I also introduce comparable across-country data to complement the within-country information and theoretically derived process tracing of the previous chapters. In the last section, I discuss in greater detail the rich jurisprudence of the Colombian Constitutional Court on the regulation of the use of force.

Legal Uncertainties in an Internal Security Crisis

The traditional war between states is nowadays rare. Yet it is not true that most states are at peace. Situations such as insurgency and counterinsurgency, or the fight against heavily armed and organized criminal organizations, challenge the traditional distinction between war and peace. In many armed conflicts of today's world, it is increasingly unlikely that a soldier will be involved in conventional combat and that, on the contrary, he or she will find him- or herself operating instead "amongst the people" (Smith 2005). The challenges of operating in this environment are enormous. Where is the line that distinguishes a "civilian" from a "combatant," especially if the armed group uses the civilians for its purposes? If a leader of an armed group is clearly identified but while walking in the city, can he be targeted with lethal force instead of being arrested?[1] Is every casualty in these conflicts a potential "homicide" that should be investigated and punished, or are many casualties acceptable "deaths in combat" or "collateral damages"?

The answer to these questions partly depends on whether there is a recognized internal armed conflict in the country because that implies the use of the IHL, also known as the law of war or the law of armed conflict. IHL is a set of rules that seeks, for humanitarian reasons, to limit the effects of armed conflict. It protects persons who are not or are no longer participating in the hostilities and restricts the means and methods of warfare. International humanitarian law applies only to armed conflict; it does not cover internal tensions or disturbances such as isolated acts of violence. The law applies only once a conflict has begun, and then equally to all sides regardless of who started the fighting. Whereas in international armed conflicts at least two states are involved, internal armed conflicts are those restricted to the territory of a single state, involving either regular armed forces fighting groups of armed dissidents, or armed groups fighting each other. The rules that apply to these conflicts are laid down in Article 3 common to the four Geneva Conventions (1949) as well as in Additional Protocol II (1977) (see Rodríguez-Villasante and Prieto 2002).

However, many governments hesitate to declare the existence of an internal armed conflict within their territories because the IHL also implies greater international oversight and sometimes also the recognition of the armed groups as parties in the conflict with certain legal privileges. Governments prefer calling these groups terrorists, extremists, subversives, or criminals and not to "tie the armed forces' hands" or their own with legal constraints. The problem is that if the IHL is not used, then the human rights law is the default framework for determining the bounds of the use of force and the civil and military criminal law is the default framework for determining the legal consequences of stepping outside of them. The civil and military criminal codes, however, set standards that are not well suited to situations of a "war amongst the people": they push to either investigate all casualties assuming they can be murders that should

[1] As Droege (2008) puts it: "Can a member of the Revolutionary Armed Forces of Colombia (FARC) be targeted when shopping in Bogotá, instead of the operation being so planned that he can be arrested?" (527).

be punished, or to look the other way and pile bodies upon bodies whose deaths are neither investigated nor punished.

Not declaring the armed conflict could also lead to the conclusion that, apart from the government's armed forces, there are only civilians in such internal crises – meaning that members of armed groups could be attacked only when they are actually conducting hostilities, but not at any other time. As Droege puts it, "from a military point of view, this is held to be unfeasible and not to reflect the reality of armed conflict. It moreover creates an imbalance between members of governmental armed forces, who could then be attacked at any time, and members of armed groups, who could not" (Droege 2008, 527). In this scenario, if members of the armed forces kill the leader of an armed group while he or she is at a party or walking in the capital city, the "crime" would not be investigated or the military officials would be processed for murder.

Even if an armed conflict is officially declared, or if the IHL is used by way of other means, there are still interesting questions regarding the regulation of the use of force. Many of them originate with the need to combine or reconcile the human rights and criminal law with the IHL. Whereas the rationale for modern human rights is to find a just relationship between the state and its citizens, to curb the power of the state vis-á-vis the individual, humanitarian law was based on the reciprocal expectations of two parties at war and on notions of chivalrous and civilized behavior mostly in the relations between states (Droege 2008, 503). Moreover, humanitarian law only applies in times of armed conflict, whereas human rights law applies at all times; traditionally humanitarian law is binding for "parties to the conflict" – that is, both state authorities and nonstate parties – whereas human rights law is understood to be binding only for states. Regarding the use of force, the standard for review is also different: human rights law starts from the premise that a death is illegal unless it is proven that extreme circumstances justify the use of force whereas humanitarian law starts from the premise that under armed conflict a death is legal unless the use of force was disproportionate or unnecessary (cf. Droege 2008, 521–5).

Combining or reconciling these legal frameworks is already difficult but there is an additional challenge in adapting them to the specific circumstances of a given country. For instance, could drug traffickers be considered a "party to a conflict"? On the one hand, drug trafficking, like any criminal enterprise, develops its own structures of protection that are in effect heavily armed groups that are trained and financed by the traffickers to protect their labs, routes, and facilities. These groups overwhelm the capacity of the police so de facto oftentimes there is not another option but to use military force against them. On the other hand, even if these armed groups defy state sovereignty by trying to control territory in order to protect their trafficking routes, they have no ideology and there is no obvious sense in which, in IHL terms, they are a "party" to anything, except to their own criminal interests (cf. Pfanner, Melzer, and Gibson 2008, 825; see also Ben-Naftali 2011). For some experts, as I will argue in the following text, the motivations of armed groups (e.g., ideological, political, or economic) are not relevant to determine whether the IHL can be applied.

In any case, as Sergio Jaramillo puts it, whenever violence within a state reaches certain levels of intensity, and those engaged have a military-like organization, governments have at least to consider "getting things in the right order and measure things with the right standard which is the IHL" (Pfanner, Melzer, and Gibson 2008, 828). In those difficult situations, what Jaramillo calls "the grey area," there are really difficult questions regarding what the appropriate legal framework is and thus the consequences of certain actions, how to balance clashing principles, and where to draw the line to the exceptions allowed by the constitution. The argument of this book is that constitutional courts could help in reducing those uncertainties, but only when they meet certain conditions as I will now show.

A Most-Similar Cases Approach on the Judicial Regulation of the Use of Force

The point of the "most-similar cases" approach is to compare cases that are alike in theoretically relevant variables but that differ in both the outcome and the main explanatory variables (e.g., Hirschl 2014; Przeworski and Teune 1970). For instance, Ginsburg (2003) is interested in explaining different levels of judicial independence in Taiwan, Mongolia, and Korea that, while similar in many relevant variables related to judicial empowerment, differ in the extent to which the incumbent regime was certain that it would remain in office. In that situation, Ginsburg argues, higher levels of uncertainty are related to a higher likelihood of judicial empowerment as a kind of insurance. Similarly, to explain why after the transition to democracy Greece did not adopt a system of constitutional review of legislation, in contrast to Spain and Portugal, Magalhaes points to the fact that among the three countries only in Greece did a single party handle the postauthoritarian stage (cited in Hirschl 2014, 220).

The outcome of interest in this chapter is the constitutional jurisprudence on the use of force and, in particular, whether that jurisprudence

Table 6.1. *Most similar cases research design: Judicial regulation of the use of force*

	Y	X_1	X_2	X_3	X_4
	Judicial regulation of the use of force	Internal security crisis, faced by the military	De jure commitment to human rights and relevant international treaties	Competitive democratic elections	High independence, access, and powers of constitutional court
Colombia	YES	YES	YES	YES	YES
Peru	NO	YES	YES	YES	NO
Mexico	NO	YES	YES	YES	NO

approaches the mediator style. I am interested in whether this happens in democratic countries with an internal security crisis faced by the armed forces. I am also interested in places where the armed forces are strong and legitimate, in order to rule out situations in which weak or heavily questioned armed forces are not called on to face the crisis or not able to resist being regulated without threatening the regime. And, of course, countries should be at least de jure committed to respecting human rights and the relevant international treaties regarding armed conflicts. Thus, I analyze the question in Colombia (since 1991), Peru (since 2002), and Mexico (since 2000), which meet the previous requirements. Table 6.1 summarizes the most similar cases approach. In what follows, I discuss in detail the variables in each of the cases.

When, Why, and How Do Courts Contribute to Regulating the Use of Force?

Sometimes cases that involve the question of whether there is an internal armed conflict in a country, and thus whether the human rights and criminal law or the IHL should be used, reach the constitutional court. In the three cases under study, we find a wide range of variation in responses of the courts. In Peru, for instance, the constitutional tribunal in 2003 decided that this is a political question beyond the judges' reach (Exp. 010-2002-AI/TC, p. 102). The Colombian Constitutional Court, in contrast, decided in 1995 that the judges, not the politicians, are the ones in charge of checking whether the requisites established in international law to declare an internal armed conflict are present, thus regulating the use of force in those situations (C-225 1995). Actually, the Colombian Constitutional Court has produced an important jurisprudential line touching on the critical issues involved in the combination of the IHL and the human rights regime. Finally, the Mexican Supreme Court has essentially remained aloof and not even discussed the question of an internal armed conflict or the possible use of the IHL.

The jurisprudence of the Colombian Constitutional Court on the regulation of the use of force will be analyzed in detail in the last section of the chapter. Let us discuss here the Peruvian and the Mexican cases. As mentioned previously, in 2003 the Peruvian Constitutional Tribunal refused to consider the declaration of an internal armed conflict and thus the use of the IHL in Peru. Two years later, the tribunal established that the international treaties related to human rights are an "integral part of the Peruvian legal order and they are situated at the same level as the constitution" (N° 00025-2005-PI/TC y N° 00026-2005-PI/TC), and built on this to establish the binding power of decisions by the Inter American Court of Human Rights (IACHR) (Exp. N° 00007-2007-PI/TC). Even though the tribunal developed interesting jurisprudence combining international and national law in areas such as the rights of the indigenous population, it did not do so in the area regarding national security.

As explained in Chapter 4, despite the negative of the Peruvian Constitutional Tribunal to consider the application of the IHL, members of the armed forces made persistent attempts at looking for a legal framework to regulate the use of force in direct negotiations with the government. As a result, the Peruvian armed forces basically started a process of self-regulation that included the training of several officials in law, human rights, and, in particular, IHL. Since 1998 the armed forces included in their curricula courses on IHL and human rights (Resolution No. 017 CCFFAA-EM-FI/DDHH), but this crystallized in 2003 when, after negotiations between the Ministry of Defense and the armed forces (through the Joint Command), the Center of International Humanitarian Law and Human Rights of the Armed Forces (that has been consolidated in recent years) was established. The problem with self-regulation is that it tends to be biased in favor of the interests of the actor that carries out the regulation and that the complex questions and dilemmas involved in using the IHL are not fully addressed. For instance, in an article by Lieutenant Coronel Roosevelt Bravo Maxdeo (from the military justice service), he considers that the IHL will give an "advantage to the Armed Forces in the fight against the subversives because they will be able to use the arms that the nation has confided to them" (Bravo Maxdeo 2009, 40).[2]

In Mexico the regulation of the use of force has received considerably less attention than in Peru and Colombia. The supreme court has been largely absent from this debate: a search for the words *International Humanitarian Law* in the court's database returns only one *tesis* that deals with gender preferences of a child in situations of conflict, not with the regulation of the use of force.[3] This is striking because, as a consequence

[2] In 2012, the Peruvian Congress passed a Law on the Use of Force but it is restricted to police forces.

[3] The supreme court's public database can be found here: http://www2.scjn.gob.mx/ConsultaTematica/PaginasPub/TematicaPub.aspx (accessed December 8, 2015). In a couple of investigations on human rights violations (the "*Caso Atenco*," Investigación Constitucional 3/2006, and "Caso *Oaxaca*," Facultad de Investigación 1/2007) the Mexican Supreme Court mentions that the use of force should be guided by basic human rights principles (see Cuéllar Vázquez 2015). However, the discussion on the use of force was not further developed and it did not include a discussion of the role of the IHL. Moreover, the court

of President Calderon's intensifying the "war on drugs" in 2006, the armed forces have long demanded "legal security" in this endeavor. Neither congress, where a law on the use of force has been dormant for years, nor the courts have responded. Without the involvement of the judicial or the legislative power, the Ministry of Defense has not done much more than publishing a "Manual of the IHL for the Armed Forces and the Police" (first published in 1999), creating a small office in 2008 to "deal with issues related to IHL," and also publishing a "Manual on the Use of Force for the Mexican Armed Forces" (published on May 22, 2014).[4] These manuals are mostly copies or summaries of applicable international law. Moreover, without an actual law (or constitutional jurisprudence) on the legitimate use of force these manuals lose much of their potential operative value.

Because Mexico's internal security crisis is more related to drug traffickers and organized crime, some lawyers argue that the IHL does not apply because, though armed, these groups cannot be considered a party in an armed conflict. However, not only does the government talk about the "war on drugs," but there are also other experts who argue that they could be a party in an armed conflict. As the editor of the *International Review of the Red Cross* puts it, "international humanitarian law does not consider the reasons why arms are taken up. The non-state actor may fight for communism, capitalism, liberalism, whatever ideology. It could therefore be an armed conflict against drug traffickers or other organized criminals as long as they fulfill [certain] objective criteria" (Pfanner, Melzer, and Gibson 2008, 825). What is noteworthy here is that the Mexican Supreme Court has not discussed this question at all, not even to "decide not to decide" on this issue area under a doctrine of a political question (see Guevara Bermúdez 2004).[5] The court has marginalized itself from this discussion, maybe because it wants to avoid making a difficult situation even worse.

did not include such mentions to human rights as guiding principles for the use of force in other decisions.

[4] This manual is applicable for the army, navy, and police forces in Mexico, substituting the previously published Manuals of the Use of Force by the Ministry of the Navy (SEMAR, published in 2009) and the Public Prosecutor's Office (PGR, published in 2012).

[5] In 2011 the so-called human rights constitutional reform in Mexico modified, among others, Article 29 that regulates the declaration of states of emergency and suspension of rights in Mexico. According to Pedro Salazar, one of the aims of the reform was to adapt the constitution to the international law in this area, including the IHL (see Salazar Ugarte 2013). The Mexican government has not declared an emergency situation since this reform. It thus remains to be seen whether, if that happens, the Mexican Supreme Court introduces the IHL framework in those situations. Thank you to Javier Martin Reyes for this observation.

Interestingly, the judicial involvement in the regulation of the use of force in Colombia has not made civilian-military relations tenser. Rather, as shown in Chapter 3, even though at first the armed forces and the civilian government resisted the constitutional court's involvement, the debates and negotiations between them since the court's intervention have had the principles, rights, and boundaries set by the Colombian Constitution as their searchlight. Similarly, declaring the regulation of the use of force through IHL a political question, as did the Peruvian Constitutional Tribunal, or simply looking the other way without even addressing the issue, as in the Mexican Supreme Court, has not made civil-military relations better and of course has not made legal uncertainties disappear. Why do some constitutional courts decide to regulate the use of force while others do not? Why, and when, can constitutional courts contribute to solving conflicts between civilian governments and their armed forces?

Political and Legal Variables Related to the Regulation of the Use of Force

During the period under study (Colombia since 1991, Peru since 2002, and Mexico since 2000) according to all existing indexes (e.g., Cheibub and Gandhi 2004), the three countries are democracies with healthy levels of political competition and no single-party unified governments. This is relevant because political fragmentation has been shown to be fertile ground for judges to make sincere decisions, given that the political organs that could react to their decisions face coordination problems (e.g., Ríos-Figueroa 2007). Political fragmentation produced by competition, coupled with public support for the court, also contributes to the enforcement of judicial rulings by increasing the costs of noncompliance (e.g., Staton 2010; Vanberg 2005). In a nutshell, the institutional incentives on judges' independence, accessibility, and powers of constitutional review that are in place are more likely to be effective in contexts of fragmented governments.

Competitive electoral dynamics also impact civilian-military relations, potentially affecting judges' behaviors in this issue area. Unrestrained electoral competition can gradually erode the armed forces' political strength because, to attract votes, politicians have sought to embrace popular causes like limiting the military's prerogatives (Hunter 1997, 454). However, depending on the context, winning votes and subordinating the military may or may not be compatible goals (Pion-Berlin 2012, 77). Under conditions of internal insecurity politicians may first respond to public demands by asking the military to address the conflict thus increasing their influence and autonomy. But as scandals of human rights violations escalate the public may start demanding scaling back of the military. In the three cases under study, political competition has brought supporters of both "iron fist" and "pro–human rights" policies, with their respective demands for latitude/constraint of the armed forces. In short, competitive democratic elections are a key variable influencing the judicial regulation on the use of force that is present in all three countries.

In the three countries, democratically elected governments have called on the armed forces to deal with internal security crises that involve fighting against armed criminal organizations such as drug cartels, guerrillas, paramilitary groups, or a mixture of these. As I detail in Chapters 3, 4, and 5, the internal security crisis starts long before the period under study in this chapter. Moreover, even though the specific characteristics of the crisis and military involvement change through time, we still find this situation in Peru since 2002 around the Valle del Rio Apurímac and Ené, in Mexico since 2000 with the war against drug-trafficking organizations and paramilitary groups in some regions of the country, and in Colombia since 2000 with the fight against the remaining guerrillas, drug cartels, and the paramilitary groups. Comparable cross-national data based on the CIRI index of the frequency of violations of physical integrity rights provides some evidence of similarities among the cases.[6] Higher values in this index indicate more instances of torture, forced disappearances, political imprisonment, and extrajudicial killings. Figure 6.1 shows that Colombia, Peru, and Mexico have had relatively high levels since the 1980s. Colombia's score is the highest, followed by Mexico's. Peru's frequency of violations has decreased since 2000, which reflects that the internal security crisis has changed from the high intensity violence of the 1980s due to the challenge posed by the Shining Path to the more localized (but no less lethal and threatening) contemporary challenge posed by the remains of the guerrilla combined with organized criminal

[6] The CIRI project collects data from 1981 to 2010. It is based on the annual *US State Department Country Reports on Human Rights Practices* and *Amnesty International's Annual Reports*. The physical integrity rights index is the sum of four variables (forced disappearance, torture, political imprisonment, and extrajudicial killing) in a country-year basis and coded on a three-part scale where 2 means that there were frequent (i.e., fifty or more) violations of the given right in that country-year, 1 means that there were some violations (i.e., between one and forty nine), and 0 means that there were no violations. The index takes values from 0 to 8, higher values mean more violations. The webpage of the project is http://www.humanrightsdata.com/ (accessed December 8, 2015).

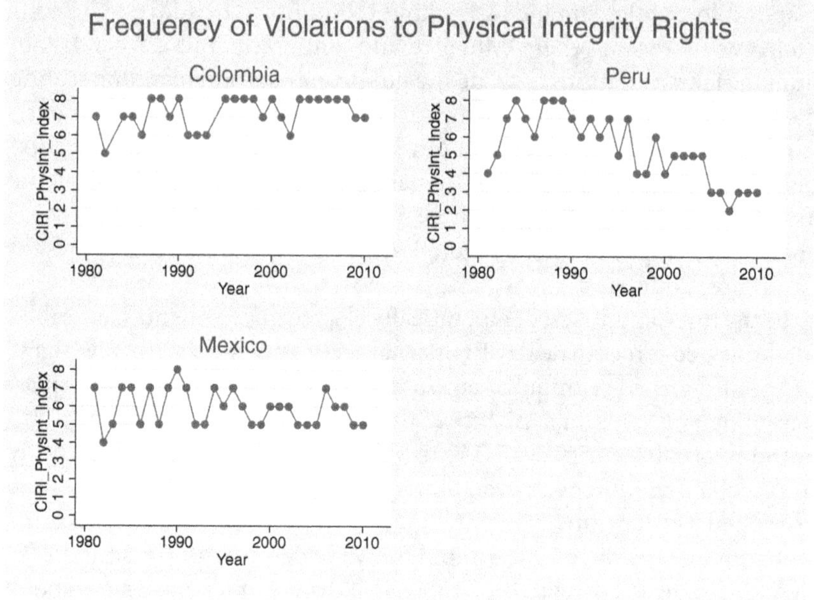

Figure 6.1. The figure shows values of the CIRI physical integrity rights index, which takes values from 0 to 8, in Colombia, Peru, and Mexico. Higher values mean more violations.
Source: Cingranelli and Richards (2010).

bands engaged in illegal mining and drug-trafficking (see Figure 6.1). The recent challenges to internal security in Peru have prompted presidential candidates in the 2016 race to campaign around increasing the role of the armed forces to face them (see Chapter 4).

In the three countries not only is the military facing the challenge of security but it has also traditionally been a strong and influential actor. Even though democratic transitions were different and processes of transitional justice have been advanced differently in the three countries (see, e.g., Gonzalez-Ocantos 2012), the military in all three countries have not lost such status. Despite the fact that there is a regional trend toward reducing the size and budgets of the armed forces (Cruz and Diamint 1988), in Colombia and Mexico (and to a lesser extent Peru), this is not the case. Colombian and Mexican armed forces have been steadily increasing in size since the 1990s, and Peru's have remained constant on average. In terms of budget, the armed forces in the three countries receive similar amounts, although they differ in what this amount represents relative to the gross domestic product.[7]

It may be argued that even though the armed forces are dealing with the challenges of security in the three countries, the differences in these challenges are not small and they condition the judicial response. For instance, Colombia has faced three sets of armed groups: right-wing paramilitaries, long-standing left-wing guerillas, and drug-trafficking organizations, whereas Peru has faced only the last two, and Mexico only the last one (see Christopher, Clarke, and Chad 2014). However, notice that the ideological motivations of the long-standing guerrillas in Colombia have been diluted since they entered the drug-trafficking business; that in Mexico paramilitary organizations have already appeared (e.g., in the states of Michoacán and Guerrero); and that in Peru the criminal organizations in the drug and illegal mining business are composed of remnants of the left-wing guerrilla that was fully operative during the 1980s. In other words, especially in the years under study in this chapter, the three countries face similar ideology-free, heavily armed groups that control territory and have elevated the hostilities to a very high level.

Colombia, Peru, and Mexico, of course, also share other relevant characteristics that are related to the behavior of constitutional judges such as a presidential system of government, the civil-law tradition, the signing and ratification of the international treaties and protocols where the IHL is specified, and the jurisdiction of the IACHR. In other words, the three countries share a commitment (de jure at least) with international human rights regimes, share a commitment with the international standards on the use of force in armed conflicts, and have accepted the jurisdiction of the IACHR. This is relevant because constitutional judges in these countries do have a legal basis on which to regulate the use of force even if this is not explicit in their respective constitutions. In other words, if the judges do not regulate the use of force it is not because the constitution, treaties, and laws in force in their respective country prevent them from doing so.

The major part of IHL is contained in the four Geneva Conventions of 1949. The conventions have been developed and supplemented by two further agreements: the Additional Protocols I and II of 1977 relating

[7] Data on army size comes from *The Military Balance*, International Institute for Strategic Studies, https://www.iiss.org/en/publications/military-s-balance. Data on armed forces budget can be found in SIPRI Military Expenditure Database 2011, http://milexdata.sipri.org (accessed December 8, 2015).

to the protection of victims of armed conflicts. Nearly every state in the world has agreed to be bound by them. Colombia, Mexico, and Peru are not the exception: although the three countries signed and ratified the four Geneva Conventions and the Additional Protocols at different points in time (Mexico in 1983, Peru in 1990, and Colombia in 1996) they are fully operative within their legal frameworks.[8] Moreover, the three countries signed and ratified (Colombia in 1973, Peru in 1978, Mexico in 1981) the American Convention on Human Rights (aka *San José* Pact), and they have also accepted the jurisdiction of the IACHR to enforce it (Peru in 1981, Colombia in 1985, Mexico in 1998).[9]

The rulings of the IACHR vary per country, and Colombia, Peru, and Mexico have received adverse sentences regarding military issues (e.g., limiting the scope of military jurisdiction and convictions for grave violations to human rights). Regarding the specific topic of the use of IHL, the IACHR in the case *Las Palmeras v. Colombia* (September 6, 2001) argued that it was not competent to hold a state accountable for violations to the IHL. However, even if that jurisprudence has not been reversed, in recent opinions and provisions since 2005 the IACHR has actually applied the IHL (Ramelli Arteaga 2009). Interestingly, the Colombian Constitutional Court's decisions on military autonomy and the IHL (which will be analyzed in detail in the following text) *precede* those of the IACHR, which actually uses the Colombian decisions in its rulings.

In sum, in the period under study, Colombia, Mexico, and Peru are politically competitive democracies with challenges of internal security faced by strong and legitimate armed forces. However, only in Colombia has the constitutional court been involved in regulating the use of lethal force and it has done so in a mediator-like way. Why? Because only the Colombian court displays the three characteristics stated in the *Theory of*

[8] Mexico, however, has not yet signed and ratified Additional Protocol II, but this arguably does not legally prevent the use of the IHL. For one, the common Article 3 to the four Geneva Conventions (ratified by Mexico) states that the most elementary form of noninternational armed conflict is present when (1) there is prolonged violence with a certain degree of intensity, between (2) two or more groups (that may or not include the state) with a certain level of organization. This arguably is a sufficient legal basis for the Mexican Court to use the IHL in the current internal security crisis. Moreover, interestingly Mexico has signed and ratified other international agreements and protocols that imply the recognition of Additional Protocol II, such as the Convention on the Rights of Children Participants in Armed Conflicts (signed in 2000 and ratified in 2002).

[9] Peru retired the recognition of the contentious competence to the IACHR in 1999. However, this does not affect the cases already decided by the Court. Moreover, Peru did not retire from the American Convention or the San José Pact thus the country is still legally linked to them (see Dulitzky 2012).

Constitutional Courts as Mediators, which argues that to the extent that constitutional courts are independent, accessible, and have ample judicial review powers they are more likely to obtain and credibly transmit relevant information to the actors in a conflict in a way that helps them reduce the uncertainties that underlie their conflict. When courts lack independence they will tend to act as delegates of the actor to which they are subordinated. When courts have independence, but they have meager powers of judicial review or access to them is very limited, they would tend to produce arbitrator-like jurisprudence: merely solving a specific case without addressing the underlying causes of the conflict.

A straightforward way to compare these variables among countries is to look at the de jure institutional incentives that promote judicial independence, powers of constitutional review, and access to the constitutional court. Table 6.2 summarizes the characteristics on appointment, tenure, and removal mechanisms that are related to independence, as well as the type, number, and characteristics of the instruments for constitutional review that are related to access and powers. According to this de jure standard, only Colombia and Mexico meet the necessary condition of independence; and Colombia gets the highest score regarding powers of judicial review and access (see Chapter 2).[10] The de jure standard is objective, in the sense that any person following the coding rules will arrive at the same result. It is also a benchmark against which we can see whether and to what extent the expectations set in the institutional incentives captured in the de jure index correspond to de facto practices. In a nutshell, the de jure indicators suggest that in Colombia it would be more likely to observe constitutional jurisprudence that approaches the mediator style of conflict resolution.

Under the period of study, as was established in the preceding text, the three countries live in a context of political competition that makes it more likely that the expectations set in de jure institutional incentives come to fruition. The widely used measure of de facto judicial independence by Linzer and Staton provides comparable data for seeing to what extent the de jure expectations produced are aligned with actual practices (see Figure 6.3). In a nutshell, de facto judicial independence is a behavioral concept that captures the capacity of judges to decide according to

[10] Under the period of study, in the de jure index of independence (0–6) of constitutional court judges Colombia gets 4, Peru 1, and Mexico 5; in the de jure index of powers of judicial review (0–8) Colombia gets 4, Peru 3, and Mexico 3 (for details on the indexes see Ríos-Figueroa 2011). In essence, the index combines the institutional features of independence and powers detailed in Table 6.1.

Table 6.2. *De jure judicial independence and powers of constitutional review in Colombia, Peru, and Mexico*

	Colombia since 1991	Peru since 1993	Mexico since 1994
Judicial Independence	New constitutional court is created.	New constitutional tribunal is created.	Supreme court is empowered.
	9 Judges, number not explicit in constitution, 8-year tenure	7 Judges, number explicit in constitution, 5-year tenure	11 Judges, number explicit in constitution, 15-year tenure
	President appoints 3, senate approves (majority vote). Council of State appoints 3, senate approves (majority vote). Supreme Court appoints 3, Senate approves (majority vote).	Congress selects all judges (two-thirds vote).	President proposes 3 candidates, senate selects 1 (two-thirds vote).
	Removal: House of Representatives votes (majority) to start impeachment process.	Removal: Permanent Committee of Congress votes (majority) to start impeachment process.	Removal: House of Deputies votes (majority) to start impeachment process.
Judicial Review Powers and Access	Public Action of Constitutionality: instrument of abstract review, with *erga omnes* effects, available to any citizen.	Action of Unconstitutionality: instrument of abstract review, *with erga omnes* effects, available to public authorities and 5,000 citizens.	Action of Unconstitutionality: instrument of abstract review, *erga omnes* effects with supermajority vote, available only to public authorities.

Tutela: instrument of concrete review, available to any citizen, *inter partes* effects, nontechnical, nonexpensive. The constitutional court receives all decisions on *Tutela*, and reviews those it considers relevant. The Court has given *erga omnes* effects to decisions on *Tutela*.	*Habeas corpus*, *Habeas data*, *amparo*: instruments of concrete review, available to any citizen, *inter partes* effects, technical and expensive. The constitutional tribunal hears these instruments in appeal.	*Amparo*: instrument of concrete review, available to any citizen, *inter partes* effects, highly technical and very expensive. The supreme court can attract *amparos* it considers relevant. A series of five similar decisions on *amparo* can give *erga omnes* effects.
Automatic Review of declarations of emergency, and decrees passed under them.		Constitutional controversy: instrument of concrete review, *erga omnes* effects with supermajority vote, available only to public authorities.

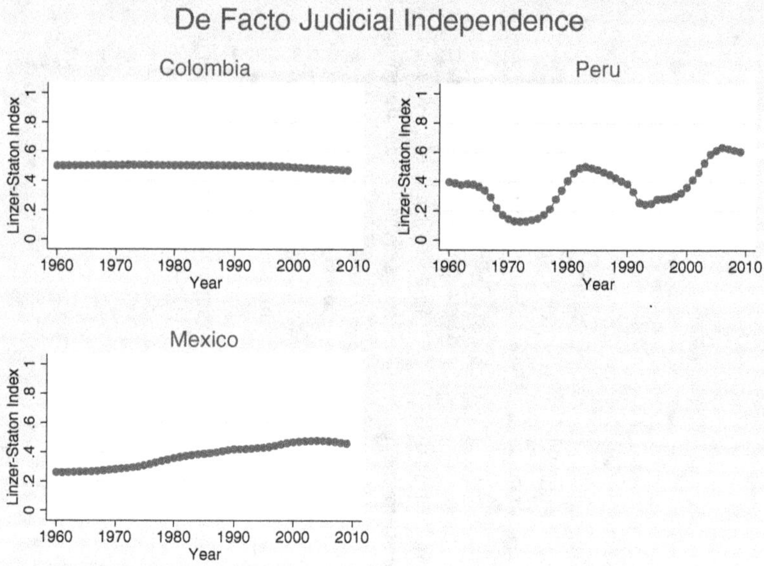

Figure 6.2. The index of de facto judicial independence [0-1] captures the latent variable underlying various extant measures of de facto independent behavior. *Source:* Linzer and Staton (2011).

their preferences and also the fact that their sincere decisions are complied with (see Ríos-Figueroa and Staton 2012). Linzer and Staton used a measurement model that captures the latent variable underlying various extant measures of de facto independent behavior, which does not distinguish between independence, powers, and access, and that encompasses a wide variety of courts and judges and comes from a diverse set of sources (Linzer and Staton 2011). Nonetheless, the story depicted in Figure 6.2 in the period from 1960 to 2010 is telling for our purposes: Colombia displays a consistent level of de facto independence slightly above .5, Mexico displays a slightly upward trend from a quite low .25 to a level similar to Colombia's in recent years, and Peru shows a zigzag pattern where the lowest values are lower than Mexico's and the highest are above Colombia's. This trend is, in general terms, consistent with the de jure expectations and the within-country narrative of Chapters 3 to 5.

Unfortunately, there are not comparable data on de facto access and powers of constitutional review. But some facts and details are worth noting. I argue that access is easier in Colombia than in Peru or in Mexico not only because only in Colombia is the abstract instrument of review open to every citizen, but also because only in this country the constitutional court receives all cases decided on concrete review (i.e., *tutelas*) by the rest of the courts and then chooses which ones it reviews. In contrast, the instruments of concrete review reach the Peruvian Constitutional Tribunal or the Mexican Supreme Court only in appeals, with the exception of the Mexican court that can attract *amparos* from lower courts if it considers them relevant (see also Gentili 2011). The numbers speak for themselves: exercising its discretionary power, the Colombian Constitutional Court from 1991 to 2013 selected to review 16,406 out of the total of 4,200,357 *tutelas* that it received (Valderrama 2015, 79). In contrast, from 1995 to 2010 the Mexican Supreme Court attracted only 810 *amparos* (and from 1995 to 2002 fewer than eighty) (Abad 2014, 63).

The Colombian Constitutional Court has also, jurisprudentially, expanded the reach of *tutela* as well as its effects. Even though the Constitution of 1991 distinguished between fundamental (e.g., life, liberty, and property) and nonfundamental rights (social, economic, and cultural) and restricted the *tutela* to addressing violations of the former, the constitutional court through jurisprudence expanded the *tutela*'s reach to nonfundamental rights directly linked to fundamental ones (see, e.g., Cepeda Espinosa 2005). The constitutional court has also jurisprudentially expanded the originally *inter partes* effects of certain *tutela* rulings that point to an "unconstitutional state of affairs," effectively protecting all persons involved in such a state (see Rodríguez-Garavito and Rodríguez-Franco 2010). Nothing remotely similar has taken place in Mexico: remember that in 2009, when ruling on the scope of the legal standing on *amparos*, the court decided that only the dead husband of Reynalda Morales was legally empowered to file the suit (see Chapter 5).[11] The Peruvian Constitutional Tribunal produced from 2002 to 2007 interesting jurisprudence expanding the effects of its decisions on *amparo*, but due to its lack of independence, this creative jurisprudence not only stopped but also was reverted (see Chapter 4).

In addition to more open access and more discretion on how to decide cases, among the three countries, Colombia also has the best figures related to the structures of legal opportunity and support for legal mobilization (Epp 1998; Smulovitz 2010): in 2004 it had 10.4 judges and 304.5 lawyers per one hundred thousand habitants; whereas in Peru the figure was

[11] However, in other issue areas the Mexican Supreme Court has been more open (see, e.g., Ríos-Figueroa 2012).

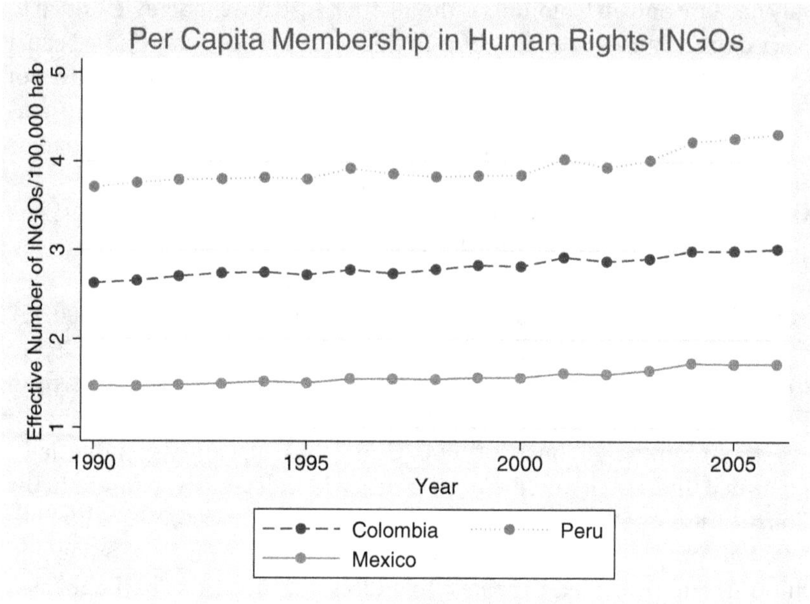

Figure 6.3. The figure shows the number of INGOs of human rights in which citizens of the state have membership per one hundred thousand habitants.
Source: Hafner-Burton (2014), Hafner-Burton, Mansfield, and Pevehouse (2013).

6 judges and 262 lawyers (Centro de Estudios de Justicia de las Américas 2007), and in Mexico in 1998 there were 0.4 federal and 3.7 state judges and 208 lawyers per one hundred thousand habitants (Pérez-Perdomo 2006, 124 and 114). Colombia, Mexico, and Peru ratified numerous human rights treaties, but Figure 6.3 shows that they vary in the number of International Non-Governmental Organizations (INGOs) of human rights in which citizens of the state have membership (Hafner-Burton 2014; Hafner-Burton, Mansfield, and Pevehouse 2013). In Figure 6.3, Mexico is again at the bottom but Colombia is slightly below Peru in the "effective number" of INGOs.

In sum, the very open access to the Colombian Constitutional Court allows it to gather a great deal of information on how the actors in a conflict are actually operating under existing rules, and on whether the application (or lack thereof) of such rules is producing the expected results. This court, through the review of different types of cases combined with its relatively higher levels of docket control and its relatively higher levels of discretion over how to decide cases, is institutionally more able to transform such information into creative and forward-looking jurisprudence. Finally, the Constitutional Court's independence makes it credible when transmitting such informative jurisprudence.

Take the Colombian case to illustrate the mechanisms through which access, review powers, and independence interact to produce mediator-like jurisprudence. The very open access to the Colombian Constitutional Court means that since 1991 the Court has been gathering a great deal of information on the different angles of the internal conflict. The court learns about specific actions of the relevant actors through its review of *tutelas* (e.g., members of the armed forces, members of the other armed groups, different types of victims, members of the government, members of civil society), as well as about laws and policies adopted by the government to deal with the conflict (through its review of actions of constitutionality and emergency decrees). Widely open access, and discretion to select cases to review in depth, means that the court should not rush a judgment but rather that it can wait for a "good case" to express its views on the deeper problem that is generating the flow of cases.[12] Open access also means that, as long as the conflict exists and the court decisions are perceived as autonomous,[13] the court knows that it will be getting a regular stream of cases on the same issue area, and thus that it can gradually build an evolving understanding and appropriate legal framework for the underlying problem, thus reducing the legal uncertainties involved in a piecemeal but progressive fashion.

As I will show in the following text, while the Colombian Constitutional Court began laying the grounds for the adoption and adaptation of the IHL in 1995 (C-225 1995 MP Alejandro Martínez Caballero), it was two years later when some key issues regarding the actual adaptation of the IHL were established (C-291 2007 MP Manuel José Cepeda). Interestingly, in this second decision the court took advantage of a very good legal challenge posed by a human rights lawyer against some articles of the Military Criminal Code (Law 522 of 1999) and the Criminal Code (Law 599 of 2000) that regulate different aspects of the legitimate use of force. Notice that this suit was possible because any citizen in Colombia can file an action of constitutionality against any law or even constitutional

12 A case may be "good," e.g., because of the quality of the arguments made by the parties, the emotional or symbolic value of the facts or actors involved, or the clarity of the evidence and applicable law and thus the relatively low or high potential for controversy.

13 Otherwise the parties would stop filing cases, or would do so knowing in advance what is the likely position that the court will take.

amendment.[14] Notice also that the suit was filed in 2006, namely six years after the challenged laws were enacted. This would not have been possible in other countries where the constitutional review powers of the court are limited, as in Mexico where an action of unconstitutionality can be filed only in the thirty days after a law is enacted. Finally, because the court is independent it keeps getting cases and its rulings and reasons are credibly made with the interests of both parties, and the country, as a guide.

A Caveat in Using a Most Similar Cases Research Design

The most similar cases research design is not without problems, especially when it is used as a tool for establishing causal inference (e.g., Goertz and Mahoney 2012; Lieberson 1991; Mahoney 2000). In the ideal "most similar cases" design the cases are identical in everything but the outcome of interest and the proposed explanatory variable. Moreover, there are not relevant omitted variables, no measurement error, and the cases selected are representative of the phenomenon under investigation in a way that allows inference. In the real instances in which this research design is used, the aim is that the cases are comparable in general terms, similar in the theoretically relevant dimensions, and different in the outcome of interest and the explanatory variables. More importantly, this design is more useful for inference when there is a representative variation in the dependent variable, and when the independent variables (i.e., the control variables, excluding the explanatory variable) are theoretically relevant and justified to be similar or comparable among the cases (Slater and Ziblatt 2013).

To the extent that this holds true in the preceding analysis of Colombia, Mexico, and Peru, the systematic comparative analysis provides evidence of the plausibility of the theory across the cases under study. In this sense, the analysis in this chapter complements the evidence provided in the chapters on case studies in which intracase variation was exploited to closely trace the process and the mechanisms through which the explanatory variables proposed in the *Theory of Constitutional Courts as Mediators* are related to the independent variable (cf. Goertz and Mahoney 2012). In Chapter 7, I analyze out-of-sample cases (Israel, Turkey, and Pakistan) in

[14] The plaintiff is Alejandro Valencia Villa. This degree of openness in abstract constitutional review, which in Colombia exists since 1910, does not exist in either Mexico or Peru. Moreover, it is still rare among civil law countries worldwide.

order to suggest the transferability value of the theory proposed in this book (Slater and Ziblatt 2013).

The Colombian Constitutional Court's Jurisprudence on the Use of Force

The "constitutional block" can be understood as a jurisprudential technique that incorporates into the constitution not only the actual constitutional text but also other normative texts and even the principles that they embody when these are related to the constitution (e.g., the international treaties signed and ratified by the state). The technique goes back to the French *Conseil Constitutionel* that in a 1971 landmark decision (71-44DC) cited the preamble of the constitution and its references to the principles laid down in the *Declaration of the Rights of Man and of the Citizen* as a reason for rejecting a law that, according to the council, violated one of these principles. Since then, it is assumed that the French "constitutional block" includes not only the Constitution, but also the other texts referred to in its preamble: the Declaration, but also the preamble of the 1946 Constitution (which adds a number of "social rights," as well as the equality of males and females) and the Environmental Charter of 2004.

In Colombia, the constitutional court introduced the IHL as part of its gradual but consistent jurisprudence building and delimiting the Colombian constitutional block. Given that the 1991 Colombian constitution restricted the use of *tutela* to fundamental rights, since the very outset the court considered that human rights present in international treaties were a valid parameter for determining exactly what rights are "fundamental" (T-02 1992 MP Alejandro Martínez Caballero). But the formal introduction of the "constitutional block" starts with a key decision (*sentencia hito*) (C-225 1995 MP Alejandro Martínez Caballero), relative to the automatic review of Additional Protocol II of 1977 to the Geneva Conventions (see Uprimny 2008).

Simply asserting that there is a "constitutional block" is not enough; it is necessary to develop exactly how it works. For instance, in C-225 1995 the court established that an international treaty or principle needed an "explicit foundation" in the Colombian Constitution in order to be included in the block, and that the treaty had to recognize a human right (thus excluding, for instance, treaties on economic cooperation), delimiting in this way the block since its conception. According to the court (C-225 1995), the treaties in which the IHL is formulated are firmly rooted in Article 214.2 of the Colombian Constitution, and they are part of the block *strictu sensu* because they are relative to rights that even under emergency or uncommon situations should be observed.[15]

The constitutional court's jurisprudence on the regulation of the use of force is rich and diverse. It touches on the most difficult questions implied by the combination of the human rights and criminal law with the IHL, and its adaptation to the Colombian context. Is there an internal armed conflict and who should declare its official existence? What are the geographic, material, and temporal limits to the application of the IHL? Who are the combatants, that is, who can be considered a lawful target of lethal force (see Ramelli Arteaga 2011)? The constitutional court has gradually developed answers to these complex questions, establishing a dialogue with the actors involved (the armed forces, the civilian government, the victims, and the citizens in general), adapting its jurisprudence to the evolving situation, as it learns from it through the facts, dispositions of the parties, *amicus curie*, international jurisprudence, and other information in the cases that reach its door.

No norm specifies which authority, national or international, should declare an internal armed conflict. In C-225 1995 the Colombian Constitutional Court did not confront this question directly, but rather argued that the rules of the IHL "are valid at all times and places."[16] Moreover, the court also said that the application of IHL does not imply recognizing the parties in conflict as belligerent combatants. This was a "juridical revolution" in its time (Ramelli Arteaga 2011, 119), because it sidelined the dilemma of giving "legitimacy" to the armed groups confronting the state by the use of IHL. Without specifying who should declare the conflict, the court nonetheless applied principles of the IHL such as the principle of distinction to situations such as the rights of the displaced population (C-251 2002 MP Eduardo Montealegre Lynett and Clara Inés Vargas). But then in another key decision (C-291 2007 MP Manuel José Cepeda), the court was explicit, arguing that the constitutional judge "can qualify a serious situation of violence in terms of an armed conflict" and thus decide that the IHL is the right legal framework in that situation.

This element of decision C-291 2007, namely that it is not up to government but to judges to declare an internal armed conflict, speaks to the level

[15] The Court ratified this view in C-148 2005 MP Álvaro Tafur Galvis, and C-307 2009 MP Jorge Iván Palacio (see Ramelli Arteaga 2011, 31).

[16] This is quite a vague statement given that the IHL is dependent upon specific factual situations (i.e., armed conflicts). As discussed in the following text, the court clarified this statement in C-291 2007. I thank Ximena Medellín for this clarification.

of independence of the court from the government. This decision took place in a context in which, according to former Vice Minister of Defense Sergio Jaramillo, the Colombian government (c. 2005) "negotiated with the paramilitary groups for their demobilization and the big drug traffickers of the *Norte del Valle* cartel started raising armies and using unheard-of acronyms in order to get their foot through the negotiation door" (cited in Pfanner, Melzer, and Gibson 2008, 826). The government, thus, was refusing to declare an armed conflict in order to avoid anybody's being able to raise, say, a few hundred young men and arm them with assault rifles thus becoming de facto a political actor, a "party" to a conflict, with all the privileges that that entails.

In that context, the constitutional court decided that it was up to the judges to declare whether an armed conflict exists. The decision, however, is a great example of mediator-like jurisprudence: while taking from the government that power the court also further incorporated international law arguing that the application of the IHL had "temporal, geographical, and material limitations" that are also up to the judges to specify. Regarding time limits, the court said that the IHL should continue from the start of the armed conflict and possibly extend beyond the cessation of hostilities, covering, for instance, peace negotiations. Regarding geographic limits, the court said that the IHL covers not only the places where the combats are taking place but also other places where events directly related to the armed conflict have occurred.[17] Thus, regarding time and geography, the court appears to apply a permissive criterion for the application of the IHL.

However, in a nice mediator-like way, regarding the material criteria the court established that not all actions (legal or not) committed within a territory and time frame characterized by an internal armed conflict are governed by the IHL, but only those "sufficiently related to the development of hostilities" (C-291 2007 MP Manuel José Cepeda). According to this original jurisprudential development, based on the peculiar Colombian conflict, it is important to consider the identity of the victims/perpetrators, an ends–means test of the use of force in a given situation, and the specific way in which force was used given the characteristics of the situation. These factors, the court argued, need to be taken in to account to establish the material delimitations of the applicability of the IHL.

An important part of the "material delimitation" of the application of the IHL is the distinction between military and civilian facilities that can

[17] In this point, the court followed criteria established by the Criminal Tribunal for the former Yugoslavia.

be targeted, as well as the distinction between civilians and combatants who are lawful targets of attack. In this regard, decision C-291 2007 also adapts criteria from international law, for instance, that the use of force would be licit when it is directed at specific military objectives, when it is proportional to the goal and does not cause excessive collateral damage, and when measures are taken to protect the noncombatant population (see also C-553 2008 MP Clara Inés Vargas). The standard developed by the court to establish whether the use of force is considered licit or illicit is crucial in determining if a war crime was committed. In that decision, the court also acknowledged the difficulty in distinguishing civilian and military facilities in internal armed conflicts, especially when the armed groups use the civilian population or civilian facilities as means to their ends.

Establishing these "material delimitations" of the use of the IHL for internal armed conflicts involves reconciling the different justifications for the use of force for human rights law and the IHL (see Ben-Naftali 2011). For the former, the use of lethal force is allowed only if there is imminent danger of serious violence that cannot be averted save by such use of force. For the IHL, the use of force is allowed in a wider set of situations but subject to the principles of necessity, distinction, precaution, and proportionality in order to avoid incidental loss of civilian life or damage to civilian objects. For instance, whereas human rights law requires that the use of force be proportionate to the aim of protecting lives, humanitarian law requires that the incidental loss of civilian life, injury to civilians, or damage to civilian objects caused by an armed attack must not be excessive "in relation to the concrete and direct military advantage anticipated" (Droege 2008, 525). In sum, combining or reconciling these legal frameworks is as hard, challenging, and changing as the internal security crisis itself.

In this type of crisis, the armed forces are put into situations for which they were not made. Historically a soldier has been trained just to defeat or kill his opponent. What they now find are situations that are much grayer, and individual soldiers and the armed forces as an institution are made to carry all the weight of those decisions. And if mistakes are made, it is their heads that will roll. As Sergio Jaramillo puts it "there is something very unfair in the modern world about the way the military is used.... A commander or a soldier on the ground needs as much help as he can get because things really are often not very clear. It's very unfair to those people who are made to make the difficult calls, and who sometimes make mistakes" (cited in Pfanner, Melzer, and Gibson 2008, 832).

At the same time, the civilian government also needs help in restoring the legitimacy of the state and in reestablishing rule of law. Again Sergio Jaramillo: "In our case, in our country, we want to strengthen the rule of law." In general, in democracies the military and the government have to learn to understand each other. The military cannot perform its duty, nor can civilians exercise their authority, unless the machinery of government allows military and civilian perspectives to mix in the formulation of policy. "The challenge in democratic government is to exercise civilian authority while satisfying the legitimate needs of the military in its pursuit of national security" (Kohn 1997). In this endeavor, a working judiciary is especially important because there is a relationship between the effectiveness of the judiciary and human rights violations. When the troops and the police see that the justice system works, they are less tempted to take justice into their own hands. Still, as Sergio Jaramillo points out, "solving the practical problems of coordination is not always easy" (Pfanner, Melzer, and Gibson 2008, 829).

The jurisprudence of the Colombian Constitutional Court has helped with the problems of coordination pointed out by Sergio Jaramillo. In particular, the jurisprudence of the court regarding the use of force has helped to reduce the uncertainties that underlie the constitutional dilemma of the armed forces (heightened by internal security challenges). By discussing under what conditions the IHL is the appropriate legal framework, the court has contributed to reducing the uncertainty over the legal consequences of certain military actions. By discussing the limitations of the use of IHL, in particular how it can be combined with the human rights law, the court has contributed to reducing the uncertainty over the bounds of the exceptions and emergencies allowed by the constitution as well as the uncertainty about how to balance clashing constitutional principles or rules in particular cases. Moreover, the jurisprudence of the constitutional court that has illuminated such complex questions, has been developed in a way that reflects what good mediators do: help the parties involved in a conflict solve their own problems through careful argumentation that avoids shaming, that announces heretofore unforeseen legal solutions in a way that helps the parties adapt to taking this proposed path.

7

Constitutional Courts as Mediators beyond Latin America

A full comparative test of the theory developed in this book would require a mixture of large-N research and case studies, together with detailed information on constitutional jurisprudence on military autonomy as well as the levels of independence, access, powers of review, and composition of constitutional courts in many countries over several years. The aim of this chapter is more limited. The aim is to identify democracies where the armed forces are dealing with internal security challenges and then to examine the constitutional court's involvement in this issue area. Given judicial independence, when the levels of access and powers of review of the court increase does the constitutional jurisprudence on military autonomy come close to the mediator style? Given judicial independence, if levels of access and powers of review are relatively low does the constitutional jurisprudence on military autonomy near the arbitrator style? If the court lacks independence, does jurisprudence reflect the interests of the regime?

I examine three countries where, at different times, democratically elected governments call on the armed forces to face security challenges: Israel since 1948, Turkey since 1961, and Pakistan since 1973. We therefore have two countries from common law and one from civil law traditions, each from different regions of the world. In all three countries, I argue that the *Theory of Constitutional Courts as Mediators* helps us explain why we observe mediator-style jurisprudence in some places – Israel since 2000 – and not others, Pakistan and Turkey. In a nutshell, an increment of access and powers of judicial review in Israel during the 1990s had a positive impact (in the mediator metaphorical sense) on the way in which the High Court became involved in the security issues surrounding the performance of the Israeli Defense Forces in the occupied territories, whereas a decrease in independence, access, and powers of review of the Turkish Constitutional Court in 1982 also had an effect, but in the opposite direction. In Pakistan, in contrast, persistent lack of judicial independence in the Supreme Court is clearly reflected in constitutional jurisprudence on military autonomy and the overwhelming role of the Pakistani armed forces in the politics of the country.

Israel

Israel is a representative parliamentary democracy that, since the 1967 Six-Day War, when it gained military control of the territories known as Judea and Samaria (the West Bank) and the Gaza Strip, has dealt with security challenges that, while not exactly "internal," are also different from the traditional kind of international conflicts. The Territories were never annexed to the sovereign state of Israel[1] and thus for many years remained governed by the military authorities of Israel and hence subject to martial law and the jurisdiction of military courts (see Weill 2007). Interestingly, based on its general jurisdiction to review executive action, the Supreme Court of Israel determined from the outset that it could accept the petitions filed by residents of the West Bank and the Gaza Strip to review actions and decisions of the military in the Territories (Kretzmer 2012, 209).[2] Uncertainty over the legal framework governing this situation arose immediately: Is Israeli law applicable even though the Territories are not part of Israel? Is this a situation that called for the application of the law of belligerent occupation? If not, should humanitarian law be applied?

The State of Israel agreed as a matter of policy to abide by the obligations of the humanitarian treaty applicable to occupied territories. Accordingly, the supreme court has routinely examined the actions and decisions of the military commander in light of the humanitarian obligations as set forth in IV Geneva Convention and any obligations in customary international law pertaining to belligerent occupation (Raguan 2011, 69). The Court, for instance, had to decide what military actions were permissible and what rights of the protected persons could be limited on grounds such

[1] The Golan Heights and East Jerusalem were annexed, although never recognized as such by the international community. I thank Udi Sommer for this precision.

[2] The Supreme Court of Israel is the court of final appeal in the country. However, it also acts in a complementary capacity as the High Court of Justice in which it has original jurisdiction over actions brought before it by individual stakeholders against public authorities, as well as matters where the court considers it necessary to grant relief in the interest of justice and in matters that do not normally fall within the jurisdiction of any other court (Hirschl 2004, 23). There is no formal instrument for abstract review of constitutionality. As in the United States, the Israeli Supreme Court addresses the constitutionality of a law based on its discussions of concrete cases.

as the "the needs of the occupying army," "imperative reasons of security," or "imperative military reasons." The Court also has to determine what actions the military are required to make in order to ensure the welfare of the local population and the order and security of the area. It is possible to distinguish two broad periods regarding the Israeli court jurisprudence in this area: from the aftermath of the 1967 War to around the mid-1990s and from then until now.

During the first period, the Israeli Supreme Court adopted, from the earliest judgments, a rather expansive approach regarding the concept of "military necessity," refusing to interfere with the commander's discretion provided that the authorities showed evidence justifying his call for national security (Kretzmer 2012, 228). Similarly, the court adopted a quite restrictive approach regarding the identity of interest holders protected under the laws of belligerent occupation (Harpaz and Shany 2010, 526). In more general terms, as Dotan and Hofnung (2005) put it, during the first three decades of its existence, the Israeli Supreme Court tended to make a sharp distinction between politics and law and to rely more often than not on a doctrine of deference to military authorities regarding strategic considerations and the managing of their own affairs. In general, the Israeli Supreme Court during that time relied on self-restraint and legal formalism regarding politically sensitive issues (see also Barzilai 1998, 94–7).

A clear example of this pattern is the decisions of the supreme court regarding the Israeli settlements in the Territories that, according to Kretzmer, are not compatible with norms of the international law of belligerent occupation: "The Court held [in the Beth El case, 1978] that if the authorities could show that a settlement was established at a strategic position and that its aim was enhancing defense of the state, then requisition of the land could be justified as being for military needs" (Kretzmer 2012, 213). In some cases, such as the Allon Moreh case (1979), the court accepted the appeal of the inhabitants of a West Bank Palestinian Village related to the confiscation of their land for the establishment of a Jewish settlement. But, as Barzilai argues, this conclusion was based on the rationale that this settlement was not considered a "military necessity." In other words, the court did not consider the settlements to be illegal (Barzilai 1998, 96). However, a few years later (1982–3) the Court rejected an attempt to further widen the term *security military needs* arguing that the "needs" are to be considered regarding the occupied area and not "national [i.e., Israel's] security interests in the broader sense. An area subject to belligerent occupation is not a field open to economic or other exploitation" (cited in Kretzmer 2012, 217).

In the late 1980s and during the decade of the 1990s, however, there was an important change in Israeli constitutional politics that eventually impacted the supreme court and its jurisprudence on the armed forces and the security challenges in the occupied territories. First, in 1988 the court liberalized its traditional rules of standing regarding direct individual petitions (e.g., the claims against public authorities where the court has original jurisdiction). Specifically, before that year the court used to demand that a petitioner show possible harm to a direct and material personal interest. In 1988 the court effectively recognized the standing rights of public petitioners and lowered the barrier of nonjusticiability. The court went as far as to declare that "whenever a petition raised an issue of important constitutional merit, or when there was a prima facie concern for significant governmental violations of the rule of law, any person was entitled to petition the High Court of Justice, regardless of his or her personal interest in the outcome of the litigation" (Hirschl 2004, 23). This change considerably expanded access to the court.

Then, in 1992, two new Basic Laws were enacted by the Knesset, Basic Law: Freedom of Occupation and Basic Law: Human Dignity and Freedom. According to Barzilai, "they entrenched rights to life, physical safety, privacy, property, human dignity, due process of law, freedom of movement, and freedom of occupation and through them the Supreme Court acquired the power to declare Knesset legislation null and void" (Barzilai 1998, 99). This amounted to a true "constitutional revolution" that effectively expanded judicial review powers by "granting the supreme court the authority both to monitor Israel's political arena closely and to hold unconstitutional primary legislation enacted by the Knesset" (Hirschl 2004, 22). In sum, by the first half of the 1990s the Supreme Court of Israel was more accessible and also had more powers of judicial review.

At this point, it is important to note that the Israeli Supreme Court has from the beginning enjoyed a good degree of independence. Supreme court judges are appointed for life (until the mandatory retirement age of seventy) by a nine-member commission composed of the president of the supreme court, two other supreme court judges, the minister of justice (who presides over the commission), another government minister, two deputies from the parliament (the Knesset), and two representatives of the lawyers. These characteristics are established in the Basic Law: The Judiciary, which, together with other Basic Laws that have been enacted piecemeal since the state's foundation, have been interpreted by the supreme court as being superior in status to "regular" laws enacted by the legislature (Raguan 2011, 67). As Sommer (2010, 57–8) argues, the fact that in *strictu sensu* the Knesset could alter the Basic Laws just like any other law has made the court fully aware of potential retaliation and its own vulnerability. The court has by and large been able to anticipate future reactions of the government and rule to serve its own goals, while not putting its institutional position and integrity in jeopardy (Sommer 2010). Linzer and Staton's (2011) index of de facto judicial independence corroborates this; the average score for Israel from 1961 to 2010 is .903.

According to the theory advanced in this book, given its independence, an increment in access and judicial review powers would lead to a change in the style of jurisprudence. Indeed, quite soon, in November 1995, the court released a ruling that has been dubbed the "Israeli Marbury v. Madison," in which the majority of the justices held that the two new Basic Laws had indeed ushered in a new era in the historic quest for a comprehensive catalogue of rights and active judicial review in Israel (Hirschl 2004, 23). At the same time, during the 1990s, as Israeli middle and upper classes liberalized (Sommer 2010, 64), it became more sensitive to human rights issues, and, "at least, a greater awareness of the rhetoric of civil rights became more prevalent" (Barzilai 1998, 101; see also Barzilai 1999, 825).[3] Accordingly, this led to amplified civilian supervision over the security establishment broadening the scope of political issues brought before the court including, of course, cases regarding security, the armed forces, and the situation in the occupied territories. The jurisprudential style in the decisions of the Israeli Supreme Court on this issue area also moved toward the mediator style.

Since late 2000 the intensity of the hostilities between the Israeli Defense Forces and organized, armed Palestinian groups have escalated considerably. As a result, the court has had to deal with an ever-growing number of petitions involving legal questions pertaining to the conduct of hostilities. At the same time, the Israeli government advanced the position that the violent clash with armed Palestinian groups, particularly with Hamas, had risen to a state of an armed conflict.[4] The Israeli Supreme Court has come to accept this position in its judgments: as early as 2001 the court started acknowledging in its decisions that the situation was of "combat," "fierce fighting," "armed struggle," and finally in a 2004 decision a

[3] The court was aware of these societal changes and was actually cultivating public opinion (see Bogoch and Holzman-Gazit 2008).

[4] Soon after violence broke out in the Territories in September 2000, the judge advocate of the Israeli Defense Forces declared that the situation there was now one of "armed conflict short of war," rather than "mere" occupation (Kretzmer 2012, 233).

"situation of armed conflict" (Raguan 2011, 73). Interestingly, this time the court addressed the developments in the challenges to security not with more deference toward the authorities but actually with more direct involvement in the deeper issues applying creatively the international framework that governs armed conflict.

The court started by adopting a so-called three-prong proportionality test developed in German law and adapted it to its doctrine on the "military necessity" invoked by the Israeli Defense Forces to justify their decisions and actions in the Territories. In the Beit Sourik case (decided in 2004) the court held that the military commander had the power to requisition land needed for the construction of a separation barrier in the West Bank because the object of barrier was security. However, the court introduced three criteria to decide whether this requisition of land was "necessary for security" as the military argued: (1) whether there was a rational connection between requisitioning the land and the legitimate purpose (security); (2) whether the route chosen was the least invasive way of achieving this purpose; and (3) whether the benefit of security of the particular route chosen outweighed the damage caused to the persons affected by that route (Kretzmer 2012, 229). This test thus established clear criteria for a judicial assessment of the commander's arguments on military necessity based on a balance of such necessity with competing interests. The deference toward military commanders was left behind and substituted with helpful judicial involvement. According to Kretzmer, the adaptation of the three-pronged test of proportionality in order to assess military necessity is a novel notion in international humanitarian law (Kretzmer 2012, 232).

The Israeli Supreme Court, given the changing nature of the security challenge, has actually combined elements from different legal frameworks to deal with the increasing number of petitions that reach its door. In particular, the Court has combined elements from the law of belligerent occupation, which had been developed by the court over decades, with international humanitarian law and the international law on human rights. In a decision that has gained international acknowledgment, the Targeted Killings case decided on December 2005, the Israeli Supreme Court sitting as High Court of Justice ruled on the normative legal framework applicable to decide who and under what circumstances it is a lawful target of lethal force, a core issue of International Humanitarian Law (IHL) (see Chapter 6). Interestingly, this case reached the court because of the previous expansion of the rules of standing: the petition was filed by an Israeli nongovernmental organization and was "public" in nature.[5] The Court actually rendered its decision despite the government's argument that this issue was inherently political and thus nonjusticiable. Moreover, the Israeli Supreme Court requested extensive briefs from the parties, addressing different points of law and facts regarding the actual situation in the field, thus complementing the information it had on all the issues surrounding the specific case at hand (see Raguan 2011, 77–8).

The decision of the "Targeted Killings" is an extraordinary example of mediator-like jurisprudence reducing legal uncertainties and delineating the boundaries of what could be considered legitimate targeted strikes. First, the court assessed whether an internal armed conflict existed and, based on the scope and degree of armed violence involved, it decided affirmatively and thus applied the IHL.[6] Second, applying human rights and proportionality principles contained in Israeli's domestic law and the court's own development of the law of belligerent occupation, the court ruled that a civilian taking direct part in hostilities could not be attacked if a less harmful means could be employed, namely arrest, interrogation, and trial, and that following an attack, "a thorough investigation regarding the precision of the identification of the target and the circumstances of the attack upon him is to be performed (retroactively)" (Raguan 2011, 79).

Another important decision, the *Physicians for Human Rights v. Prime Minister* decided in January 2009, also exemplifies the recent mediator-like jurisprudence of the Israeli Supreme Court. This case was about the balance between the military objectives when hostilities are taking place and the military's obligations (as occupation force) to ensure the welfare of the local civilian population. In this decision the court again rejected the government's argument that due to the ongoing hostilities the petition was nonjusticiable. The court instead, as Raguan argues, "applied to the facts in question the obligations found in customary international law … adding that 'the fundamental rules of Israeli public law also apply'" (Raguan 2011, 83). Interestingly, this decision was delivered within days and while the operation was still ongoing.

[5] "The central benefit of the Court's liberal approach to standing is the fact that interest groups can now file petitions challenging military action in the Territories regardless of whether or not they represent a particular individual whose interest has been or could be affected by a particular policy. The petition challenging Israel's targeted killing policy best illustrates this. The petition was filed by two human rights groups and challenged the general policy of Israel to target those individuals considered to be terrorists" (Raguan 2011, 90).

[6] The court did not thoroughly examine, however, the degree of organization behind the armed violence (Kretzmer 2012, 233).

There is no doubt that the Israeli Supreme Court has been more involved since the late 1990s and early 2000s in regulating the use of force and the performance of the armed forces in the complex security challenges that Israel faces. The mediator-like approach taken by the court has meant that the conduct of security policies takes place "under the shadow" of the court's jurisprudence, which attempts to combine into a legal framework that reduces uncertainties both military needs to face the security challenges and the human rights and democratic principles that guide the country. As Raguan points out, "to date, the military has responded to and argued all petitions challenging its policies. Hence, it seems that the accessibility of the court alone has an impact on the implementation of the military's policy" (see Raguan 2011, 84–5). In a nutshell, the development of Israel's Supreme Court jurisprudence can be understood in the light of the theory developed in this book: given the independence of Israel's Court, the expansion of access and judicial review powers owed to the liberalization of the standing doctrine and the "constitutional revolution" of the 1990s has facilitated the production of mediator-like jurisprudence since the early 2000s.[7]

Turkey

Since the 1960s Turkey has dealt with an internal security crisis triggered by separatist Kurdish nationalism. At that time Kurdish intellectuals, politicians, journalists, and activists began defying the Turkish state by publishing Kurdish-language periodicals, publicly debating the status of the country's Kurdish communities, and founding new organizations to articulate Kurdish grievances and further Kurdish ethnonational interests (Watts 2007, 2). The "Kurdish question" became more violent with the creation and rise of the Kurdistan Workers Party (PKK) in 1978, which has been actively involved in attacks on multiple targets and armed clashes with Turkish security forces since then.[8] The conflict, however, reached levels of full-scale insurgency beginning in the mid-1980s through 1999, and then again since 2004.[9] To deal with the challenge, the Turkish state

[7] Of course, further investigation on the complexities of this case and other relevant variables would be required to fully assess the case in light of the theory.

[8] Turkey, the United States, and NATO consider the PKK a terrorist organization. The European Union Court of First Instance removed its consideration of the status of a terrorist organization in April 2008. Although attacks have taken place in many regions of Turkey, the security crisis posed by the PKK insurgency is concentrated in southeastern Turkey.

[9] In August 1984 the PKK initiated an uprising that lasted until September 1999 when it declared a unilateral cease-fire. The armed conflict was later resumed on June 1, 2004,

turned to the military and effectively placed the focus of the conflict, the region of Southeastern Anatolia as well as other parts of the country, under military rule (martial law was lifted in all provinces in 2002). The conflict, according to the Uppsala Conflict Data program,[10] has produced between twenty-five thousand and thirty thousand casualties (from 1984 to date), thousands of internally displaced people, and numerous complaints of violations of rights by both sides.

The internal security crisis in Turkey has produced the types of uncertainties highlighted in this book, raising questions regarding the acceptable limits to emergency situations and the military's involvement; the appropriate scope of the military jurisdiction and of military autonomy; the legal consequences of actions by Turkish military officers and Kurdish insurgents; the rights of the victims and civilians in these conflicts; and so on. In general terms, the Turkish Constitutional Court has not been directly involved in contributing answers to these questions but, interestingly, this does not mean that it has been a passive actor with regard to Turkish armed forces and national security. On the contrary, the Turkish Constitutional Court was a faithful "guardian of the regime" (Shambayati 2008; Shambayati and Sütçü 2012, 211) closer to what I have labeled an "arbitrator," from 1961 to 1980 and then a "delegate" from 1983 until at least 2010. Both periods start with the enactment of a constitution drafted under a period of military rule (a brief one from 1960 to 1961, and then another from 1980 to 1983). In what follows, I explain the performance of the Turkish Constitutional Court during these two periods in further detail.

Since the establishment of the Republic of Turkey in 1923, the state- and nation-building processes have been historically lead by the Turkish army and have revolved around the mission of building a unitary and secular republic in the face of "divisive" forces, such as Islam, sectarianism, and separatist Kurdish nationalism. This turned the Turkish Army into the political symbol of nationhood and the instrument for preserving the nation, with sufficient freedom to make and change civilian allies in line "with its self-perceived image of being above social dissent, party politics, and particular interests" (Cizre 1997, 154; see also Heper 2011,

when the PKK declared an end to its cease-fire. Since the summer of 2011, the conflict has become increasingly violent with resumption of large-scale hostilities. In 2013 the Turkish government and the jailed PKK leader Abdullah Öcalan started a new process regarding the Kurdish question. On March 21, 2013, Öcalan announced the *end of armed struggle* and a cease-fire with peace talks.

[10] See http://www.pcr.uu.se/research/UCDP/. Accessed December 10, 2015.

245–51). Between the establishment of the Republic in 1923 and the transition to multiparty politics in 1950, Turkey was ruled by the Republican People's Party (RPP) under the leadership of two distinguished military officers and founders of the Republic, Mustafa Kemal Atatürk (1923–38) and Ismet Inönü (1938–50). In 1950 the hegemonic RPP lost the elections to the newly establish Democrat Party (DP) that was not considered to be a part of the founders' "state elite" (composed of the army, the universities, and other state institutions that embodied Atatürk's legacy)[11] and that tried to limit the authority of the military. This led to a backlash: in 1960 the Turkish military removed the elected government in an attempt to reunify the state elite and to revive the project of modernization that, in the opinion its members, had been interrupted under the DP (Heper 2005, 218; Shambayati and Kirdis 2009, 770; see also Tachau and Heper 1983).

The military government, before leaving power in 1962, convened a bicameral constituent assembly consisting of the military junta, officially known as the National Unity Committee, and the National Assembly. The assembly was composed primarily of the supporters of the RPP and representatives of various professional groups associated with the RPP.[12] Interestingly, this unilateral constituent assembly created what is known as the Turkish "liberal Constitution of 1961" because it contains a bill of rights and constitutional guarantees of judicial independence: after having been opposed for a decade in, the RPP and its allies empowered the courts and created the constitutional court as a vehicle for protecting the secular and republican regime (Shambayati and Kirdis 2009, 769–70). Of course, the Constitution of 1961 maintained military autonomy, also liberating the military from punishment for the coup, and it recognized the universities, the broadcast media, and the judiciary as semiautonomous institutions, members of the state elite and beyond the reach and control of elected governments.

The Turkish Constitutional Court was created by the Constitution of 1961. It began operations in 1962 with fifteen members, appointed for life (until mandatory retirement at sixty-five years of age) by different actors: three appointed by the national assembly (one nominated by the universities), two by the senate (one nominated by the universities), four

[11] Since that election there has been a "distinction between what the Turkish public identifies as the state (*devlet*, which includes the military, security agencies, and the judiciary), and the government (*hükümet*, composed of the parliament and the cabinet)" (Shambayati 2008, 114).

[12] "By one account, 200 of the 265 members of the assembly were members of the RPP" (Shambayati and Kirdis 2009, 770).

by the court of cassation, three by the council of state, one by the court of accounts, and two by the president (one nominated by the military court of cassation). Thus, even though no single actor appoints the majority of the judges, actors from the "state-elite" nominate or appoint the majority of the Turkish Constitutional Court judges, a fact that guarantees similitude of preferences between the Turkish Constitutional Court and the "regime" or state elite (Articles 145 and 146 of the Constitution of 1961). Thus, while de jure independence of the Turkish Constitutional Court is not bad, its factual limitation is reflected in Linzer and Staton's (2011) de facto index: an average of .531 from 1960 to 1980 (the index goes from 0 to 1).

The powers of judicial review and access of the Turkish Constitutional Court were also limited (see Articles 147–52 of the Constitution of 1961). The Turkish Constitutional Court could exercise both concrete and abstract review in its original jurisdiction. However, any abstract challenge to the constitutionality of a law or bylaw had to be filed within sixty days after the law was published, and the Turkish Constitutional Court had no more than three months to decide on the issue. Moreover, Article 152 states that no allegation of unconstitutionality shall be made with regard to the same legal provision until ten years have elapsed since a decision by the Turkish Constitutional Court on it was published in the *Official Gazette*. Regarding access, only political actors could file constitutionality suits before the Turkish Constitutional Court. Abstract review could be requested by the president of the republic, the parliamentary group of the main party in government, the main opposition party, or a minimum of one-fifth of the total number of the members of parliament, the political parties that had won at least 10 percent of the vote in the last election (the supreme council of judges, the court of cassation, the council of state, the military court of cassation, and the universities could ask for abstract review of laws that affected their own functions). In concrete review, the supreme administrative and military courts, and the trial courts, could refer a case to the court if during the resolution of a case the applicable law/decree was deemed unconstitutional (the parties may suggest that this is the case). In sum, the Turkish Constitutional Court had limited independence and powers of judicial review, and access to it was also limited.[13] Given these institutional features, the *Theory of Constitutional Courts as*

[13] In the Constitution of 1983 the levels of independence, access, and powers of the Turkish Constitutional Court were further reduced. This is why some authors mention the high levels of these features of the Turkish Constitutional Court in the Constitution of 1961 (cf. Shambayati 2008; Shambayati and Kirdis 2009).

Mediators suggests that we should observe this Turkish Constitutional Court making decisions that comes close to the arbitrator style, and there is some evidence supporting this expectation.

The constitution was ratified in a referendum in July 1961 by 61.7 percent of the votes with almost 17 percent of voters abstaining. As Shambayati and Kiridis (209, 772) argue, this "defeat" was repeated in the parliamentary elections in October when the parties close to the defunct DP garnered 48 percent of the vote. In the elections of 1965, the RPP lost the majority and became the main opposition party. The newly elected government was not reacting properly to what the military considered an increase in the pro-Kurdish separatism propaganda and other activities, and in 1971 the military issued a memorandum warning of the threat posed by Kurdish separatism, which led to the resignation of the government (Watts 2007, 25). The military-supported technocratic government in the early 1970s then imposed martial law in many regions (mostly in the southeast) and set up state security courts to deal with "crimes against the state" and provided for trial by panels consisting of both civilian and military judges and with far less protection than that available in civilian courts.

The Turkish Constitutional Court, which had been somewhat active since 1962, mostly favoring the "state-elite" preferences, was occasionally willing to annul some of the more restrictive legislation favored by the state elite (see Belge 2006). For our purposes, the most relevant decision came in 1976 when the court ordered the closure of the state security courts, which had been established a few years earlier, on the grounds that the legislation that created them was not properly debated in the senate (Shambayati and Kirdis 2009, 773). However, the Turkish Constitutional Court and other lower courts often deferred to the security forces in the many cases involving allegations of violations of individual rights and civil liberties related to the fight against Kurdish separatism and Islamic fundamentalism (Shambayati 2008, 125; see also Kogacioglu 2004). In general, the state elite had in the Turkish Constitutional Court (and the courts in general) an ally in their quest for building a secular and united Turkey along the lines of Atatürkism (Tachau and Heper 1983).[14] In this endeavor, with limited independence, powers, and access, the Turkish Constitutional Court behaved more like an arbitrator: solving specific disputes without

[14] According to Shambayati, between 1962 and the September 1980 military coup, the constitutional court received an average of nineteen cases per annum for abstract review. It found grounds for unconstitutionality in 37 percent of these cases. Moreover, since its foundation in 1962 until 2008 the Turkish Constitutional Court had closed twenty-four political parties, most of them with ties to Islamists (Shambayati 2008, 119, 125).

participating in helping the diversity of Turkish political actors solve their own informational problems.

The levels of political violence at the end of the 1970s increased rather than decreased, and the Turkish military decided to intervene directly in politics again in September 1980. The first order of business for the military regime was to reestablish law and order in the strife-torn country. Martial law was extended to all the provinces. Suspicious militants of all political persuasions, as well as trade union and student activists, were arrested, and party leaders were taken into custody along with a large number of deputies. The military regime did not openly interfere with the constitutional court that had been in place since 1962, although it did appoint some new members to the court. The military regime, however, suspended the constitution and exempted its own decisions from review by the court (Shambayati 2008, 117). The Turkish armed forces appointed a small constituent assembly of military officers, like-minded law professors, and high-level bureaucrats that created a new Constitution of 1982 (the current constitution) that was ratified in a highly controlled referendum before the military handed power over to civilians in 1983.

The Constitution of 1982 was drafted to maintain the military's sway over politics. On the security front, "reserve domains in power," immunity against prosecution, the reestablishment (at the constitutional level this time) of the State Security Courts, a strong and influential National Security Council, and other related mechanisms were in place (Shambayati 2008, 147–8). The Turkish Constitutional Court was another piece in the puzzle with the function to guard this regime: its independence, judicial review powers, and access were further restricted. The new constitution reduced the number of constitutional judges to eleven and stripped the parliament of any role in the appointment process: now the president of the republic freely appoints all judges.[15] Again, only political actors and the political parties of the governing coalition and the main opposition party (no longer other political parties, nor the judiciary, nor the universities with respect to laws that affected their functioning) could file actions of constitutionality (Article 150).[16] Moreover, sooner rather than later, the

[15] Article 146 specifies that the eleven judges must be chosen by the president as follows: two from the high court of appeals, two from the council of state, two from the military courts, one from the audit court, three from senior bureaucrats, and one from the board of higher education.

[16] Time restrictions for challenging the constitutionality of laws and decrees were maintained, as well as the time restriction for the Turkish Constitutional Court to decide on the constitutionality of a law as applied to a case referred by another court (Articles 151–3).

military regime assured that the preferences of the Turkish Constitutional Court judges were close to their own: "While there was no overt attempt to pack the courts, due to mandatory retirement at age sixty-five, the military regime had numerous opportunities to make judicial appointments and named ten new justices to the TCC between 1980 and 1982" (Shambayati and Kirdis 2009, 775; see also Shambayati and Sütçü 2012, 111–14).

In 1983 elections were held and civilians returned to power to implement liberal economic policies including freer flow of capital, privatization, and integration into the European Union customs union, which produced middle classes that began to come into their own in the 1990s (Özel 2003, 83–4).[17] Although there were economic ups and downs, the liberalization reinvigorated the political arena and the democratization process. Interestingly, the emerging middle class was favoring accession to the European Union along with the political Islam that successfully moderated and eventually won the majority of parliament in 2002. But the 1980s and 1990s were also years of internal turmoil on the security front. Faced with massive terrorism in the southeast the government recurred again to a declaration of a state of emergency, the passage of an antiterror law, and the framing of military intervention in terms of needs of national security, which actually increased the levels of violence related to the "Kurdish problem" (Cizre 2003, 217; Narli 2011). In fact, the violations of human rights produced by the "Kurdish issue" were among the main obstacles to the accession of Turkey to the European Union.

The Turkish Constitutional Court, designed to be a "delegate court," was deferent to the regime and the military regarding the military's iron-fisted security policies. In this regard, it was the European Court of Human Rights, not the Turkish Constitutional Court, that decided in 1999 that the composition of the state security courts had to be civilianized (the Constitution of 1982 mandated a mixed composition of civilian and military judges) and further reformed them in 2002 (Cizre 2003, 222). A faithful servant of the regime but not necessarily of the government, the Turkish Constitutional Court did get involved in controversial rulings in the political arena and the "civilizing mission of the state" supervising political parties. The Turkish Constitutional Court was particularly harsh with allegedly Islamist and pro-Kurdish political

Furthermore, until 2001, the constitution specifically barred the constitutional court from reviewing some of the more restrictive laws and regulations that were legislated by the military regime (Shambayati 2008, 123).

[17] Although technically Turkey had returned to civilian rule in 1983, the leader of the military coup remained president of the republic until 1990.

parties: "between 1962 and 1982 the Court closed six political parties, another eighteen have been closed since 1983" (Shambayati and Kirdis 2009, 776).[18] With the 1999 capture of PKK leader Abdullah Öcalan and the partial winding-down of the internal war, Islamism came to replace Kurdish nationalism as the primary security threat in the eyes of the military (Cizre 2003).[19] Nonetheless, the Islamist Justice and Development Party (JDP) won the majority of the seats in parliament in 2002.

The victory of the JDP brought tension with the constitutional court and the whole judiciary. In 2005, there was a charged public exchange between the then president of the Turkish Constitutional Court and the speaker of the Parliament: "in response to the Chief Justice's public warning that any attempt to lift the ban on headscarves in universities could result in a new decision of closure by the TCC, the speaker noted that the parliament had the power to shut down the TCC" (Shambayati and Sütçü 2012, 114). Three years later, the Turkish Constitutional Court fined the JPD "for undermining the secular basis of the Turkish Republic" (Shambayati and Kirdis 2009, 767). In part due to these tensions, the JDP passed a major amendment to the constitution in 2010 that directly challenged the Turkish Constitutional Court: the number of judges was increased to seventeen (from eleven) and three of them were to be selected by the parliament. Furthermore, future justices would be drawn from a much wider pool than had been the case so far. That year the JDP government also started to take action against the military by initiating a series of trials in which many officers and generals were accused of planning a coup against the government.

Against all expectations, as Metin Heper puts it, the relationship between the military and the JDP government has been essentially another example of concordance between politicians and officers in Turkey (Heper 2011; see also Narli 2011). "It seems from 2002 onwards, the High Command has arrived at the conclusion that the military should no longer play a guardian role" (Heper 2011, 254). It remains to be seen if, given the amendment of 2010 that modified the appointment of Turkish

[18] In other words, the Turkish Constitutional Court was an activist/deferent court depending on the regime's preferences on different issues: in national security cases the court was deferential, but in cases involving political Islam the court was activist. This ambivalence is captured in an increase in de facto judicial independence according to Linzer and Staton's (0–1) index: the average from 1983 to 2009 is .66 (somewhat higher than in the period from 1960 to 1980).

[19] However, even up until 2005 some generals still publicly mentioned that "separatist terror is the most critical problem Turkey faces" (Heper 2011, 253).

Constitutional Court judges, the constitutional court starts playing a different role in Turkish politics regarding the military, the challenges of internal security, and secularism.

Pakistan

The nation- and state-building processes in Pakistan have taken place in the midst of complex security challenges since its independence in 1947. The new country's geographical divide (between East and West Pakistan, with India in the middle), reinforced by political and ideological splits, eventually triggered a civil war that culminated in the independence of West Pakistan that became Bangladesh in 1971. Pakistan has also dealt from the outset with tense international relations with India over the territory of Kashmir, with the belligerent Baloch nationalism (in the Balochistan region, the southwest of the country bordering Iran), and more recently with Taliban terrorism. These security-related concerns caused the nascent parliamentary democracy to lean heavily on the armed forces, which undertook their mission by asserting their responsibility to protect the state's unity, identity, and ideology including its Islamic character (Kalhan 2013, 21). Within a decade of Pakistan's independence, in 1958, the military effectively interrupted democratic governance and has since directly ruled for more than half of Pakistan's time as an independent state and indirectly exerted its political influence for the rest, casting a long and dense shadow over democracy and civilian politics (Shah 2014a, 2014b).

Repeated military *coup d'états* (1958, 1977, and 1999) and long episodes of military or military-led governments that have followed each coup have led the military to entrench its prerogatives in politics and reinforced its praetorian propensities. Moreover, one consequence of the preeminence of the military is not only the securitization of Pakistan's politics but also the blurring of internal and external threats, with the military and its allies often deeming "all internal political opposition as somehow instigated by outside forces" (Kalhan 2013, 21). However, democracy and civilian rule are also part of Pakistan's history. Even if since Pakistan gained independence only once has an elected government completed its tenure and peacefully transferred power to another elected government (Shah 2014b), the cycles between civilian and military rule have strengthened not only the military and its prerogatives but also, albeit to a lesser extent, civil society and political parties. Since 2008 Pakistan has been a parliamentary democracy that has been dealing with the constitutional dilemma of the armed forces amidst complex internal security challenges. The history of Pakistan is thus marked by questions of the limits to democracy and the rule of law, of the relationship between law and order, constitutionalism and security, *raison d'état* and citizen's rights. What role has the Pakistani Supreme Court played in this story?

According to the theory developed in this book, the role of the court depends on its levels of independence, access, and powers of judicial review. According to the Constitution of 1973 (still in force), after a convoluted process that involves many individuals closely related to the executive power, ultimately the preferences of the president prevail for appointments of all judges to the supreme court for an unlimited period (until mandatory retirement at sixty-five years).[20] Regarding powers, the Pakistani Supreme Court is the highest court of appeals in concrete matters that require the interpretation of the constitution (Article 185), and it also has original jurisdiction on disputes between levels of government and on matters involving a question of "public importance" with reference to the "enforcement of any of the fundamental rights" of the citizens of Pakistan that the court can take up (commonly referred to as *suo motu*) or that can be filed before it at the request of a party in a case (Article 184). In addition, the court has so-called advisory jurisdiction through which the president may refer a question of law that he or she considers to be of public importance to the court (Article 186). The Pakistani Supreme Court would then have low de jure independence and medium levels of powers and access. In the de facto index of judicial independence, the court gets an average of .24 (out of 1) from 1960 to 2009 (Linzer and Staton 2011).[21] In a nutshell, given the low levels of independence (which have been fairly constant since Pakistan became a country) we would expect the court to produce jurisprudence more as a "delegate" than as "arbiter" or "mediator."

There is evidence showing that indeed the Pakistani Supreme Court has behaved as a delegate of those in power and as a guardian of the

[20] A Judicial Commission of nine members (the chief justice, the four most senior members of the supreme court, one former chief justice or supreme court judge, the minister of justice, the attorney general, and a lawyer appointed by the bar) nominate one person for a vacancy in the supreme court; the nomination goes to a committee of eight legislators that confirms the nomination; then the nomination goes to the president, who appoints the judge (Article 175A). In 2010 an amendment modified judicial appointment giving the chief justice more clout in the process.

[21] Kalhan adds: "Outside the military's formal institutional boundaries, the strength of Pakistan's deep state ensures that other elites and institutions – often including its judges and courts – independently share the military's interests in that dominance, frequently without any need for formal collaboration, coordination, or coercion" (Kalhan 2013, 23).

regime. However, the Pakistani Supreme Court has done so in an interesting way: instead of sidelining itself from politics, it has got involved in producing jurisprudence around the debates that have been present in Pakistan's political development. While the Pakistani Supreme Court (in particular that of Chief Justice Chaudhry) along with Pakistani lawyers gained international notoriety for its recent participation in the fall of the latest military regime led by Pervez Musharraf (e.g., Ghias 2010), it has also produced interesting decisions regarding the relationship between law and power, the legitimacy and legality of military interventions and acts of military regimes (e.g., Mahmud 1993, 1994). Despite the role of the Pakistani Supreme Court during Chief Chaudhry's tenure, in general the court has been instrumental for validating military interventions and facilitating the military's political influence even when civilian rule had formally returned (cf. Kalhan 2013, 24).

Just two months after the first military coup in 1958, the Pakistani Supreme Court issued a decision that proved to be very influential in countries with political problems similar to those of Pakistan (Mahmud 1993). The case involved the question on whether a military coup interrupts legal continuity and whether the new military government has the legitimacy and authority to enact valid laws. The court turned to Hans Kelsen's theory of revolutionary legality, adopting the proposition that the efficacy of a *coup d'etat* is the basis of its validity: "The court held that the coup having been successful satisfies the test of efficacy and thus became a law creating fact.... In the aftermath of a successful coup the new national legal order must depend for its validity upon the new law-creating organ ... therefore under the new legal order any law may at any time be changed, and there being no restriction on the coup-makers' law making power, the fundamental rights test to determine the validity of the laws and fetters on the power of the legislature to make laws have both disappeared" (Mahmud 1994, 55).

In 1972, after the Civil War and the Independence of West Pakistan, a government elected under laws enacted by the previous military regime was challenged before the Pakistani Supreme Court. This time the court first declared the previous military regime (no longer in power) an usurper. Then the court rejected its previous doctrine of "revolutionary legality" and instead developed a doctrine of "implied mandate," "according to which courts may validate certain necessary acts of an usurper made in the interest of preserving the state because the lawful sovereign would have also wanted these acts to be undertaken" (Mahmud 1994, 75; see also Mahmud 1993). In 1977 another military coup deposed the elected prime minister, and this prompted a suit asking the court to be consistent with its previous doctrine and to declare the military government a usurper. The court, in a new twist, did not declare the new military regime a usurper and instead produced a doctrine of "constitutional deviation dictated by necessity": the court argued that though the coup was an "extra constitutional step, it was obviously dictated by the highest considerations of State necessity" (Mahmud 1994, 78).[22] According to Mahmud (1993, 1225–8) the last doctrine in this saga is one of "executive unfettered" that the court has built since 1985 when the military regime declared the revival of the Constitution of 1973 (see also Kalhan 2013).

After a period of civilian rule in the 1990s, the military seized direct control again in 1999 and Pervez Musharraf assumed the presidency. The coup followed Pakistan's extra constitutional script of military interventions to the letter: suspending the constitution and issuing a "Provisional Constitutional Order" under which all judges were required to take new oaths of office. Six supreme court judges who refused to take the oath were replaced. Among the replacements was Judge Chaudhry, who also behaved as a regime judge: "In May 2000, Justice Chaudhry was on the twelve-member bench that validated the coup on grounds of necessity; in 2002, he was on the nine-member bench that upheld General Musharraf's extra-constitutional referendum to become the president; in 2003, he was on the five-member bench that upheld Musharraf's amendments to the constitution; and in 2005, he was on the five-member bench that allowed Musharraf to continue being the army chief during his presidential term. Chaudhry was elevated to chief justice in June 2005" (Ghias 2010, 11).

Coincident with the appointment of Chaudhry as chief justice, the supreme court began to assert an unusual degree of autonomy from Musharraf's regime, which had challenged military dominance. The regime's efforts to constrain the court in response found some limited short-term success, but also triggered the anti-Musharraf movement, which ultimately brought opponents of the regime to power (Kalhan 2013, 11). The Chaudhry court increasingly challenged the regime, expanding its use of public interest litigation and *suo moto* powers. The court intervened to regulate commodity prices, canceling corrupt public-sector

[22] The court insisted that the 1973 Constitution "still remains the supreme law of the land and that the superior courts continue to have the power of judicial review" but it also admitted that the "legislative capacity of the military regime included the power to amend the constitution" (Mahmud 1994, 79).

privatization contracts and, more relevant for our purposes, also pursuing the cases of hundreds of "disappeared" persons, mostly terrorist suspects illegally detained by military intelligence agencies since Pakistan joined the U.S.-led war on terrorism in 2001 (Shah 2014a, 9; see also Ghias 2010).[23] In an unprecedented show of independence, Chief Justice Chaudhry, leading the bench, summoned high-level military intelligence officials before the supreme court and ordered them to explain the legal basis for the detention of the "disappeared" persons. The court also ordered the military to physically produce the "disappeared" persons before the court.[24]

Not surprisingly, facing an increasingly assertive judiciary, the regime tried to constrain the court more tightly. In March 2007, Musharraf confronted Chaudhry with a raft of misconduct allegations and put pressure on him to resign. When Chaudhry refused, Musharraf suspended him and referred him for disciplinary proceedings. Chaudhry was detained and, later, physically mistreated by police while television cameras rolled. Outraged lawyers and bar associations responded by mobilizing in support of Chaudhry's reinstatement and judicial independence, which soon triggered a broader anti-Musharraf movement advocating civilian democratic rule (Kalhan 2013, 44). The incident sparked a mass movement, led by lawyers and judges, demanding the reinstatement of Chief Justice Chaudhry and the return of constitutional order. Protests went on for months and on July 20, 2007, the movement prevailed with the supreme court setting aside the supreme judicial council's investigation into the alleged misconduct and restoring the chief justice to the bench. Following Chaudhry's reinstatement in 2009, the lawyers' movement pushed the judiciary to consolidate and further assert its autonomy. The court remained active, proceeding with its existing inquiries into disappearances and the regime's privatization initiatives, and – venturing still closer to core military interests (see Ghias 2010; Kalhan 2013). That year,

[23] The court took note of human rights groups that had argued that the missing persons were mostly political adversaries from Baluchistan, as opposed to members of the Taliban or al-Qaeda. The regime had been involved in a conflict with the Bugti tribe in Baluchistan over natural gas revenues. In other words, Musharraf saw the tactics of the "war on terror" useful in this conflict as well (Ghias 2010).

[24] As Kalhan notes, functionally, the court's actions were not unprecedented because its use of public interest litigation and *suo moto* powers built upon mechanisms that had initially been used to enhance its power and autonomy under civilian rule during the 1990s. What was an innovation, given the court's institutional history, was its use of these mechanisms to challenge Pakistan's military and broad state interests, as opposed to civilian institutions (Kalhan 2013, 44).

the supreme court delivered a decision on a petition, sending a powerful and clear message against military rule.

> [M]ilitary rule, direct or indirect, is to be shunned once and for all. Let it be clear that it was wrongly justified in the past and it ought not to be justified in [the] future on any ground, principle, doctrine or theory whatsoever.... Unless such an approach is firmly entrenched into the body politic and the jurisprudence of this country, military takeovers previously in the name of martial law, and later in the garb of proclamation of emergency will continue to recur as heretofore, there will be nothing stopping.... (cited in International Commission of Jurists 2013, 85)

The armed forces remain a key political actor in Pakistan. Military prerogatives have remained high and they have curtailed the autonomy of the party in power since 2008. As Shah explains, they act as an independent source of democratic weakness by virtue of the undue power they endow on the military (Shah 2014a, 14). The Pakistani Supreme Court has managed to exert some pressure on the government and the military (including the investigative security agency) but at the same time is careful not to prompt an aggressive reaction from them. For instance, in a recent case on illegal campaign financing that involved some generals, the court, rather than take the risk of antagonizing the generals, vaguely instructed the government to take "necessary legal action" against them (Shah 2014a, 21). After a recent massacre of schoolchildren by Taliban gunmen (in Peshawar at the end of 2014), the government passed a constitutional amendment considerably expanding the scope of the military jurisdiction in trying suspected Islamist militants, opening the way for a rapid but roughly hewed judicial process that could move defendants from arrest to execution in a matter of weeks (Walsh 2015). A number of suits have been filed before the Supreme Court challenging the constitutionality of this empowerment of military courts. The court first delayed the hearings, then a legal battle started that is still ongoing (December 2015), but meanwhile some executions after summary judgments at military courts have already taken place.[25]

The military in Pakistan is an actor that still exerts a disproportional influence. The armed forces allowed the supreme court's involvement in public interest litigation, but they strongly reacted when the court's decisions started to affect them directly. This is similar to what Moustafa reports

[25] See the reports at the Global Military Justice Reform Blog, http://globalmjreform.blogspot.mx/ Accessed December 11, 2015.

in Egypt, where the High Court that had enjoyed "limited independence" was dismantled when it started meddling with politically sensible areas such as public security (Moustafa 2007). In this context, a decrease in the power or standing of the military can open up a space for a more stable jurisprudential turn regarding the military.[26]

Conclusion

This chapter has shown the ways in which the supreme or constitutional courts in Israel, Turkey, and Pakistan have made decisions in cases regarding the involvement of the armed forces in fighting an internal security crisis. In all three countries, the key to whether the court produces mediator-like jurisprudence that helps the military and the civilian government solve (at least some of) their informational problems is its level of independence, access, and powers of judicial review. In Israel, where the Supreme Court had enjoyed healthy levels of independence, after the "constitutional revolution" that entrenched rights and an increase in access to the court, we observe jurisprudence that approaches the mediator style. In Israel, as in Colombia, broadening access to an already independent court changed litigation dynamics and the court's jurisprudence in a substantial manner. In contrast, in Turkey and Pakistan low degrees of independence make the constitutional and supreme courts, respectively, behave more like delegates and "faithful servants" (Brinks 2011) of their respective regimes. In both countries the gravitational force that the armed forces exert over the whole political system makes itself felt in the court's jurisprudence, sometimes in creative and influential ways such as in the Pakistan Supreme Court's "jurisprudence of treason" (Mahmud 1994).

[26] The influence of the ups and downs in the armed forces' capacity, strength, and legitimacy in the supreme court's jurisprudence can also been seen in Argentina. Specifically, in a context of "limited democracy," instability, and military strength the supreme court in *Caso Rodríguez* (Fallos 254:116, October 1962) argued that civilians could be judged in military courts under emergencies. After the transition to democracy when the military was being accused of gross violations of human rights, economic mismanagement, and bad judgment for having gone to war with England for the Malvinas/Falklands islands, the Supreme Court of Argentina limited the scope of the military jurisdiction in *Caso Bignone* (Fallos 306:655, June 1984) and *Caso Videla* (Fallos 306:2101, December 1984). Then, again, after the *carapintadas* military rebellion took place, in *Caso Rico* the court broadened again the military jurisdiction (Fallos 312:312, March 1989). In 2008 the Argentinean Congress abrogated the military jurisdiction.

8

Constitutional Courts and Democratic Conflict Solving

Ordinary courts help solve conflicts. Constitutional courts do more than help in solving specific conflicts: their authoritative interpretation of the constitution is a means for adapting existing institutions and rules of the political game to changing conditions. Constitutional jurisprudence also helps political actors and regular citizens learn what the constitutional framework and principles are and to adapt their views and preferences accordingly. I have advanced an informational theory of constitutional review arguing that to the extent that the source of a conflict is uncertainty,[1] constitutional courts acting as third-party mediators in conflict resolution can obtain and credibly transmit through jurisprudence conflict-relevant information to the parties, which reduces the uncertainly underlying their conflict. The theory rests on the interrelation of three features of constitutional courts: access (so that judges obtain conflict-relevant information), powers of judicial review (to transform the received information into jurisprudence), and independence (to credibly transmit the information). Independence is a necessary condition: when courts are not independent they tend to act as delegates of whoever controls them. But when courts are independent their jurisprudence approaches the mediator model of conflict resolution to the extent that they are more accessible and have greater powers of judicial review.

Existing theories of the role of courts in producing desired outcomes emphasize the importance of judicial independence. In the theory advanced in this book independence is a necessary condition for courts to produce informative, mediator-like jurisprudence. But of most critical importance is access to constitutional justice. When people cannot get their cases to the court, not only is justice denied to them but also the court does not get enough information about the underlying causes that

[1] Specifically, as mentioned in Chapter 1, uncertainty about the legal consequences of actions, over the bounds of the exceptions and emergencies permitted by the constitution, or uncertainty about how to balance clashing constitutional principles or rules in particular cases.

drive particular parties to file or contest a suit. The court then tends to solve that particular case, with a narrower approach than if it had had the opportunity to learn that the specific case at hand is part of a larger social or political or economic problem that is producing grievances among parties. Of course, judges as persons may have an idea of those underlying socioeconomic factors, depending on their personal characteristics and their degree of political information or interest in politics. But only if their courtroom is filled with cases that they can interrelate to each other will they learn, as judges, about the underlying causes of conflict and be able to act upon them. Increasing access also gives independent judges the chance to surf the political waves more effectively, waiting for the "right" case and the "right" time to make a decision, or to produce a stream of decisions, on a given issue. In short, augmenting access to justice (and to constitutional justice in particular) strengthens citizenship, the courts, and democracy.

Broad judicial review powers are also key. Constitutional courts not only need the possibility to craft by themselves good monitoring mechanisms of decisions that are made by judges all over the country, but also they need to be granted discretionary powers to pick and choose the cases to be reviewed. This discretionary capacity is paramount when looked at in tandem with generous and open accessibility to constitutional justice: without discretion to pick and choose cases the constitutional court would be paralyzed under a pile of files. Moreover, constitutional judges also require the capacity to give to their decisions, in the cases they select, effects that go beyond the parties in the case. Otherwise increasing access can turn into a strategy to inundate the court and make it inefficient. It may seem paradoxical, but one of the messages of this book may be stated as follows: granting to the constitutional court more independence, more powers of judicial review, more discretion to choose cases and to decide them without time or other substantive limits, and making it more accessible would allow the court to intervene politically in a subtler, less obstructive, yet more helpful way.

In the cases analyzed in this book, Colombia and Israel, the two cases that come closest to representing the ideal type of court as mediator, a true revolution in access to already independent courts precedes the production of the type of jurisprudence that I have labeled "informational." These two courts also have broad judicial review powers. These two accessible, powerful, and independent constitutional courts have been helpful actors in democratic conflict solving in their respective societies. In contrast, when access is lacking, courts become irrelevant actors even in the midst of a national tragedy. The case in point is Mexico, where the difference between the thousands of complaints filed before the National Human Rights Commission and the relatively few cases that have reached the Supreme Court tells it all: a lack of access is key to understanding why the court has been absent from the debates on (and possible solutions to) the violence that has been spreading throughout the country. The marginal role played by the Peruvian Tribunal of Constitutional Guarantees (1980–2002) during one of the bloodiest and more violent periods in the history of the country can also be explained by the existence of several obstacles to bring cases against the agents in charge of the state security for human rights violations.

In the informational theory of constitutional review, independence, of course, also matters but less, or rather in a slight different way than has been stressed in the literature. When independence under democracy is slight, and the tribunal has a good deal of power and is accessible, as in Peru since 2001, we see jurisprudential U-turns that reflect the interests of incumbent governments that can more easily exert influence on the content of jurisprudence. When independence is good, but levels of access and powers are relatively low, the courts tend to focus on solving specific cases with a narrow approach closer to the arbitrator role as in Colombia (roughly 1958–91), Peru (1980–93), or Mexico (1917–40). In other words, independence in democracies does matter but not in isolation: as stressed in the theory developed in this book we need to consider how independence relates to other key features of courts, notably access and powers of judicial review, to make sense of exactly how and when it matters. Finally, when independence is completely absent, as in Mexico (1940–94) or in Pakistan, the constitutional court becomes a delegate of whoever pulls the strings of power. Though nonindependent courts can exist in democracies, they are a defining feature of authoritarian regimes (Svolik 2012) that are no mere window dressing but can actually play a key role in the dilemmas of control and power sharing faced by autocrats (Aguilar and Ríos-Figueroa 2014).

Courts as Mediators Beyond Civil-Military Relations

The *Theory of Constitutional Courts as Mediators* was empirically evaluated in the issue area of military autonomy. But it is conceived as a general theory of constitutional review that can be useful in explaining jurisprudence in other issue areas, especially those where the types of uncertainty discussed in this book are an important source of conflict between parties. Consider, for example, an old conflict that has been reframed given the recently gained visibility of marginalized indigenous groups in Latin America.[2] The conflict is between governments (and businesses), on the one hand, and indigenous communities, on the other, due to the attempts by the former to promote development through the extraction of natural resources or the construction of megainfrastructure projects in lands inhabited by the latter. Indigenous communities used to have few or no means for either stopping or at least benefitting from those development efforts. However, in 1989 the International Labor Organization adopted *Convention 169 on Indigenous and Tribal Peoples* that includes a right to prior consultation, which essentially requires that indigenous and tribal peoples be consulted on issues that affect them. In the Latin American countries that have ratified *Convention 169*, the old conflict has been reframed as one pitting governments seeking to encourage private investment with a view to promoting development against indigenous peoples asserting their rights to use and enjoy their lands and to protect and manage them according to their own worldview. In this conflict, governments and indigenous communities claim to act according to their constitutional prerogatives and obligations.

In a nutshell, in this conflict both governments and indigenous communities are pursuing good ends and both claim to act as required by the constitution and the international legal norms. How can these conflicting views be properly accommodated? How to promote economic development without jeopardizing the rights and the identity of indigenous peoples? The *right of prior consultation* presumably can help to reconcile these two aims. But what constitutes a "free and prior" consultation? Who should organize the consultation and how? Does the right to prior consultation imply veto power? What proceeds if an agreement is not reached after the consultation? How should the different interests involved be balanced? Should they always be balanced or are there circumstances under which one of the interests outweighs the other?

Notice that in this issue area we are also talking about uncertainty about the legal consequences of certain actions, uncertainty on the bounds of the exceptions and special circumstances allowed by the constitution, and uncertainty about how to balance clashing constitutional principles or rules in particular cases. If we look at the jurisprudence on the right of prior consultation in Colombia, Peru, and Mexico, we see that only Colombia has produced mediator-like jurisprudence in this case, as well, despite the fact that the three countries have substantial indigenous

[2] This example is taken from Pozas-Loyo and Ríos-Figueroa (2016).

populations that have challenged state or private development projects, and also a de jure commitment to the right to prior consultation.[3] Since 1992 (T-428 1992 MP Ciro Angarita) the Colombian Constitutional Court established that conflicts between a community and the government (that was trying to build a road) were not about "particular interests versus the general interest," but involved a clash between two collective interests." Moreover, it stated that given that "the interest of the indigenous community . . . was grounded on fundamental rights extensively protected by the Constitution," it should be given full consideration, and could not be dispatched merely by the utilitarian argument that the project had a positive impact on a larger number of people, thus reducing the uncertainty regarding the consequences of omitting prior consultation.

In a series of other decisions, the Colombian Constitutional Court has produced a line of informative jurisprudence on the right to prior consultation. In a case in which the U'wa community claimed it had not been consulted before an environmental license for seismic prospecting activities with the goal of finding oil fields was granted, the court determined that the government had thirty days to initiate a consultation with the U'wa community and that this process ought to comply with the criteria established in the decision (SU-039 1997 MP Antonio Barrera Carbonell). In this case, the court took decisive steps forward in defining what constitutes prior consultation, for instance, arguing that "informative workshops" did not constitute prior consultation. In other decisions (e.g., C-208 2007 MP Rodrigo Escobar Gil; C-030 2008 MP Rodrigo Escobar Gil) the court continued to build a doctrine that attempted to balance the differing rights of the communities and the developmental state, reducing the uncertainties that surround this issue area (see Pozas-Loyo and Ríos-Figueroa 2016 for further discussion).

In contrast, the Peruvian Constitutional Tribunal and the Mexican Supreme Court have produced strikingly similar jurisprudence in this issue area as in the area of military autonomy. In Peru, lack of consistency (produced by low independence) has produced erratic jurisprudence on the right to prior consultation. For instance, the Peruvian Tribunal first accepts that some contracts for a development project violate indigenous community rights but when the community requests their nullification, the tribunal does not nullify them based on convoluted arguments (see

[3] The Colombian Constitutional Court has more than forty decisions that refer to *Convention 169 on Indigenous and Tribal Peoples* 169 of the International Labor Organization. See International Labor Organization (ILO) 2009, 9.

06316-2008-PA/TC and Resolution N06316-2008-AA). In the case of Mexico, a country with a large number of indigenous communities and numerous developmental projects, the jurisprudence on prior consultation is rare, which again can arguably be explained by the lack of access to the supreme court. And when a case reaches the court, it has managed to discourage further litigation. For instance, in a recent *amparo* suit 631/2012 in which the Yaqui community challenges the construction of an aqueduct promoted by the government of the state of Sonora, the supreme court first recognized that the right to prior consultation of the Yaqui community had been violated; but then in a statement issued as a clarification of its decision, the supreme court permitted the aqueduct to continue functioning without the required permissions and before the mandated consultation had concluded.

The *Theory of Constitutional Courts as Mediators* is more applicable to the extent that the source of conflict is informational, that is, when underlying the conflict between two or more parties there is one of the types of uncertainty discussed in this book. Of course, there are other sources of conflict between parties such as distributional sources. In a postelectoral conflict when two parties are claiming to have won the election, any resolution involves clear winners and losers. In these cases, according to the literature on conflict resolution, an arbitrator (disposing authoritatively who wins and loses the particular dispute) is a better approach. Of course, many conflicts have both informational and distributional causes. An interesting avenue for future research is to evaluate whether courts, such as the Colombian Constitutional Court or the Costa Rican *Sala Cuarta* that are independent, highly accessible, and have substantial powers of judicial review, vary their kinds of decisions depending on whether the source of the underlying conflict is mainly distributional or informational.

Conflicts in democratic societies are processed in a way that respects the rights of the individuals involved as well as the moral and political principles established in the constitution. These may be everyday conflicts important mostly to the parties involved, but they can sometimes turn bloody, cruel, lasting, and harmful for the society at large, threatening the democratic regime itself. This book has argued that even under dramatic circumstances constitutional courts can contribute in pointing out solutions, serving as lighthouses that signal a possible way out to navigate the trouble and uncertain waters created in the fog of war, building bridges across conflictive actors, and eventually easing the pain on suffering citizens under the framework of constitutionalism and the rule of law.

REFERENCES

Abad, Alberto. 2014. *La Protección de los Derechos Fundamentales en la Novena Época de la Suprema Corte de Justicia de la Nación*. México, D.F., México: IIJ-UNAM/Porrúa.

Abad Yupanqui, Samuel, and Carolina Garcés Peralta. 1993. "El Gobierno de Fujimori: Antes y Después Del Golpe." In *Del Golpe de Estado a la Nueva Constitución*. Lima: Comisión Andina de Juristas, 85–190.

Ackerman, Bruce. 2002. "Don't Panic: States of Emergency." *London Review of Books* 24(3): 15–16.

Agüero, Felipe. 1995. *Militares, Civiles y Democracia: La España Postfranquista en Perspectiva Comparada*. Madrid: Alianza Editorial.

2001. "Institutions, Transitions, and Bargaining: Civilians and the Military in Shaping the Post-Authoritarian Regimes." In *Civil-Military Relations in Latin America: New Analytical Perspectives*, ed. David Pion-Berlin. Chapel Hill: North Carolina University Press, 198–222.

Aguilar, Paloma, and Julio Ríos-Figueroa. 2014. *Judicial Institutions and the Dilemmas of Power Sharing and Control in Authoritarian Regimes*. Documento de Trabajo, CIDE, México, DTEP 271.

Aguirre Roca, Manuel. 1991. "La Razón Principal Del Fracaso Del TGC." *Themis* 20: 7–12.

Alegría Varona, Ciro. 2003. "Bases Para Un Modelo de Relaciones Entre el Poder Político Y El Mando Militar Desde Una Perspectiva Democrática." In *Bases Para Un Control Civil Democrático de la Fuerza Armada en el Perú*, ed. Ciro Alegría Varona, Narcís Serra, and Ana María Tamayo Flores. Lima: Instituto de Defensa Legal, 29-74.

Andrade Becerra, Oscar David. 2012. "Relaciones Cívico-Militares en Colombia: Apuntes Para Un Estado Del Arte." *RAI. Revista de Análisis Internacional* 6: 145–71.

Ansolabehere, Karina. 2010. "More Power, More Rights? The Supreme Court and Society in Mexico." In *Cultures of Legality: Judicialization and Political Activism in Latin America*, ed. Javier Couso, Alexandra Hunneus, and Rachel Sieder. New York: Cambridge University Press, 78–111.

Ariza, Librado. 1999. "Fuerzas Armadas, Justicia Penal Militar Y Discurso Judicial: Entre El Garantismo Y El Eficientismo." In *Derecho Constitucional: Perspectivas Críticas*. Bogotá: Siglo del Hombre/Universidad de los Andes, 3–38.

Ariza, Librado, Felipe Cammaert, and Manuel Iturralde. 1997. *Estados de Excepción y Razón de Estado Colombia*. Bogotá: Universidad de los Andes.

Aydın, A. 2013. "Judicial Independence across Democratic Regimes: Understanding the Varying Impact of Political Competition." *Law and Society Review* 47(1): 105–34.

Barak, Aharon. 2002. "A Judge on Judging: The Role of a Supreme Court in a Democracy." *Harvard Law Review* 116(16): 19–162.

Barany, Zoltan. 2012. *The Soldier and the Changing State: Building Democratic Armies in Africa, Asia, Europe and the Americas*. Princeton, NJ: Princeton University Press.

Barreto Rozo, Antonio. 2011. *La Generación del Estado de Sitio: El Juicio a la Anormalidadinstitucional en la Asamblea Nacional Constituyente de 1991*. Bogotá: Universidad de los Andes.

Barros, Robert. 2002. *Constitutionalism and Dictatorship: Pinochet, the Junta, and the 1980 Constitution*. New York: Cambridge University Press.

Barzilai, Gad. 1998. "Political Institutions and Conflict Resolution. The Israeli Supreme Court and the Peace Process." In *The Middle East Peace Process*, ed. Ilan Peleg. Albany: SUNY University Press, 87–106.

1999. "War, Democracy, and Internal Conflict. Israel in Comparative Perspective." *Comparative Politics* 31(3): 317–33.

Bejarano, Ana María, and Eduardo Pizarro. 2005. "From 'Restricted' to 'Besieged': The Changing Nature of the Limits of Democracy in Colombia." In *The Third Wave of Democratization in Latin America: Advances and Setbacks*, ed. Frances Hagopian and Scott Mainwaring. New York: Cambridge University Press, 235–60.

Belge, Ceren. 2006. "Friends of the Court: The Republican Alliance and Selective Activism of the Constitutional Court of Turkey." *Law and Society Review* 40(3): 653–91.

Ben-Naftali, Orna. 2011. *International Humanitarian Law and International Human Rights Law: Pas de Deux*. New York: Oxford University Press.

Bickel, Alexander. 1962. *The Least Dangerous Branch: The Supreme Court at the Bar of Politics*. New Haven, CT: Yale University Press.

Bland, Douglas. 1999. "A Unified Theory of Civil-Military Relations." *Armed Forces and Society* 26(1): 7–25.

Blomquist, William, and Elinor Ostrom. 2008. "Deliberation, Learning, and Institutional Change: The Evolution of Institutions in Judicial Settings." *Constitutional Political Economy* 19(3): 180–202.

Boaventura de Sousa, Santos, and Mauricio García Villegas, eds. 2001. *El Caleidoscopio de las Justicias en Colombia*. Bogotá: Siglo XXI.

Bogoch, Bryna, and Yifat Holzman-Gazit. 2008. "Mutual Bonds: Media Frames and the Israeli High Court of Justice." *Law and Social Inquiry* 33(1): 53–87.

Bonilla, Heraclio. 2006. *La Trayectoria del Desencanto. El Perú en la Segunda Mitad del Siglo XX*. Lima: Arteida Editores.

Botero, Sandra. 2014. *Judicial Impact and Court-Promoted Monitoring in Argentina*. Paper presented at the Latin American Studies Association Annual Congress, Chicago, IL, May 21–24.

Bovino, Alberto. 1998. "El Juzgamiento de Civiles." In *Justicia Militar y Estado de Derecho*, ed. Jorge Mera Figueroa. Santiago, Chile: Universidad Diego Portales, 47–71.

Bravo Maxdeo, Roosevelt. 2009. "El Derecho Internacional Humanitario y la Sentencia del Tribunal Constitucional Sobre la Ley de Empleo de la Fuerza." *Revista de Análisis Jurídico Especializado (RAE)* 18(2): 3–45.

Brinks, Daniel. 2011. "'Faithful Servants of the Regime': The Brazilian Constitutional Court's Role under the 1988 Constitution." In *Courts in Latin America*, ed. Gretchen Helmke and Julio Ríos-Figueroa. New York: Cambridge University Press, 128–53.

Brunneau, Thomas C. 2013. "Civilians and the Military in Latin America: The Absence of Incentives." *Latin American Politics and Society* 55(4): 143–60.

Bush, Robert A. Baruch, and Joseph P. Folger. 2004. *The Promise of Mediation: The Transformative Approach to Conflict*. San Francisco: Jossey-Bass.

Bybee, Keith J. 2010. *All Judges Are Political – Except When They Are Not: Acceptable Hypocrisies and the Rule of Law*. Stanford, CA: Stanford University Press.

Caballero, José Antonio. 2010. "Amparos Y Abogánsters. La Justicia En México Entre 1940 Y 1968." In *Del Nacionalismo al Neoliberalismo (1940–1994)*, ed. Elisa Servín. Mexico, D.F.: CIDE-FCE, 45–73.

Cabarcas Maciá, Gina. 2011. *Militares, Política y Derecho. Sobre los Silencios de la Constituyente de 1991*. Bogotá: Universidad de los Andes.

Cabrera Acevedo, Lucio. 1998. *La Suprema Corte de Justicia Durante los Gobiernos de Portes Gil, Ortiz Rubio y Abelardo L. Rodriguez (1929–1934)*. Mexico, D.F.: Suprema Corte de Justicia de la Nación.

Cabrera Ortiz, Fabricio. 2005. "Relaciones Civiles-Militares Durante el Periodo Comprendido Entre 1994 y 2002, y Su Impacto en la Seguridad Nacional." Tesis de Maestría en Estudios Políticos, Bogotá, Colombia: Universidad Javeriana.

Cameron, Charles M. 2002. "Judicial Independence: How Can You Tell It When You See It? And, Who Cares?" In *Judicial Independence at the Crossroads: An Interdisciplinary Approach*, ed. Steven B. Burbank, and Barry Friedman. New York: Sage Publications Inc., 134–47.

Carbonell, Miguel. 2002. "El Rol de las Fuerzas Armadas en la Constitución Mexicana." *Ius et Praxis* 8(1): 35–51.

Carpizo, Jorge. 2000. "Otra Reforma Constitucional: La Subordinación del Consejo de la Judicatura Federal." *Cuestiones Constitucionales* 2(2): 209–18.

Carrubba, Clifford James. 2009. "A Model of the Endogenous Development of Judicial Institutions in Federal and International Systems." *The Journal of Politics* 71(1): 55.

Castagnola, Andrea, and Aníbal Pérez-Liñán. 2009. "Presidential Control of High Courts in Latin America: A Long Term View (1904–2006)." *Journal of Politics in Latin America* 2(1): 89–115.

Castillo Sánchez, Camilo. 2015. "Cooptación Judicial e Impunidad. El Caso de la Junta Militar de 1957 En Colombia." Tesis de Doctorado en Derecho, Bogotá, Colombia: Universidad del Rosario.

Centro de Estudios de Justicia de las Américas. 2007. *Reporte Sobre la Justicia en las Américas 2006–2007*. Santiago, Chile: CEJA.

Cepeda Espinosa, Manuel José. 2005. "The Judicialization of Politics in Colombia: The New and The Old." In *The Judicialization of Politics in Latin America*, ed. Rachel Sieder, Line Schjolden, and Alan Angell. Oxford: Palgrave Macmillan, 95–130.

2008. "La Constitución de 1991 Y Sus Orígenes." In *Polémicas Constitucionales*, ed. Manuel José Cepeda Espinosa. Bogotá: Legis, 335–417.

Cepeda Ulloa, Fernando. 2008. "Colombia: The Governability Crisis." In *Constructing Democratic Governance in Latin America*, ed. Jorge Domínguez and Michael Shifter. Baltimore, MD: Johns Hopkins University Press, 193–219.

Cheibub, José Antonio, and Jennifer Gandhi. 2004. "Classifying Political Regimes: A Sixfold Classification of Democracies and Dictatorships." Paper presented at the *Annual Meeting of the American Political Science Association*, Chicago, IL, April 3–6.

Christopher, Paul, Colin P. Clarke, and Serena Chad. 2014. *Mexico Is Not Colombia: Alternative Historical Analogies for Responding to the Challenge of Violent Drug-Trafficking Organizations.* Washington, DC: Rand Corporation.

Cingranelli, David L., and David L. Richards. 2010. *The Cingranelli Richards (CIRI) Human Rights Database Coding Manual.* Available at http://www.humanrightsdata.com/

Cizre, Ümit. 1997. "The Anatomy of the Turkish Military's Political Autonomy." *Comparative Politics* 29(2): 151–66.

2003. "Demythologizing the National Security Concept: The Case of Turkey." *Middle East Journal* 57(2): 213–29.

Clark, T. S., and A. B. Strauss. 2010. "The Implications of High Court Docket Control for Resource Allocation and Legal Efficiency." *Journal of Theoretical Politics* 22(2): 247–68.

Clark, Tom S., and Jeffrey K. Staton. 2013. "Optimal Dockets." Working paper on file with author.

Conaghan, Catherine M. 2005. *Fujimori's Peru: Deception in the Public Sphere.* Pittsburgh, PA: University of Pittsburgh Press.

Cossío, José Ramón. 2010. "El Fuero Militar: Alcances y Limitaciones." *Cuestiones Constitucionales* 22(2): 321–62.

Couso, Javier. 2010. "The Transformation of the Constitutional Discourse and the Judicialization of Politics in Latin America." In *Cultures of Legality: Judicialization and Political Activism in Latin America*, ed. Javier Couso, Alexandra Hunneus, and Rachel Sieder. New York: Cambridge University Press, 141–59.

Cruz, Consuelo, and Rut Diamint. 1988. "The New Military Autonomy in Latin America." *Journal of Democracy* 9(4): 115–27.

Cuéllar Vázquez, Angélica. 2015. *La SCJN: Sus Ministros, la Política, y el Agravio Social*. Mexico, D.F.: Universidad Nacional Autónoma de México.

Dahl, Robert. 1985. *Democracy and Its Critics*. New Haven, CT: Yale University Press.

Dargent, Eduardo. 2009. "Determinants of Judicial Independence: Lessons from Three 'Cases' on Constitutional Courts in Peru (1979–2007)." *Journal of Latin American Studies* 41(2): 251–78.

Díez, Jordi. 2008. "Legislative Oversight of the Armed Forces in Mexico." *Mexican Studies/Estudios Mexicanos* 24(1): 113–45.

2012. "Civic-Military Relations in Mexico: The Unfinished Transition." In *The Oxford Handbook of Mexican Politics*, ed. Rodric Ai Camp. New York: Oxford University Press, 265–85.

Díez, Jordi, and Ian Nicholls. 2006. *The Mexican Armed Forces in Transition*. Carlisle, Pennsylvania: Strategic Studies Institute, US Army War College.

Dixon, Rosalind. 2007. "Creating Dialogue About Socioeconomic Rights: Strong-Form versus Weak-Form Judicial Review Revisited." *International Journal of Constitutional Law* 5(1): 391–430.

Dotan, Yoav and Menachem Hofnung. 2005. "Legal Defeats–Political Wins: Why Do Elected Representatives Go to Court?" *Comparative Political Studies* 38(1): 75–103.

Droege, Cordula. 2008. "Elective Affinities? Human Rights and Humanitarian Law." *International Review of the Red Cross* 90(871): 501–48.

Dulitzky, Ariel. 2012. "El Retiro del Reconocimiento de la Competencia Contenciosa de la Corte Interamericana de Derechos Humanos por Parte de Perú." *Pensamiento Constitucional* 6(6): 705–27.

Easton, David. 1975. "A Re-Assessment of the Concept of Popular Support." *British Journal of Political Science* 5(4): 435–57.

Eguiguren Praeli, Francisco. 1989. "El Estado de Emergencia y Su Aplicación en la Experiencia Constitucional Peruana, 1980–1988." In *La Constitución Diez Años Después*, ed. Enrique Bernales. Lima: Fundación Friedrich Naumann, 261–87.

1990. *Los Retos de Una Democracia Insuficiente. Diez Años de Régimen Constitucional en el Perú, 1980–1990*. Lima: Comisión Andina de Juristas/Fundación Friedrich Naumann.

Epp, Charles R. 1998. *The Rights Revolution: Lawyers, Activists, and Supreme Courts in Comparative Perspective*. Chicago: University of Chicago Press.

Epstein, Lee, and Jack Knight. 1998. *The Choices Justices Make*. Washington, DC: CQ Press.

2013. "Reconsidering Judicial Preferences." *Annual Review of Political Science* 16: 11–31.

Epstein, Lee, Jack Knight, and Olga Shvetsova. 2001. "The Role of Constitutional Courts in the Establishment and Maintenance of Democratic Systems of Government." *Law and Society Review* 45: 362–77.

Eto Cruz, Gerardo, Cesar Landa Arroyo, and José Palomino Manchego. 1997. "La Justicia Militar En El Perú." In *Jurisdicción Militar y Constitución En Iberoamérica*, ed. Germán Bidart and Josçe Palomino. Lima: Grijley, 353–463.

Favretto, Katja. 2009. "Should Peacemakers Take Sides? Major Power Mediation, Coercion, and Bias." *American Political Science Review* 103(2): 248–63.

Feaver, Peter D. 1999. "Civil-Military Relations." *Annual Review of Political Science* 2: 211–41.

Ferejohn, John. 2002. "Judicializing Politics, Politicizing Law." *Law and Contemporary Problems* 65(3): 41–68.

Ferejohn, John, and Pasquale Pasquino. 2003. "Constitutional Courts as Deliberative Institutions: Towards an Institutional Theory of Constitutional Justice." In *Constitutional Justice, East and West*, ed. Saduurski Wojciech. London: Kluwer International, 21–36.

2010. "The Countermajoritarian Opportunity." *University of Pennsylvania Journal of Constitutional Law* 13(2): 353-95.

Ferejohn, John, and Lawrence Sager. 2002. "Commitment and Constitutionalism." *Texas Law Review* 81(7): 1927–75.

Fey, Mark, and K. W. Ramsay. 2010. "When Is Shuttle Diplomacy Worth the Commute? Information Sharing through Mediation." *World Politics* 62(4): 529–60.

Fisher, Roger, William L. Ury, and Patton Bruce. 2011. *Getting to Yes: Negotiating Agreement without Giving In*. New York: Penguin Books.

Fix-Fierro, Héctor. 2003. "Judicial Reform in Mexico: What Next?" In *Beyond Common Knowledge: Empirical Approaches to the Rule of Law*, ed. Erik G. Jensen and Thomas C. Heller. Stanford, CA: Stanford University Press, 240–89.

Friedman, Barry. 1993. "Dialogue and Judicial Review." *Michigan Law Review* 91(4): 577–682.

2009. *The Will of the People: How Public Opinion Has Influenced the Supreme Court and the Meaning of the Constitution*. New York: Farrar, Straus and Giroux.

García Belaúnde, Domingo. 1990. "El Constitucionalismo Peruano en la Presente Centuria." *Derecho: Pontificia Universidad Católica de Perú* 43–4: 59–101.

García-Godos, Jemima, and Knut Andreas O. Lid. 2010. "Transitional Justice and Victims' Rights before the End of a Conflict: The Unusual Case of Colombia." *Journal of Latin American Studies* 42(3): 487–516.

García Villegas, Mauricio, and Rodrigo Uprimny. 2005. "La Normalization de l´exceptionnel: Sur le Contrôl Jurisdictionnel des États d'urgence en

Colombie." In *Justice et Démocratie en Amérique Latine*, ed. Marie Julie Bernard and Michel Carraud. Grenoble: PUG, 117–43.

Gargarella, Roberto. 2008. "Un Papel Renovado Para la Corte Suprema. Democracia e Interpretación Judicial de la Constitución." In *Tribunales Constitucionales y Democracia*. Mexico City: Suprema Corte de Justicia de la Nación, 573–90.

Garrido, Luis Javier. 2005. *El Partido de la Revolución Institucionalizada (1928–1945)*. Mexico, D.F.: Siglo XXI.

Gauri, Varun, and Daniel M Brinks. 2008. "Introduction: The Elements of Legalization and the Triangular Shape of Social and Economic Rights." In *Courting Social Justice: Judicial Enforcement of Social and Economic Rights in the Developing World*, ed. Varun Gauri and Daniel M Brinks. New York: Cambridge University Press, 1–37.

Gentili, Gianluca. 2011. "A Comparative Perspective on Direct Access to Constitutional and Supreme Courts in Africa, Asia, Europe and Latin America: Assessing Advantages for the Italian Constitutional Court." *Penn State International Law Review* 29(4): 705–57.

Ghias, Shoaib A. 2010. "Miscarriage of Chief Justice: Judicial Power and the Legal Complex in Pakistan under Musharraf." *Law and Social Inquiry* 35(4): 985–1005.

Gibson, James, and Gregory A. Caldeira. 1995. "The Legitimacy of Transnational Legal Institutions: Compliance, Support, and the European Court of Justice." *American Journal of Political Science* 39(2): 459–89.

Gibson, James L. 2008. "Judicial Institutions." In *Oxford Handbook of Political Institutions*, ed. Sarah A. Binder, R. A. W. Rhodes, and Bert A. Rockman. New York: Oxford University Press, 514–34.

Gibson, James L., Gregory A. Caldeira, and Vanessa A. Baird. 1998. "On the Legitimacy of National High Courts." *American Political Science Review* 92: 343–58.

Gilligan, Michael J., and Leslie Johns. 2012. "Formal Models of International Institutions." *Annual Review of Political Science* 15(1): 221–43.

Ginsburg, Tom. 2003. *Judicial Review in New Democracies: Constitutional Courts in Asian Cases*. New York: Cambridge University Press.

Ginsburg, Tom, and James Melton. 2013. "Does De Jure Judicial Independence Really Matter? A Reevaluation of Explanations for Judicial Independence." *Journal of Law and Courts* 2(2): 187–217.

Glennerster, Rachel, and Kudazai Takavarasha. 2013. *Running Randomized Evaluations: A Practical Guide*. Princeton, NJ: Princeton University Press.

Goertz, Gary, and James Mahoney. 2012. *A Tale of Two Cultures: Qualitative and Quantitative Research in the Social Sciences*. Princeton, NJ: Princeton University Press.

Goldberg, Stephen B., Frank E. A. Sander, Nancy H. Rogers, and Sarah Rudolph Cole. 2012. *Dispute Resolution: Negotiation, Mediation, and Other Processes*. New York: Wolters Kluwer Law and Business.

Goldstein, Judith O., and Robert O. Keohane. 1993. "Ideas and Foreign Policy: An Analytic Framework." In *Ideas and Foreign Policy: Beliefs, Institutions, and Political Change*, ed. Judith O. Goldstein and Robert O. Keohane. Ithaca, NY: Cornell University Press, 3–30.

González Ocantos, Ezequiel. 2012. "The Collapse of Impunity Regimes in Latin America: Legal Cultures, Strategic Litigation and Judicial Behavior." PhD Dissertation in Political Science, University of Notre Dame.

González Oropeza, Manuel. 2006. "El Fuero Militar En México: La Injusticia En Las Fuerzas Armadas." In *Estudios en Homenaje a Marcia Muñoz de Alba Medrano. Estudios de Derecho Público y Política*. Mexico, DF: Instituto de Investigaciones Jurídicas – UNAM, 177–95.

Graber, Mark. 1998. "Establishing Judicial Review? Schooner Peggy and the Early Marshall Court." *Political Research Quarterly* 51(1): 221–39.

Guevara Bermúdez, José A. 2004. *México Frente al Derecho Internacional Humanitario*. México, D.F.: Universidad Iberoamericana.

Gutiérrez Sanín, Francisco. 2007. *Lo Que el Viento se Llevó. Los Partidos Políticos y la Democracia en Colombia, 1958–2002*. Bogotá: Editorial Norma.

Gutiérrez Sanín, Francisco, and Luisa Ramírez Rueda. 2004. "The Tense Relationship between Democracy and Violence in Colombia, 1974–2001." In *Politics in the Andes: Identity, Conflict, Reform*, ed. Joe-Marie Burt and Philip Mauceri. Pittsburgh, PA: Pittsburgh University Press, 228–46.

Hafner-Burton, E. M. 2014. "A Social Science of Human Rights." *Journal of Peace Research* 58: 273–86.

Hafner-Burton, Emilie M., Edward D. Mansfield, and Jon C. W. Pevehouse. 2013. "Human Rights Institutions, Sovereignty Costs and Democratization." *British Journal of Political Science*, 45(1): 1–27.

Harpaz, Guy, and Yuval Shany. 2010. "The Israeli Supreme Court and the Incremental Expansion of the Scope of Discretion under Belligerent Occupation Law." *Israeli Law Review* 43(3): 514–50.

Helmke, Gretchen. 2005. *Courts under Constraints*. Cambridge: Cambridge University Press.

Helmke, Gretchen, and Jeffrey K. Staton. 2011. "The Puzzle of Judicial Politics in Latin America." In *Courts in Latin America*, ed. Gretchen Helmke and Julio Ríos-Figueroa. New York: Cambridge University Press, 306–31.

Heper, Metin. 2005. "The Justice and Development Party and the Military in Turkey." *Turkish Studies* 6(2): 215–31.

2011. "Civil-Military Relations in Turkey: Toward a Liberal Model?" *Turkish Studies* 12(2): 241–52.

Hilbink, L. 2012. "The Origins of Positive Judicial Independence." *World Politics* 64(4): 587–621.

Hilbink, Lisa. 2007. *Judges beyond Politics in Autocracy and Democracy: Lessons from Chile*. New York: Cambridge University Press.

Hirschl, Ran. 2004. *Towards Juristocracy: The Origins and Consequences of the New Constitutionalism*. Cambridge, MA: Harvard University Press.

2014. *Comparative Matters: The Renaissance of Comparative Constitutional Law*. New York: Oxford University Press.

Holmes, Oliver Wendell. 1992. "The Path of the Law." In *The Essential Holmes*, ed. Richard A Posner. Chicago: The University of Chicago Press, 160–77.

Human Rights Watch World Report. 2013.New York: Human Rights Watch.

Hunneus, Alexandra. 2012. "Courts Resisting Courts: Lessons from the Inter-American Court's Struggles to Enforce Human Rights." *Georgetown International Law Journal* 44(2): 101–56.

Hunter, W. 1997. "Continuity or Change? Civil-Military Relations in Democratic Argentina, Chile, and Peru." *Political Science Quarterly* 112(3): 453–75.

Huntington, Samuel. 1957. *The Soldier and the State: The Theory and Politics of Civil-Military Relations*. Cambridge, MA: Harvard University Press.

International Commission of Jurists. 2013. *Authority without Accountability: The Search for Justice in Pakistan*. Geneva.

James, T. M. 2006. "Law and Revolution in Mexico. A Constitutional History of the Amparo Suit and Social Reform during the Mexican Revolution." PhD Dissertation in History, The University of Chicago.

Justicia Viva. 2008. *Balance Al 2008 Del Tribunal Constitutional Peruano: El TC Que Se Nos Fue y el TC Que Se Nos Viene*. Lima: Instituto de Defensa Legal.

2010. *Nuevo Çódigo Penal Militar Cierra Círculo de Impunidad en Derechos Humanos*. Lima: Instituto de Defensa Legal.

Kalhan, Anil. 2013. "'Grey Zone' Constitutionalism and the Dilemma of Judicial Independence in Pakistan." *Vanderbilt Journal of Transnational Law* 46(1): 3–96.

Kapiszewski, Diana. 2012. *High Courts and Economic Governance in Argentina and Brazil*. New York: Cambridge University Press.

Kogacioglu, Dicle. 2004. "Progress, Unity, and Democracy: Dissolving Political Parties in Turkey." *Law and Society Review* 38(4): 433–62.

Kohn, Richard. 1997. "How Democracies Control the Military." *Journal of Democracy* 8(4): 140–53.

Kornhauser, Lewis A. 2002. "Is Judicial Independence a Useful Concept?" In *Judicial Independence at the Crossroads: An Interdisciplinary Approach*, ed. Steven B Burbank and Barry Friedman. Thousand Oaks, CA: SAGE, 45–55.

Kretzmer, David. 2012. "The Law of Belligerent Occupation in the Israeli Supreme Court." *International Review of the Red Cross* 94(885): 207–36.

Kydd, Andrew H. 2003. "Which Side Are You on? Bias, Credibility, and Mediation." *American Journal of Political Science* 47(4): 597–611.

2006. "When Can Mediators Build Trust?" *American Political Science Review* 14(3): 319.

2010. "Rationalist Approaches to Conflict Prevention and Resolution." *Annual Review of Political Science* 13(1): 101–21.

Kyle, B. J., and A. G. Reiter. 2013. "Militarized Justice in New Democracies: Explaining the Process of Military Court Reform in Latin America." *Law and Society Review* 47(2): 375–407.

Landa Arroyo, Cesar. 2007. *Tribunal Constitucional y Estado Democrático*. Lima: Palestra.

Law, David S. 2009. "A Theory of Judicial Power and Judicial Review." *Georgetown Law Journal* 97: 723–801.

Leiras, Marcelo, Guadalupe Tuñón, and Agustina Giraudy. 2015. "Who Wants an Independent Court? Political Competition and Supreme Court Autonomy in the Argentine Provinces (1984-2008)." *The Journal of Politics* 77(1): 175–87.

Lieberson, Stanley. 1991. "Small N's and Big Conclusions: An Examination of the Reasoning in Comparative Studies Based on a Small Number of Cases." *Social Forces* 70(2): 307–20.

Linzer, Drew A., and Jeffrey K. Staton. 2011. "A Measurement Model for Synthesizing Multiple Comparative Indicators: The Case of Judicial Independence." Unpublished manuscript.

López Medina, Diego Eduardo. 2009. *El Derecho de los Jueces*. Bogotá: Legis.

Lovatón Palacios, David. 2007. *Tribunal Constitucional y Reforma de la Justicia Militar*. Lima: Palestra.

Loveman, Brian, and Thomas M. Davies, Jr. 1997. *The Politics of Antipolitics: The Military in Latin America*, ed. Brian Loveman and Thomas M. Davies, Jr. Wilmington, DE: Scholarly Resources.

Madrazo, Alejandro, and Estefanía Vela. 2011. "The Mexican Supreme Court's (Sexual) Revolution?" *Texas Law Review* 89(7): 1863–94.

Magaloni, Beatriz. 2003. "Authoritarianism, Democracy and the Supreme Court: Horizontal Exchange and the Rule of Law in Mexico." In *Democratic Accountability in Latin America*, ed. Scott Mainwaring and Christopher Welna. New York: Oxford University Press, 266–306.

Magaloni, Beatriz, Arianna Sánchez, and Eric Magar. 2011. "Legalists vs. Interpretativists: The Supreme Court and the Democratic Transition in Mexico." In *Courts in Latin America*, ed. Gretchen Helmke and Julio Ríos-Figueroa. New York: Cambridge University Press, 187–218.

Magaloni Kerpel, Ana Laura, and Ana María Ibarra Olguín. 2008. "La Configuración Jurisprudencial de los Derechos Fundamentales. El Caso del Derecho a Una Defensa Adecuada." *Cuestiones Constitucionales* 19(1): 107–47.

Mahmud, Tayyab. 1993. "Pretorianism and Common Law in Post-Colonial Settings: Judicial Responses to Constitutional Breakdowns in Pakistan." *Utah Law Review* 4: 1226–1305.

1994. "Jurisprudence of Successful Treason: Coup d'Etat and Common Law." *Cornell International Law Journal* 27(1): 49–140.

Mahoney, James. 2000. "Strategies of Causal Inference in Small-N Analysis." *Sociological Methods and Research* 28(4): 387–424.

Malleson, Kate, and Peter H. Russell. 2003. *Appointing Judges in an Age of Judicial Power*. Toronto: University of Toronto Press.

Marván Laborde, Ignacio. 2010. "La Revolución Mexicana, 1908–1932." In *Historia Crítica de las Modernizaciones en México*, ed. Clara García Ayluardo and Ignacio Marván Laborde. Mexico, D.F.: CIDE-FCE, 1-40.

McCubbins, Matthew D., and Thomas Schwartz. 1984. "Congressional Oversight Overlooked: Police Patrols versus Fire Alarms." *American Journal of Political Science* 28(1): 165–79.

Mejía Garza, Raúl. 2011. "Jurisdicción Militar: Leyes Y Tribunales Especiales." In *Sentencias de la Suprema Corte de Justicia de la Nación Desde la Perspectiva de los Derechos Humanos*. Mexico, DF: Suprema Corte de Justicia de la Nación, 801–38.

Milgrom, Paul, Douglass C. North, and Barry Weingast. 1990. "The Role of Institutions in the Revival of Trade: The Medieval Law Merchant, Private Judges, and the Champagne Fairs." *Economics and Politics* 2(1): 1–23.

Montesquieu. 1977. *The Spirit of the Laws (A Compendium of the First English Edition)*. London: University of California Press.

Motta Ferraz, Octavio. 2011. "Harming the Poor through Social Rights Litigation: Lessons from Brazil." *Texas Law Review* 89(7): 1643–68.

Moustafa, Tamir. 2007. *The Struggle for Constitutional Power: Law, Politics, and Economic Development in Egypt*. New York: Cambridge University Press.

Narli, Nilüfer. 2011. "Concordance and Discordance in Turkish Civil Military Relations, 1980–2002." *Turkish Studies* 12(2): 215–25.

Negretto, Gabriel. 2013. *Making Constitutions: Presidents, Parties, and Institutional Choice in Latin America*. New York: Cambridge University Press.

Nielson, Daniel L., and Matthew Soberg Shugart. 1999. "Constitutional Change in Colombia: Policy Adjustment through Constitutional Change." *Comparative Political Studies* 32(3): 313–41.

North, Douglass, and Barry Weingast. 1989. "Constitutions and Commitment: The Evolution of Institutions Governing Public Choice in 17th Century England." *Journal of Economic History* 49(4): 803–32.

Nunes, Rodrigo. 2010. "Ideational Origins of Progressive Judicial Activism: The Colombian Constitutional Court and the Right to Health." *Latin American Politics and Society* 52(3): 67–97.

Özel, Soli. 2003. "After the Tsunami." *Journal of Democracy* 14(2): 80–94.

Palmer, David Scott. 1980. *Peru: The Authoritarian Tradition*. New York: Praeger.

Pedroza de la Llave, Susana Thalía. 2011. "La Reinterpretación Constitucional del Fuero de Guerra o Militar en el Marco del Estado Democrático." *Cuestiones Constitucionales* 25(1): 152–98.

Perdomo, Marta Patricia. 2012. "La Militarización de la Justicia. Una Respuesta Estatal a la Protesta Social (1949–1974)." *Análisis Político* 76(2): 83–102.

Pereira, A. W., and Jorge Zaverucha. 2005. "The Neglected Stepchild: Military Justice and Democratic Transition in Chile." *Social Justice* 32(2): 115–31.

Pérez-Perdomo, Rogelio. 2006. *Latin American Lawyers: A Historical Introduction*. Stanford, CA: Stanford University Press.

2010. *Justicia e Injusticias en Venezuela. Estudios de Historia Social del Derecho*. New Orleans, LA: Quid Pro Law Books.

Pfanner, Toni, Nils Melzer, and Kathleen Gibson. 2008. "Interview with Sergio Jaramillo Caro." *International Review of the Red Cross* 90(872): 823–33.

Pion-Berlin, David. 1992. "Military Autonomy and Emerging Democracies in South America." *The Journal of Comparative Politics* 25(1): 83–102.

2010. "Informal Civil-Military Relations in Latin America: Why Politicians and Soldiers Choose Unofficial Venues." *Armed Forces and Society* 36(3): 526–44.

2012. "The Latin American Military." In *Routledge Handbook of Latin American Politics*, ed. Peter Kingstone and Deborah J. Yashar. New York: Routledge, 76–87.

Ponce, Aldo, and Lydia Tiede. 2014. "Evaluating Theories of Decision-Making on the Peruvian Constitutional Tribunal." *Journal of Politics in Latin America* 6(2): 139–64.

Popova, Maria. 2012. *Politicized Justice in Emerging Democracies: Courts in Russia and Ukraine*. New York: Cambridge University Press.

Posner, Eric, and Adrian Vermeule. 2007. *Terror in the Balance: Security, Liberty, and the Courts*. New York: Oxford University Press.

Pou Giménez, Francisca. 2012. *Judicial Review and Rights Protection in Mexico: Assessing the Recent Amparo Constitutional Reforms*. Unpublished manuscript on file with author.

Pozas-Loyo, Andrea, and Julio Ríos-Figueroa. 2007. "When and Why 'Law' and 'Reality' Coincide? De Jure and De Facto Judicial Independence in Chile and Mexico." In *Evaluating Transparency and Accountability in Mexico: National, Local and Comparative Perspectives*, ed. Alejandra Rios-Cazares and David Shirk. San Diego, CA: University of San Diego Press, 127–64.

2010. "Enacting Constitutionalism: The Origins of Independent Judicial Institutions in Latin America." *Comparative Politics*, 42(3):293–311.

2011. "The Politics of Amendments Processes: Supreme Court Influence in the Design of Judicial Councils." *Texas Law Review* 89(7): 1807–33.

2016. "Constitutional Courts as Third-Party Mediators in Conflict Resolution. The Case of the Right to Prior Consultation in Latin America." In *A New Perspective on Conflict Solving in Latin America*, ed. Jorge Gordin and Lucio Renno. London: ECPR Press.

Przeworski, Adam. 2011. *Self-Government in Our Times*. New York: Cambridge University Press.

Przeworski, Adam, and Henry Teune. 1970. *The Logic of Comparative Social Inquiry*. New York: John Wiley & Sons.

Raguan, Galit. 2011. "Adjudicating Armed Conflict in Domestic Courts: The Experience of Israel's Supreme Court." In *Yearbook of International Humanitarian Law* 2010. Amsterdam: Springer, 61–95.

Ramelli Arteaga, Alejandro. 2009. "El Derecho Internacional Humanitario Ante La Corte Interamericana de Derechos Humanos." *Anuario Mexicano de Derecho Internacional* 9: 35–68.

2011. *Jurisprudencia Penal Internacional Aplicable en Colombia*. Bogotá: Universidad de los Andes.

Rath, Thomas. 2013. *Myths of Demilitarization in Postrevolutionary Mexico, 1920–1960*. Chapel Hill: University of North Carolina Press.

Rauchhaus, Robert W. 2006. "Asymmetric Information, Mediation, and Conflict Management." *World Politics* 58(2): 207–41.

Revenga Sánchez, Miguel, and Emilia Girón Reguera. 2004. "La Corte Constitucional Colombiana Ante las Medidas de Seguridad y Defensa Nacional del Gobierno de Uribe." *Estudios Socio Jurídicos* 6(1): 29–57.

Ríos-Figueroa, Julio. 2007. "Fragmentation of Power and the Emergence of an Effective Judiciary in Mexico, 1994–2002." *Latin American Politics Society* 49(1): 31–57.

2011. "Institutions for Constitutional Justice in Latin America." In *Courts in Latin America*, ed. Gretchen Helmke and Julio Ríos-Figueroa. New York: Cambridge University Press, 27–54.

2012. "Sociolegal Studies on Mexico." *Annual Review of Law and Social Science* 8: 307–21.

2015. "Judicial Institutions." In *Routledge Handbook of Comparative Political Institutions*, ed. Jennifer Gandhi and Rubén Ruiz-Rufino. New York: Routledge, 195–208.

Ríos-Figueroa, Julio, and Jeffrey K. Staton. 2012. "An Evaluation of Cross-National Measures of Judicial Independence." *Journal of Law, Economics and Organization* 30(1): 104–37.

Roberts, Kenneth. 2006. "Do Parties Matter? Lessons from the Fujimori Experience." In *The Fujimori Legacy: The Rise of Electoral Authoritarianism in Peru*, ed. Julio Carrión. University Park: Pennsylvania State University Press, 126–49.

Rodríguez-Garavito, César. 2011. "Beyond the Courtroom: The Impact of Judicial Activism on Socioeconomic Rights in Latin America." *Texas Law Review* 89(7): 1669–98.

Rodríguez-Garavito, César, and Diana Rodríguez-Franco. 2010. *Cortes y Cambio Social. Cómo la Corte Constitutional Transformó el Desplazamiento Forzado en Colombia*. Bogotá: DeJusticia.

Rodríguez-Raga, Juan Carlos. 2011. "Strategic Prudence in the Colombian Constitutional Court, 1992–2006." PhD Dissertation in Political Science, University of Pittsburgh.

Rodríguez-Villasante, and José Luis Prieto. 2002. *Derecho Internacional Humanitario*. Valencia: Cruz Roja Española/Tirant lo blanch.

Rogers, James R. 2001. "Information and Judicial Review: A Signaling Game of Legislative-Judicial Interaction." *American Journal of Political Science* 45(1): 84–99.

Ronfeldt, David. 1985. *The Modern Mexican Military: Implications for Mexico's Stability and Security*. Santa Monica, CA: Rand.

Rubio Correa, Marcial. 1990. "Fuerzas Armadas y Constitución en el Perú: 1979–1988." In *La Constitución Diez Años Después*. Lima: Constitución y Sociedad, 223–60.

Saín, Marcelo Fabián. 2010. *Los Votos y Las Botas. Estudios Sobre la Defensa Nacional y las Relaciones Civiles-Militares en la Democracia Argentina*. Buenos Aires: Prometeo Libros.

Sajó, András. 1999. *Limiting Government: An Introduction to Constitutionalism*. Budapest: Central European University Press.

Salazar Ugarte, Pedro. 2013. "Estado de Excepción, Suspensión de Derechos Y Jurisdicción." In *Derechos Humanos en la Constitución. Comentarios de Jurisprudencia Constitucional e Interamericana*, ed. Eduardo Ferrer McGregor, José Luis Caballero Ochoa, and Christian Steiner. Mexico, D.F.: Universidad Nacional Autónoma de México, SCJN, Konrad Adenauer Stiftung, 231–57.

Salazar Villalobos, Rossy. 2006. "¿Mantenimiento o Ampliación de la Justicia Militar?" In *Operaciones Conjuntas. Civiles y Militares en la Política de Defensa*, ed. José Huerta. Lima: Instituto de Defensa Legal, 311–404.

San Martín, César. 2006. *Derecho Procesal Penal*. 2nd ed. Lima: Grijley.

Schedler, Andreas. 2013. *The Politics of Uncertainty: Sustaining and Subverting Electoral Authoritarianism*. New York: Oxford University Press.

Scheppele, Kim Lane. 2003. "Constitutional Negotiations Political Contexts of Judicial Activism in Post-Soviet Europe." *International Sociology* 18.

Schiff, Rebecca. 1995. "Civil-Military Relations Reconsidered: A Theory of Concordance." *Armed Forces and Society* 22(1): 7–24.

Seawright, J., and J. Gerring. 2008. "Case Selection Techniques in Case Study Research: A Menu of Qualitative and Quantitative Options." *Political Research Quarterly* 61(2): 294–308.

Segal, Jeffrey A., and Harold J. Spaeth. 2002. *The Supreme Court and the Attitudinal Model Revisited*. Cambridge: Cambridge University Press.

Serra, Narcís. 2010. *The Military Transition: Democratic Reform of the Armed Forces*. New York: Cambridge University Press.

Serrano, Mónica. 1995. "The Armed Branch of the State: Civil-Military Relations in Mexico." *Journal of Latin American Studies* 27(2): 423–48.

Sgubini, Alessandra, Mara Prieditis, and Andrea Marighetto. 2013. *Arbitration, Mediation and Conciliation: Differences and Similarities from an International and Italian Business Perspective*. Available at http://www.mediate.com/articles/sgubinia2.cfm (accessed December 11, 2015).

Shah, Aquil. 2014a. "Constraining Consolidation: Military Politics and Democracy in Pakistan (2007–2013)." *Democratization* 21(6): 1007–33.

2014b. *The Army and Democracy: Military Politics in Pakistan*. Cambridge, MA: Harvard University Press.

Shambayati, Hootan. 2008. "The Guardian of the Regime: The Turkish Constitutional Court in Comparative Perspective." In *Constitutional Politics in the Middle East*, ed. Saïd Amid Arjomand. Portland, OR: Hart Publishing, 99–122.

Shambayati, Hootan, and Esen Kirdis. 2009. "In Pursuit of 'Contemporary Civilization': Judicial Empowerment in Turkey." *Political Research Quarterly* 62(4): 767–80.

Shambayati, Hootan, and Güliz Sütçü. 2012. "The Turkish Constitutional Court and the Justice and Development Party." *Middle Eastern Studies* 48(1): 107–23.

Shapiro, Martin M. 1981. *Courts: A Comparative and Political Analysis*. Chicago: University of Chicago Press.

Singer, Linda. 1994. *Settling Disputes: Conflict Resolution in Business, Families, and the Legal System*. New York: Westview Press.

Slater, Dan, and Daniel Ziblatt. 2013. "The Enduring Indispensability of the Controlled Comparison." *Comparative Political Studies* 46(10): 1301–27.

Smith, Alistair, and Allan Stam. 2004. "Bargaining and the Nature of War." *Journal of Conflict Resolution* 48(6): 786–813.

Smith, Rupert. 2005. *The Utility of Force*. London: Allen Lane.

Smulovitz, Catalina. 2010. "Judicialization in Argentina: Legal Culture or Opportunities and Support Structures?" In *Cultures of Legality: Judicialization and Political Activism in Latin America*, ed. Javier Couso, Alexandra Huneeus, and Rachel Sieder. New York: Cambridge University Press, 234–53.

Sommer, Udi. 2010. "A Strategic Court and National Security: Comparative Lessons from the Israeli Case." *Israel Studies Forum* 25(2): 54–80.

Staton, Jeffrey K. 2010. *Judicial Power and Strategic Communication in Mexico*. New York: Cambridge University Press.

Stephenson, Matthew C. 2003. "When the Devil Turns: The Political Foundations of Independent Judicial Review." *Journal of Legal Studies* 32(1): 59–90.

Stone Sweet, Alec. 2012. "Constitutional Courts." In *Oxford Handbook of Comparative Constitutional Law*, ed. Michael Rosenfeld and András Sajó. New York: Oxford University Press, 816-30.

Sutter, Daniel. 1997. "Enforcing Constitutional Constraints." *Constitutional Political Economy* 8(1): 139–50.

Svolik, Milan. 2012. *The Politics of Authoritarian Rule*. New York: Cambridge University Press.

Tachau, Frank, and Metin Heper. 1983. "The State, Politics, and the Military in Turkey." *Comparative Politics* 16(1): 17–33.

Tanaka, Martín. 2005. "Peru 1980–2000: Chronicle of a Death Foretold? Determinism, Political Decisions, and Open Outcomes." In *The Third Wave of Democratization in Latin America. Advances and Setbacks*, ed. Frances Hagopian and Scott Mainwaring. New York: Cambridge University Press, 261–89.

Tobler, Hans Werner. 1971. "Las Paradojas del Ejército Revolucionario: Su Papel Social en la Reforma Agraria Mexicana, 1920–1935." *Historia Mexicana* 21(1): 38–79.

Toche Medrano, Eduardo. 2008. *Guerra Y Democracia. Los Militares Peruanos Y La Construcción Nacional*. Lima: CLACSO.

Uprimny, Rodrigo. 2003. "The Constitutional Court and Control of Presidential Extraordinary Powers in Colombia." *Democratization* 10(4): 46–69.

2004. *Orden Democrático y Manejo de Conflictos*. Bogotá: Universidad Pedagógica Nacional.

2006. "Entre El Protagonismo, La Precariedad Y Las Amenazas: Las Paradojas de La Judicatura." In *En la Encrucijada. Colombia en el Siglo XXI*, ed. Francisco Leal Buitrago. Bogotá: Editorial Norma, 81–111.

2008. *Bloque de Constitutionalidad, Derechos Humanos y Proceso Penal*. Bogotá: Consejo Superior de la Judicatura.

Valderrama, César. 2015. "El Papel de las Audiencias en la Protección de Derechos y la Construcción de la Legitimidad. Los Casos de Colombia y México." Tesis de Doctorado en Ciencias Sociales, FLACSO-México.

Vanberg, Georg. 2005. *The Politics of Constitutional Review in Germany*. New York: Cambridge University Press.

2009. "Establishing and Maintaining Judicial Independence." In *Oxford Handbook of Law and Politics*, ed. Gregory A Caldeira, R. Daniel Kelemen, and Keith E. Whittington. New York: Oxford University Press, 1–29.

Vergara, Alberto. 2013. *Ciudadanos Sin República. ¿Cómo Sobrevivir en la Jungla Política Peruana?* Lima: Planeta.

Walsh, Declan. 2015. "New Courts Offer Pakistan's Generals the Power They Used to Seize." *The New York Times*.

Watts, Nicole F. 2007. "Silence and Voice: Turkish Policies and Kurdish Resistance in the Mid XX Century." In *The Evolution of Kurdish Nationalism*, ed. Mohammed Ahmed and Michael Gunter. Costa Mesa, CA: Mazda Press, 68–89.

Weill, Sharon. 2007. "The Judicial Arm of the Occupation: The Israeli Military Courts in the Occupied Territories." *International Review of the Red Cross* 89(866): 395–419.

Weingast, Barry. 1997. "The Political Foundations of Democracy and the Rule of Law." *American Political Science Review* 91(2): 245–63.

Whittington, Keith E. 2001. *Constitutional Construction: Divided Powers and Constitutional Meaning*. Cambridge, MA: Harvard University Press.

2003. "Legislative Sanctions and the Strategic Environment of Judicial Review." *International Journal of Constitutional Law* 1: 446–74.

Wilson, B. M. 2006. "Legal Opportunity Structures and Social Movements: The Effects of Institutional Change on Costa Rican Politics." *Comparative Political Studies* 39(3): 325–51.

Wilson, Bruce. 2009. "Institutional Reform and Rights Revolutions in Latin America: The Cases of Costa Rica and Colombia." *Journal of Politics in Latin America* 1(2): 59–85.

INDEX

www.ingramcontent.com/pod-product-compliance
Lightning Source LLC
LaVergne TN
LVHW011522200926
848484LV00001B/115
* 9 7 8 1 1 0 7 0 7 9 7 8 6 *